THE NATURE OF HONOUR

DAVID McBRIDE

THE NATURE OF HONOUR

SON, DUTY-BOUND SOLDIER, MILITARY LAWYER, TRUTH-TELLER, FATHER

VIKING
an imprint of
PENGUIN BOOKS

VIKING

UK | USA | Canada | Ireland | Australia
India | New Zealand | South Africa | China

Viking is part of the Penguin Random House group of companies
whose addresses can be found at global.penguinrandomhouse.com

First published by Viking in 2023

Cover photography by Michelle Kaldy at Urban Dystopian
Cover design by Christabella Designs © Penguin Random House Australia Pty Ltd
Typeset in 12/16 pt Goudy Old Style by Midland Typesetters, Australia

Printed and bound in Australia by Griffin Press, an accredited
ISO AS/NZS 14001 Environmental Management Systems printer

 A catalogue record for this
book is available from the
National Library of Australia

ISBN 978 1 76089 799 4

penguin.com.au

We at Penguin Random House Australia acknowledge that Aboriginal and
Torres Strait Islander peoples are the Traditional Custodians and the first storytellers
of the lands on which we live and work. We honour Aboriginal and Torres Strait
Islander peoples' continuous connection to Country, waters, skies and communities.
We celebrate Aboriginal and Torres Strait Islander stories, traditions and
living cultures; and we pay our respects to Elders past and present.

To Sarah, James and Georgie
and
a God of my own understanding

And to Jake
A dog of my own understanding

CONTENTS

INTRODUCTION

Ground Zero

In the deserts of South Asia there is a snake that lives in amongst the rocks and hunts under the stars. As it ages, its eyesight and reflexes grow weaker, and it begins to strike in ever more desperate attempts to survive. Despite striking at nothing, the action of striking sets off receptors in its brain that make it strike even more. In such a frenzy it can sometimes bite its own tail, thinking that it's a rodent scurrying away behind it. Strangely, when it bites its tail, rather than let go in pain – realising its mistake – it grips all the tighter, because the endorphin rush received from feeling that it's finally got some prey, that it's finally going to eat something, overpowers the pain from being bitten.

It believes the pain is something to be endured for its ultimate survival, and, if anything, it simply drives the snake to bite all the harder. At a certain point, the pain becomes unbearable, and the tail goes into spasms, twisting and turning uncontrollably. This, in turn, encourages the head and teeth to grip still more implacably, as it feels 'the rodent' must surely soon die. The dance goes on – neither teeth able to cease biting, nor tail able to stop writhing – until the snake is dead. At no point does it ever realise it is, in fact, killing itself.

I remember exactly where I was standing. It was about nine at night, and I was in a spartan white corridor, lit by strip lights, or what looked like a corridor from the inside. It was actually a number of cargo containers assembled like huge Lego blocks to make buildings – an ingenious invention by some Dutchman or German called 'Dreh'. No doubt, they filled an immediate need and cost the Australian military huge amounts of money.

Whoever the mysterious 'Dreh' was, the bases all over Afghanistan were made up of hundreds of such containers. Each container housed a different unit or section of the Special Forces, and had heavy reinforced steel doors that could be locked. An officer like me might have a Drehtainer to himself, or might share it with someone else: I had my own. The commanding officer had two of them put together.

By the thirteenth year of the war, this iteration of Drehtainers was the third or fourth. They had lights, air conditioners and even separate corridors. Most had flatscreen TVs. The ones for officers had carpets, but generally the troops didn't care for such luxuries. Their decorations were more earthy – whiteboards with timings for missions, with some cryptic coded numbers in the corners.

There were corridors which linked these office blocks and made a sort of large capital 'T' shape, with a corridor down the middle and various different offices off to each side. Some were joined together to make operations rooms. These were behind still more locked doors and punch-codes, all of which we memorised.

The roof was reinforced steel, which got thicker each year in response to Taliban rockets that were able to pierce the original buildings and kill the occupants. Overall, the scene looked a little like a police station on the moon, its staff policing some very mean aliens – which in many ways was exactly what it was.

Outside the office block was a dining hall and then a perimeter fence about twelve feet high, with another four feet of razor wire on the top. The perimeter was lit with bright lights, which would have made it a hard climb, at any hour. A high tower in the centre of the base gave an additional all-round view of the roughly two football-pitch-sized hexagon. It was never manned. It wasn't necessary: no-one was foolish enough to want to break in.

Outside that perimeter wall was where the general population, the normal soldiers, lived. And outside that fence was another fence beyond which the Afghan soldiers lived. And outside *that* fence was another fence up to which the Afghan contractors could bring trucks. Each of the walls had security checkpoints and patrols on the perimeter. So, I stood in the epicentre of a large number of circular perimeter fences. The bullseye on a dartboard. The eye of the storm.

I was outside the office of the commanding officer of Task Force 66, the most successful – and at the same time notorious – of the Special Forces groups fighting the Taliban for control of the country. He had sent a 'runner' for me, who had first gone to the gym, where I usually was, and then to my room, and had only come to my office as an afterthought.

I wasn't normally in the office, because there was nothing much to do in it, except make phone calls, and interview people after something had gone seriously wrong. Typically, I didn't do much of that, but lately it had been my focus. I went to the gym, but that was to process what I had just heard. And to relieve the anger that was growing within me. I was also in uniform, the greyish pattern that only the Australian Special Forces wore on this base. It was comfortable, and being allowed to wear light-weight hiking shoes made it more so.

It was still a uniform, though, and it meant something to me. I was part of TF66. I was also an officer in the Australian Army.

These were positions of power, but with power comes responsibility, which means doing tough things. Despite the fact there were no rank badges or insignia on them, you could tell who was who by the way they wore their uniform.

Like every single person on the base, I was armed, with a 9mm pistol strapped to my side at all times. It came to the toilet, and it came to bed. Of late, we had lost as many people shot in the back while on base by the Afghan soldiers we were trying to train, as we had being wounded in the heat of battle.

'Green on blues', they were called: the US-led forces being the blue, and the local Afghan forces we were training, the green. It meant we were getting shot by the people we were meant to be assisting. Sometimes, it was by Taliban sympathisers who had infiltrated their ranks deliberately, sometimes by those who had been turned by the Taliban while on leave, and sometimes by those who simply decided they hated us.

Despite a lot of research into the issue, there was no clear answer. The person smiling at you and shaking your hand one minute could be taking a bead on you the next. I'd seen the same in Northern Ireland, so I wasn't that bothered by it. But there, like here, it was worth keeping your wits about you and your pistol ready.

The fact that the CO had sent a runner to find me usually meant we were either about to try to kill someone, or one of our own had been killed. Tonight, it was neither. I walked steadily to his door. There was no need to run, but no excuse not to go there immediately. By the look on the runner's face, and his body language, the news was obviously not good, which meant both the CO and the regimental sergeant major (RSM) would be waiting for me to arrive. To keep him waiting would mean risking whatever emotions he was feeling being directed at me; but more importantly, losing his respect.

As expected, the RSM was there as well, and when I came in I acknowledged them both. The CO didn't ask me to close the door. It seemed it was going to be a short meeting, and, in any case, there was a long corridor that meant no-one would hear what was being said.

The CO looked at me and uttered just one short sentence. I thanked him for the information and exchanged a quick glance with the RSM. I didn't swear out loud, as I had during what he'd told me a couple of hours earlier. I held my breath and then respectfully excused myself. I walked out of the office, and waited in the corridor for a few seconds. I knew then that I was about to go to war against my own country. Not just my own country, but in a complex set of alliances and dependencies, it ultimately would likely, in effect, include the Pentagon and the various US security agencies. People who I knew played for keeps. I looked at the python slithering in its cage – the SAS had adopted it as a mascot – which seemed to be looking at me. For once, I paid it no attention.

Strange as it might seem to a civilian, I didn't think too much about how many people I was up against. Like any military decision, you don't reflect upon how hard it's going to be, you just do it. It would be impossible for the military to operate any other way. The way I saw it, it was simply me doing my job, exactly as I was trained to do. I was a soldier. I had a mission. The obstacles in front of me were relevant, but only in so far as being problems to be solved.

I wasn't trained to *not* do something because I thought it was going to be hard. In some strange ways, I felt alive and was looking forward to the coming battle, even though I also knew it would be totally 'shite', to use the black humour employed by soldiers. The phrase 'living the dream' – another black-humour joke for all occasions in the military – seemed to encapsulate that dark ambiguity.

If my own generals and political masters – and their political masters – insisted on doing the wrong thing, and trashing everything the West was meant to stand for, as well as the lives of millions of people in South Asia, simply to win elections back home, then they had become the real enemy. I was going to do my best to expose them, and defeat them.

I knew I was far from alone. I was just the person on the spot with the right information, and the wherewithal to try to make it happen. I was backing myself, even if the fight took the rest of my life, which I knew it might. Righteous anger is out of fashion today, but it is a great motivator. There is no greater gift in a fight than a truly despicable enemy. That factor alone probably won the Second World War for the Allies. Being right matters.

I accept that my actions will seem strange to many, and likely seem quite mad to some. My enemies have often painted me that way. Someone who was vaguely supportive of me once said, 'You're pathologically honest. You have an overdeveloped sense of duty.' They didn't mean it as a compliment.

However, the way I see it, you don't have a sense of duty. You have a duty. You do it, or you fail to do it. If you're trying to work out which outcome will be best for you in the long run, it can be complex, indeterminate, a grey area. But if you make decisions based on what you consider to be right and wrong, it's not so hard.

And so I did what my conscience, my training and my life experience told me to do. Which brings me to the present day, and the purpose of this story. I'm now facing the harsh consequences of my decisions, but I felt like I had to blow the whistle. In fact, I've never liked myself more or felt more my authentic self, if that is a thing. I have no idea whether I will go to prison or not; and if I do go to prison, how long it's going to be.

I've never met anyone who says they would have done what I've done, and the way that I've done it. But this book simply describes who I was, and how I came to be that person.

CHAPTER 1

One Last Question

In all of us, there's a history we know, and a history we don't know. It's the history we don't know which is the most important. Ironically enough, if my story was, in effect, to end with a trial, it had also begun with a trial.

I've always been aware of those who came before me. Even as a kid, I knew I was lucky. My parents' house was much bigger than my grandparents'. My ancestors weren't rich, and it wasn't too far back in time that they couldn't even read. But I knew a few things about them, two of which stayed with me. Firstly, this country gave them opportunities they previously didn't have in Britain, and that this country wouldn't be the way it was without people like them fighting bit by bit for its improvement. Also, that if they could see me now, they'd want me always to make the most of my opportunities – opportunities they'd endured great hardship for, just so I could experience this life. And, where necessary, they'd want me to stand up for what is right.

I never had a good picture of who my ancestors were. They weren't wealthy landowners, and there were no family portraits.

Instead, I pictured what they 'saw': a tall ship on a light blue
Pacific sea; white sails contrasting with dark wood masts; creaking
rigging; then, once they'd landed, rough hands hammering a
chisel into sandstone, cutting deep tunnels in the landscape, in
searing heat, inch by inch. Even before I was aware of my convict
ancestry, this type of image was at the back of my mind.

It wasn't so much that I had been lucky, although I had been.
I was simply the last in a long line of people who had sacrificed,
fought and survived to get me here. They wouldn't begrudge me
my life, but my position in that line came with certain responsi-
bilities: don't waste our work, and don't go backwards. But what
would they want me to do in this situation?

My nationality as Australian is more than simply a passport.
It's part of who I am, and defines my character, good and bad.
While I claim the shared heritage of the beginnings of democracy, and freedom of thought and religion, that emerged in
Britain over the course of a thousand violent years, my particular
spirit didn't start until it arrived in Australia, infused with those
ideals of fairness, or at least improvement in one's circumstances.

My relationship to this country started a little over two centuries ago, in 1816 – in the Old Bailey, the largest criminal court in
the largest empire in the world. The Battle of Waterloo had been
fought the year before, but rather than winning glory with the
forces of the Duke of Wellington, my ancestor James Freeman
was facing a trial of a different sort.

The first witness that day was one James Judd. He was a two-
penny post letter carrier, the equivalent of a mailman. During
that era, those receiving mail paid for it on receipt, which meant that
at the end of his shift, he was carrying a fair amount of cash.

While it's mostly speculation on my part based on a few hints,
I imagine him to be a largish man, sensibly dressed and sober of
habit. The precision with which he speaks on the court transcript
suggests he is the sort of person who is middle class; a town-
crier type. He is sure of his position in life, and dismissive of the

riff-raff through whom he must navigate as he travels between the houses and businesses of the gentry. Judd's no fool, however, and he is clearly not afraid of the criminal gangs of London either. His evidence is as follows:

> In the late afternoon of the 5th November, between 5 and 6 o'clock I was in Bell Lane, Spitalfields. I had delivered my letters and had received 10 Pounds for them, consisting of eight one-pound bank notes, and the rest in silver and copper, with some 'half-crowns' among them. I was stopped by three men, one of them held my right hand down, and the other, that is the prisoner [pointing to James Freeman, who was standing in the dock], robbed me of the money in my pocket. The notes were in my right breeches pocket, the silver in my left, and the copper in my coat-pocket, which he tore when taking the copper out. The third stood watch. They were about five minutes, and they ran away. I gave the information at the police office, and described the men. I then saw the prisoner again at Lambeth Street [police station] on the 21st, I recognised him immediately. I'm sure the prisoner is the man, I picked him out from a 'line-up' of several others. There was good light, because of a factory lamp above us at the time, and it was by the factory lamp that I was robbed.

All in all, it was a pretty good evidence-in-chief. It was now the turn of my ancestor to try to catch him out in cross-examination. He didn't have a lawyer – the only lawyer being the prosecutor – but he was permitted to ask questions himself. By now, James Freeman had been held on remand for two weeks, and while he was only twenty-one years old, it may not have been his first time among those who knew a thing or two about law.

He opened with a fair gambit. 'Was you intoxicated?' he asked, a mixture of fear and bravado undoubtedly in his voice.

'No' came Judd's reply – disdainfully, I'd imagine.

The next witness was the constable from Lambeth, Samuel Miller, who claimed that he'd recognised the defendant 'from the description I was given by Judd. I found [Freeman] walking along Whitechapel [a major and busy road, some distance from the scene of the robbery]. I told him I wanted him for robbery, and I arrested him for the robbery of the postman in Bell Lane . . .'

It was not looking good for James Freeman, but he had some tricks up his sleeve: an alibi witness, and not just one, but two.

The first of these was a Mrs Dianna Elliot. She gave evidence that Freeman lived with her as a lodger in Dog Row and that he was a rope-maker by trade. 'I remember the 5th of November well,' she said. 'Mr Freeman came home at about half past one, and nailed his shoes. It was a wet day, and he was nailing his shoes nearly all afternoon. He drank tea with myself and my friend, who came to my house around 3 o'clock, as she does every day.'

Thanks to Mrs Elliot, the 'rope' now seemed a little further away from the rope-maker. He then called his next witness, a Miss Hannah Carr.

Miss Carr said she was in the silk trade and confirmed Mrs Elliot's story. After coming to tea with her around three o'clock, she'd stayed till about eight. All that time, she claimed, Mr Freeman was also there, tapping away on his shoes.

While Judd was sure it was Freeman who'd robbed him, there were no other witnesses. The fact that Freeman had not one, but two alibi witnesses would seem to have given him hope he may be acquitted. His freedom – in fact, his life, and the course of the lives of all his descendants – came down to the final question from the Crown Prosecutor to Miss Carr.

Having closed the gates, as they say in courtroom technique, by asking her the finer detail of what happened that day, he got Miss Carr to confirm she seemed to remember everything – from the exact time she'd arrived and left, to what the trio had discussed.

Noting that, according to her testimony, Freeman 'could not have possibly committed this robbery because he was with you, fixing his shoes, while you drank tea with your good friend Mrs Elliot, Freeman's landlady', he finished with this:

One last question, if I may, Miss Carr. What day of the week was the 5th of November that you remember so well?

Apparently, Miss Carr's response was less than satisfactory. The only other words on the transcript are: 'Verdict: guilty, Sentence: death.' However, as it turns out, the day of the trial, 15 January, was in many ways James Freeman's lucky day – not that he would have thought it at the time. While found guilty and sentenced to hang, his sentence was later commuted to transportation for life to New South Wales. Whether this indicated some sort of leniency, or whether more manpower was needed to build the new colony, it was a stroke of luck for my ancestor. He survived the trip, and a further ten years of hard labour, which quite likely meant cutting stone while in shackles, day after day.

After completing his sentence – with only one minor aberration of 'insubordination' – he was sent north of Sydney to work as an indentured labourer to a dairy farmer at the frontiers of the colony. It was on this farm, working as a supervisor of some sort, that he had his second stroke of luck: meeting his future wife, the remarkable Mary Ann Smith in 1831.

Back in England two or three years earlier, Mary Ann, then about eighteen years old, had met an habitual, but apparently charming, criminal named Matthew Kirkman. He was well known as a 'great thief', even described in the local papers as such, and by the time Mary Ann met him in 1829 he had already served a two-year jail term for theft. The pair seemed to become a team both on and off the field, eschewing the convention of marriage.

In January 1830, Matthew and Mary Ann were before the court as co-defendants on the charge of stealing clothes from Matthew's brother's shop. Kirkman evaded conviction, but Mary Ann, who had taken the stolen garments to the local pawnbroker, and was caught in possession of the duplicate key to the shop, was not so lucky. The court records that it was her second offence, and she was therefore sentenced to seven years' transportation.

While in prison awaiting the voyage, she gave birth to Kirkman's son, who she named John, and who accompanied her on the long journey to her new home. She sailed on the all-female convict ship *Kains*.

On arrival, she was assigned to work at the dairy. She and James Freeman were married in November 1831 and seemed to have a happy and adventurous life together, eventually buying their own farm. She bore another ten children, and she and James stayed together until his death.

She must have been something of a local identity in that part of the world, given that, while in her nineties, she was interviewed by the *Newcastle Herald* about her life. Reading her responses it's not hard to imagine her as optimistic and energetic, as well as appreciative of the new country in which she'd found herself.

She recounts the night a notorious local bushranger gang came to their farmhouse, asking for shelter and a loan of fresh horses. James was not there at the time, and she states that the gang leader, Davis, made 'unwelcome advances' towards her, which were only stopped by a second gang member threatening him with a pistol. After her husband returned and defused the situation, she and James lent the bushrangers some horses. They were left in the place they said they would be, true to their word.

This country, and its wild spirit, gave my ancestors a life, and it is as much a part of my character as any one relation. While, as I've said, I'm proud to claim the development of the rule of law in the UK as part of my heritage, I don't claim the relatives of Smith and Freeman – those who stayed in the UK – as my family. My family history starts with transportation.

The fact that Freeman was recognised in London, a city of a million people even then, not by the victim of the robbery but by someone who had been given only a verbal description, seems improbable. It's hard not to see it as an act of fate.

CHAPTER 2

Myrine and Jack

I'm not sure how much my grandmother, Myrine Griffith, knew of her convict forebears, as in those days – only a few generations away from prisons, illiteracy and humiliating treatment at the hands of their gaolers – her family history was likely considered quite shameful. James and Mary Ann were her great-grandparents, and while their lives were, in many ways, probably not very similar, they certainly all faced huge challenges.

Myrine's mother, Eliza, had died a few months after her birth. Her father, Tom, remarried not long afterwards, and she'd grown up believing that her stepmother was her birth mother. Myrine was eventually told, apparently by mischievous cousins at a family gathering, presumably without any attempt to soften the blow.

From anecdotal family histories, her grandfather Edwin lived with them, in Bexley in the south of Sydney, and both he and her father played in the local brass band. Music was a big part of their lives, and no doubt Myrine spent a lot of time watching the band practise and perform. She had grown into a striking young woman, almost six feet tall, and was comfortable singing and playing the piano to an audience.

Socialising in these rather formal times was highly scrutinised, and my grandmother and grandfather met as a result of him, John 'Jack' McBride, playing in the same brass band. Jack was born in 1892, five years before Myrine, and his parents, James and Alice McBride, had immigrated from Northern Ireland. They were Protestants, which would have pleased the stiff and aspirational Griffiths, and the fact that he was a member of the band seemed to make him the ideal candidate to marry Myrine. Unfortunately, the First World War intervened.

Jack went off to war badged as a bandsman, medic and stretcher bearer, as apparently did many of those who played in brass bands. He was a few inches shorter than Myrine, and a lot quieter, but he was strong. He was sent to the Western Front and was wounded carrying out his duties, bringing back the wounded and the dying through the mud of Ypres and Passchendaele. After a few months in hospital in Aldershot in England, he returned to the front for more of his grim, but necessary work. One can only imagine what he saw. He experienced artillery barrages so long and intense that his hearing never properly returned.

The war provided grim work back home for his own father, James McBride, as well. James was a newsagent. In those days, the job involved the delivery of the daily papers to houses in each suburb, by a flat trailer piled high with stacked newspapers tied together like hay bales - loaded singlehandedly by James - and pulled steadily by a draft horse. During the war years, the job took on an ominous edge as often the first a family knew of the death of their son was reading about it in the casualty lists. My grandfather was known as a kind man, and I can only imagine what it was like to be the daily deliverer of such news.

Jack and Myrine were married in 1920. They had a son, Ken, in 1922, a daughter, Betty, in 1924, and their youngest child, my father, William, was born in 1927. James McBride died when Bill was only two, and Jack inherited the newsagency. Once transport became mechanised, he developed it into a small trucking firm.

The McBrides weren't wealthy, but they lived in a nice house on a corner block, with a piano, and Dad noticed that when he went to school during the Depression, he was one of the few kids who had shoes. Theirs was a typical middle-class home, of which his parents were immensely proud. As I remember from my childhood, there was a rose garden at the front, complete with concrete figures of Indigenous people and flamingos, elaborate dark brickwork, large but uncomfortable sofas, pictures of Asian women on the walls, and a pet cockatoo.

If the memories of the war haunted him, Jack didn't show it, although he had a constant reminder. He carried a piece of shrapnel from the war in his body all his life, until it eventually worked its way out of his leg, one day in the garden.

Myrine might not have been so lucky. It is said that traumatic events are cumulative – in that, rather than the brain recovering after one, they pile up on top of each other, no matter how many intervening years there might be of relative calm. While the facts are shrouded in mystery, Myrine suffered a number of nervous breakdowns. These breakdowns were serious, and as a result, my father spent many of his primary school years living in the country with his cousins, attending a tiny ten-person school.

While the exact causes will never be known, there are plenty of strong possibilities. There was the shock of finding out that her birth mother was dead, and that her birth may have contributed to it; the four years during which she never knew whether Jack was coming home from the war; the Depression years, when times were so tough for everybody; and finally, in the late 1930s, as war again approached, and the prospect loomed that both her sons might be killed, leaving her alone in her old age.

In fact, in her older years, while I never experienced anything but kindness from my grandmother, she was in and out of hospital, and was at times both angry and delirious.

Despite his war experience, Jack didn't lose his faith in the 'idea' of Australia, and remained quietly patriotic to his core. When war was declared again in 1939, he was under no illusions about the realities that his son would likely face. Like most of his compatriots, although he'd been through it all himself he didn't think of stopping his eldest son from doing his duty, whatever his private fears. Jack seemed to quietly accept that Australia was worth fighting for, and even having your eldest son die for.

In January 1943, while Ken was off at war, my father Bill, who was now sixteen years old, won a Commonwealth scholarship to study Medicine at Sydney University. Bill was the first person on either side of the family to go to university, but it's unclear whether his father was particularly excited about it. Maybe his life experience knew it was too early to celebrate.

Jack never stopped caring for Myrine, patiently pushing his lawnmower, and pruning their roses. When he finally died in 1972, Myrine never left hospital and died soon after in 1973.

CHAPTER 3

Thalidomide

Distaval can be given with complete safety to pregnant women and nursing mothers without adverse effect on mother or child.

Advertising of Distaval (thalidomide), 1958

Until they met at medical school, Bill McBride and Patricia Glover led roughly parallel lives. Both had been the first members of their families to go to university, and both did so on Commonwealth scholarships. Outwardly, perhaps they seemed ordinary, but both had their fair share of childhood trauma. In some ways they were polar opposites. Bill never worried; Pat rarely stopped. They'd both liked the beach growing up, but Bill could only recall the good times he had in the surf club, and Pat only the day she was washed off the rocks and broke her leg.

Bill seemed to know exactly what he was going to do with his life from an early age, and he was lucky enough to have parents who were just financially comfortable enough to enable him, but not *so* comfortable that he was faced with distractions. While

Pat appeared less set on Medicine, it certainly provided her with an unparalleled opportunity to be independent, and to help others.

They were in the sweet spot for professionals: growing up just outside the inner circles of society, and with both the desire and ability to enter that club. Most of their friends were the same. Their lives, in many ways, began at the doors of the medical school, as if it was a school of magic, which to them it was.

Bill was a pragmatist, and, with his entry to the medical faculty at sixteen years of age, he was a young man in a hurry. Although his mother's psychological difficulties can't have made life easy for him, he was given every opportunity to shine. As early as primary school, he had both his major life goals in mind: become a renowned medical specialist, and buy a farm. As with all plans, sometimes it's the same things that can both make and break us; or, to put it another way, be careful what you wish for.

Bill seemed to have taken to school early on. Being born in late May meant he was the youngest in his academic year. While he was never dux of his school, he was born with qualities that are even more useful than being top of the class: optimism, drive, a love of learning and a single-minded pursuit of his goals. His first real hero was Howard Florey, an Australian who had gone to the UK and changed the world by the development of antibiotics for the treatment of infection. Bill hoped to make a similar splash. Given that no-one in his family had ever been to university, the boy from Bexley had fairly big dreams.

Bill's first memories were of the Depression and the effect it had on the collective consciousness of Australia at that time. In later life he claimed to have remembered the opening of the Harbour Bridge, and the sound of so many feet marching simultaneously. Maybe it seems a stretch as he was only four years old in 1932, but it's certainly possible, as he seemed to have matured early in many other ways.

He also remembered that he was one of the few kids at school during the Depression who had either shoes or schoolbooks.

Like most boys who grew up in Australia in the 1930s, his other heroes were the national cricket team, especially Donald Bradman, as they took on the English, who were widely considered a sinister force. While it seems laughable now that cricket produced such emotions, for Australians still living in the shadows of Gallipoli and the Depression, it seems this was a very real battle of good vs evil, plucky underdog colonials taking on those who considered them somehow 'less than'. While Bill was not a great sportsman himself (although he tried his hand at both rugby league and surfboat racing), this patriotic underdog spirit seemed to be very much a part of who he was.

After my grandmother's nervous breakdown when he was a boy, he was sent to the country to live with her half-sister, Lily. Lily had grown up in the city in a middle-class home, with pianos and brass instruments, then marrying a dairy farmer and going to live in Dungog, about 130 miles north of Sydney.

Strangely, for a boy who loved learning, and idolised the great medical scientists of the day, Bill fell in love with the Australian bush, the country lifestyle, and the people he met there. The life of a dairy farmer had a carefree quality about it that was very different from the house on the corner block in Bexley, with a war-veteran father, who kept his ghosts largely to himself, and a mother suffering from a mental illness. Perception is everything, and rather than see the harsh privations of rural life in the 1930s in a negative light, he seemed to picture it all very romantically. It was a perception that stayed with him all his life.

Bill spent a year or two in Dungog, walking the two miles from the dairy farm to a tiny one-teacher school, with only about ten students aged from seven to twelve. Outside of school hours, there was little for them to do, except swim in the river and ride horses. He and his cousin of a similar age would spend each day exploring the farm, and would run terrified from huge snakes, cranky bulls and what they were sure were ghosts in nearby haunted houses.

My father returned to Sydney, gaining entry into Canterbury Boys High School – an academically selective school – as a second world war was about to erupt. Aged sixteen, he was then admitted to Sydney University. Medicine seemed to be almost a sacred calling for him, similar to how I felt on entering Sandhurst military academy forty-five years later.

Once he graduated, he set off for England for further study in London. He didn't have the money for a ticket, by either plane or ship, so he got to the UK by working as a doctor on a merchant navy vessel. His parents came to see him off at Circular Quay, tall and skinny in his white naval style uniform, complete with peaked hat.

In London, he barely had enough money to eat, and would live off a single chocolate bar for lunch. He worked as a junior doctor in some of the famous teaching hospitals, and was in awe of the senior physicians, who were household names for those in that world. These physicians were stoic individuals who had lived through World War II, either as doctors or soldiers, and they had a military air about them. They likely recognised in him someone completely devoted to the job, as they had been during their training.

My father picked up a saying at that time that never left him, something the senior doctors would say when a baby was born not breathing: 'We've got three minutes before we need to panic.' It summed him up in a crisis. I never saw him flustered, although maybe in retrospect some fear might have been good for him. Like many larger-than-life characters, the seeds of their downfall are often sown in their rise.

On returning to Australia, he became the superintendent of Crown Street Women's Hospital in Sydney. This position was like being an adjutant in the military, in that, even though you were a relatively junior doctor yourself, you had to supervise and discipline the other junior doctors. They worked long hours, and their one pleasure was going across the road to the Dolphin

Hotel to drink a single beer before closing time, which was then at the early time of six o'clock.

It was around this time that he met and became engaged to Patricia, who was doing her internship at the hospital. She had been two years below him at university, and, while they had noticed each other, there was no romance until they met again at Crown Street.

After they became engaged, Pat took a round-the-world trip to Japan, England and Spain, to reflect upon their relationship and ensure marriage was the right decision for her. While in Spain she had a serious car accident driving a friend's car, rolling a number of times, before they found themselves upside down in a ditch, surrounded by shocked local villagers. It shook her up, and seemed to precipitate her decision to return to Australia and marry Bill.

The real world and its prejudices of the time, however, didn't allow things to go smoothly. Pat was a Roman Catholic, and Bill's grandparents couldn't tolerate having a Catholic in the family, despite the fact that she was a beautiful young doctor. But Bill insisted. While he respected his elders, they were clearly of a generation he had left behind. Fortunately, in the end they agreed to the marriage.

The wedding was in Pat's local Catholic church and was modest by modern standards. The presents were largely cheap kitchen utensils, such as spoons, forks and plates. Having grown up with their major luxury being simply their education, they were grateful. And, in any case, it was the fifties – the postwar boom – and they felt that the world was their oyster.

They moved first to Carss Park, a modest waterside suburb close to where Bill had grown up, and the couple had three children in quick succession – I arrived later, in 1963. Bill became a specialist in obstetrics and gynaecology and got his PhD equivalent, with Patricia then going back to work as a doctor, to allow him to finish his PhD.

When Bill's practice began to take off, they upgraded to a big house in neighbouring Blakehurst, with sweeping lawns and a tennis court. It was a lifestyle their grandparents would have only dreamed of. Actually, I like to think it was exactly what they did dream of: that their children's children might have all the opportunities that they hadn't had; and when they had them, that they should grip them with both hands. If that was the case, the ghosts of the past would have been very happy with Bill and Pat's home in Sydney's southern suburbs.

Fate, however, was to intervene, and a quiet life in the suburbs was not what awaited them. My father had enormous stores of energy, being up early each morning and working late each night, often having sleep interrupted to deliver babies, a job that gave him enormous satisfaction, and sense of purpose. That sense of purpose was tested one day in May 1961, when his world was to change forever.

The story, as I understand it, is that a patient he had nurtured for a number of years was having her first child. A gynaecologist only has a limited number of patients who are expecting at one time, and they know them all personally: their names, their husbands, their joys and their fears. Tragically, the baby was born without arms or legs, and some of its other vital organs weren't able to support life. It died a few hours after being born. In the London teaching hospitals after the war, Dad had been taught to be stoic, but his feeling of grief for the parents was strong.

His hunch was that this heartbreaking event was out of the ordinary. A few weeks later, he delivered a baby with similar deformities and results. He sensed it wasn't right. However, as a doctor you can have difficulty proving that numbers alone are indicative of a major issue. There is always a one in 100,000 chance of something happening. Even of it happening twice. But Bill 'knew'. He just needed to work out why.

The first thing he did was to get a wall map of Sydney and plot the suburbs in which the affected mothers lived, to see if it was related to some sort of toxic waste or radiation. Sydney had a new nuclear facility in the south, near where he lived, and perhaps that was the culprit? But there was no correlation between where the mothers lived. A second problem was the fact that the mothers were perfectly healthy. If they had been somehow poisoned by the environment, they should have shown signs of ill health themselves.

This was the trick of the morning-sickness drug thalidomide, and it took Dad's hunch to work it out. A 'wonder drug' made by the West German company Chemie Grünenthal, thalidomide had been introduced into the local market in 1957, and the UK and Australia the following year. Although some in the medical profession had their suspicions about a link between thalidomide and these deaths and birth deformities, there had never previously been a drug that affected the foetus in such a devastating way without also poisoning the mother. Nor, strictly speaking, did the drug even poison the foetus; it just sometimes had a disastrous effect on the limb development.

The situation was complicated by two other factors. Firstly, not everybody who took thalidomide was affected. Secondly, not everybody who took the drug had it recorded on their medical files, as it was easily available. It required a prescription, but that could have been given by the family GP, or any doctor the patient may have seen during the pregnancy. In the days before online records were able to piece together someone's medical records, it wasn't always easy to determine exactly what a patient had ingested. After all, these were the days when it was commonplace for women to continue to drink and smoke during pregnancy.

The one person who was able to give him a clue was a midwife at the Crown Street Hospital. She told him that the one thing the patients had in common was being prescribed the drug Distaval – a brand name for thalidomide – for morning sickness. During the June long weekend, when Bill had time off from seeing his patients in the day, he resisted the temptation to have a relaxing time at home, or to take Pat and the three toddlers on a family excursion. He was driven to find out why the tragedies had happened, and to make sure they never happened again.

I'm not sure what he did during those three days. I assume it was to apply his medical knowledge and experience to other studies that suggested that thalidomide could damage the nerve endings of adults in their hands and feet (peripheral neuritis), if taken for extended periods, with other cases of birth defects.

While he couldn't solve the riddle of why it affected some but not others, his hunch was that it might be related to ingestion during the weeks of limb development. He might have been wrong, of course, and it was a bold claim to make against a big drug company. It could easily have destroyed his career, which was for him everything that he had worked for since he was a small boy.

As someone who'd prescribed the drug himself, his situation also involved some feelings of guilt. However, on the Sunday of that weekend he made his decision to act: the healthy birth of future babies was more important than either the risks to himself, or his ego, and he was satisfied he could defend his decision. On the Monday he called in at the hospital and asked the pharmacy to take the thalidomide off the shelves. They did.

Having acted on a hunch, he now needed to prove his hunch to the satisfaction of others, to prepare for the likely backlash from the manufacturers, their own medical specialists, and other more experienced doctors who hadn't made the connection, and would likely dismiss him because of the lack of hard proof.

It seems quite comical now, but Dad bought some rabbits from a local pet shop, and put them in makeshift hutches assembled by the maintenance team at the hospital. He then tried to get the rabbits to eat the thalidomide pills, with the aim of seeing whether they subsequently had deformities in their developing foetuses. Unfortunately, they had limited success, largely because the rabbits didn't want to eat the drug.

He relayed his concerns to salespeople, but of course they neither knew he was right, nor were prepared to withdraw the drug on his word alone.

One thing Dad could do was write to the world's leading medical journal. His five-line letter was published in *Lancet* in December 1961, and while its wording was polite and deferential, its meaning, and risk for his career, was clear. Bill's letter is considered by *Lancet* to be one of the most important published in the journal's two-hundred-year history.

A year later, an eminent German scientist, Professor Widukind Lenz, confirmed through thorough laboratory testing what Bill had been saying for some time: thalidomide had the ability to stop the development of limbs due to its effect on certain blood vessels in the foetus. Lenz had the good grace to credit the young doctor from the other side of the planet with being the first to alert the world to the dangers. Another 'Australian underdog world first' story was born.

It's not that difficult to stand up when you're backed by unassailable evidence, but it's much harder when it's simply a hunch. There was some luck in Bill's story. However, considering his family background – his father going to the Great War; his older brother, the second; growing up through the Depression; his mother suffering from severe mental health issues all her life; and him gaining entry to the medical faculty by scholarship, the first in his family to do so – he was hardly undeserving of some luck in his life.

A second key factor in the story of thalidomide was the rise of investigative journalism teams in the large broadsheet newspapers. In this, too, there was an Australian element, in that a key reporter for the London *Sunday Times* Insight team, Phillip Knightley, was not only Australian but a fellow Canterbury High graduate. Another UK-based reporter, John Pilger, a graduate of Sydney Boys High and ten years younger than Phillip and my father, also took up Bill's cause.

It took several years of investigating, and various battles along the way, before a series of articles in the early 1970s exposed the lack of oversight in the pharmaceutical industry. Phillip would later co-write a book about the scandal, *Suffer the Children*, published in 1979.

While the manufacturers could be forgiven for not anticipating the unprecedented effects on the foetus, the marketing of the drug had encouraged people to take it. Safety concerns hadn't been highlighted.

Bill McBride was lucky that he had such a strong journalistic team on his side. In the future he wouldn't be so lucky. As the 1960s began, when he was still in his early thirties, Bill had achieved what he'd set out to achieve as a small boy. He even bought part of the farm in Dungog that had given him such happy memories.

One thing that could never be taken away from my father was his unfailing love of Australia. Unlike his hero, Florey, and many others who achieved international success, Dad had no desire to move to either the UK or the US. Australia had given him all his opportunities, and as far as he was concerned, it was the best country in the world. He was never happier than when swimming at a Sydney beach with his children or grandchildren. That, for him, was better than any other place, and he kept that love to the day he died. He wanted his children to grow up as Australians, and to give them the best possible opportunities – like his ancestors before him.

CHAPTER 4

Passion, Patton, Paris, Prayer

I was born post-thalidomide in 1963. We'd recently moved to that bigger house in Blakehurst, as there were now four children under seven years of age. For my parents, life largely revolved around kids and work.

The first thing that happened to me, straight after coming out of the hospital with my mother, wrapped in a towel, was a trip to the country; that is, the much-loved family farm at Dungog. This involved a five-hour trip with three toddlers in the back seat – every available space in the car crammed with food and toys, Dad driving manically, and Mum cradling me on her lap. It was a heatwave and about 40 degrees Celsius, and air-conditioning consisted of twisting the funny triangular section of the front side windows outwards, and Dad driving as fast as he could, with dust raining in on the car, on the many dirt roads on the way to Dungog.

It was a mythical place. We used to go there a couple of times a year, nearly every Easter and Christmas. We rode horses and motorbikes around the paddocks, without any skill or safety precautions, and the shops still sold lollies for one cent (they were more expensive in the city). For little boys it was heaven, just like my father had experienced thirty years before.

I don't remember any trauma in my early years. In fact, being the youngest of four children with a father who was living his dream, and a mother who was very compassionate and considerate, was a pretty good gig. I spent most of my first years largely accompanying my mother on her various outings to the local greengrocer, relatives, and, best of all, David Jones – and then at kindergarten and school. I didn't particularly like either. After my first day at kindy, I told my family I wanted to 'resign'.

Blakehurst was a nice, if unfashionable, suburb. It was typical of Australia at the time: we walked around the neighbourhood freely, and played in the houses of our neighbours as they played in ours. We weren't the richest people in our street by any means. That was the 'millionaires' up the road, who not only had a red Ferrari Dino, but a polar-bear rug (although we'd never actually seen it) and a *full-sized pool table*.

Our tastes were quite simple, and the family across the road had a 'Pirates of the Caribbean' themed wine cellar, complete with gold coins lying in rock pools, and mini-waterfalls, and my brother John and I thought it the most amazing thing we'd ever seen. Like most other kids at the time, we had the usual diet of American TV, and occasionally the Australian wrestling on a Saturday morning with our grandfather, Jack. He'd let us hold him down while he 'slapped the mat', begging for mercy.

There's a saying that what you want to be when you're seven years old is what you really want in life. It was true with my father, with his dreams of Florey and being a respected doctor, and it was equally true of me. While there were many examples of 'snakes and ladders' in my life to come, I think it's fair to say that from the age of seven I had the blueprint of my life, or least my character, in my head, even if the harder part, *the practice*, didn't come till much later.

There were a few formative experiences for me during these years. I didn't see much of my father, who worked until past my dinnertime each night, and left the house long before I woke up most mornings. I accepted that this was the price to be paid for the life we lived. I don't remember ever resenting him for not being present.

I also understood that his job was to help people and that he was good at it. I knew this because people from the newspapers would occasionally come to take our photos as a family. As well, when we walked down the street together, former patients of his would sometimes come up to him and thank him for the birth of their child, and even children would shake his hand. He delivered over fifteen hundred babies in Crown Street alone and this was his greatest pleasure.

Despite his work commitments, he tried to be as present as possible for us as a father. One photo illustrates this well: it's Christmas Day in the mid-1960s, and Dad is sitting on the bed surrounded by kids holding up their favourite present. He's probably just returned from the hospital, delivering a child, and looks absolutely exhausted.

He wasn't a warm fuzzy dad – most fathers weren't in those days – but he was certainly there for me, and was keen to spoil me. He travelled a lot and would always bring home exotic presents, especially for me as the youngest. When I was about four years old, I was one of the first kids to have a motorised toy car – a mini-Formula 1 powered by motorcycle battery – which I sat in and drove around the house with great gusto. It was quite big and heavy, yet he'd insisted on buying it, and bringing it on the plane to Sydney as carry-on luggage, oblivious to any possible inconvenience to other passengers. He never took check-in luggage, and would have all his clothes in a huge suit bag, much to the flight attendants' bemusement.

It was times like this that his enthusiasm and complete lack of practicality was a gift; later, not so much. He seemed to enjoy watching me drive that ride-on car as much as I enjoyed it myself. He was clearly happy to be able to give me the sort of things he'd only dreamed of, growing up in Bexley during the Depression.

He was forever frugal in some things, though, refusing to buy shaving cream, saying that soap was just as good, and reusing disposable razors for what seemed like years. His travelling bags were always full of the tiny shampoos and soaps from hotels he'd stayed in.

I knew that our lifestyle came from his hard work. He had a study downstairs, with a bay window that looked out onto the garden. Usually, when he was at home, he was in there, working late into the night reading and writing scientific papers. His method of filing was unusual, but one I was also to adopt: lay all the papers you are using out on the floor like a carpet of snow. Also, he never worked on just one project at a time: there'd be everything from decades-old medical journals to Hereford bull pedigrees strewn across the floor. Naturally, he frequently misplaced things, but Mum always knew where to find them.

The study had a distinct smell of old wood and stale papers. I'd try to read some of them but they were in dry scientific language, with lots of tables with figures and strange symbols, interspersed with Latin medical terminology like 'teratogens': the creation of monsters. There were photos of babies with malformed limbs as well, and plates of undefined foetuses.

Even as a kid, I knew I was lucky to be healthy, and perhaps had an overdeveloped sense of guilt for my good fortune. But Dad set an example of giving something back. We never spoke about it, but we didn't have to. He could be brusque at times; however, his heart was in the right place. I was about to start at school. There, I'd encounter people who were the opposite of that, and I'd come to appreciate his way even more.

Aged six, I went with my mother and brother to be measured up for my boarding-school uniforms and belongings. Even being measured for the uniforms had an air of joining the army about

it, but only the boring bits. In January 1971, my brother and I –
with our suitcases with our initials painted on them – boarded
an old train at night, and set off for school. We were heading for
Tudor House in Moss Vale, in the Southern Highlands, about
80 miles away. It was the first of many institutions of which I'd
become a member. In many ways this was the beginning of the
formation of my adult personality.

I hated the first few weeks of boarding school and remember
crying a lot. I'm not sure it was because I missed my parents; it was
probably more that I missed my television and general freedom.
While not quite Dickensian, it was certainly regimented. It
seemed fairly humourless, although there were soon rays of light
as I discovered things about the place that I actually liked.

The first was 'competition', which was basically polite and
organised fighting, either in the classroom, or on the sports field.
In those days it was quite acceptable for teachers to organise
games where the boys had to hop on one leg and knock each
other over, until only one was left standing. This was more
exciting than home life with a couple of older sisters.

I was also read stories of the great acts of daring of World War II:
The Wooden Horse and *Escape from Colditz*. Once I began to see
school not as some sort of holiday camp, but rather a military
prison camp in which the teachers were to be defied, and games
were to be won, it became far more enjoyable.

A second major thing that was to shape my outlook on life
happened that year. Dad had been awarded a prize by a new
French organisation called the Institut de la Vie, which seemed
to be some sort of Gallic answer to the Nobel Prize. At the same
time, he was sponsored for a trip for the whole family by the oil
company BP, as some sort of ambassador, so we were taken out of
school for about six weeks during the European summer. Off we
went to places unknown.

Our first stop was Bangkok and I remember getting off the
plane at night and feeling the humidity and excitement of being

in the Far East. This place felt alive. The terminal was rudi-
mentary, and my brother and I were fascinated to see stuffed
cobras arranged upright, with flashing fangs and glass eyes, as
if they were fighting a mongoose to the death. It was a real-life
re-creation of Kipling's 'Rikki Tikki Tavi', which our teacher had
read to us at school.

We got Dad to buy us snakeskin belts, to go with the suede
Easy Rider-style tassel jackets we'd been given for Christmas and
which I treasured. Back on the plane we were transfixed by the
beautiful and elegant French air hostesses, who fussed over my
brother and me, and handed out sweets to us from a big bag.

Sometime during the long trip – which included a second refu-
elling stop in Bahrain – the family looked around and couldn't
find me. I'd seen flashes of the movie in the next section, through
the curtain that opened a little, and I snuck in to investigate.
I stood transfixed, and eventually one of the hostesses moved
me to an empty seat so I could settle in to watch. My feet didn't
even reach the floor, so I must have looked comical. The movie
was *Patton*, the story of the controversial US general, George S.
Patton, starring George C. Scott. I was already fascinated by the
military, but this seemed to be exactly what I wanted in life.

Once I returned to the family, who were quite bemused by
my choice of movie, I finally got some sleep, and I woke up as we
descended into Paris. We arrived at Charles de Gaulle Airport
and from there journeyed to a once-grand hotel on the Left Bank,
notorious for being the headquarters of the Gestapo during
World War II.

The Institut de la Vie ceremony was every bit as grand as its
would-be competitor. It was held in the historic Hall of Mirrors
in the Palace of Versailles, with everyone dressed in black tie and
my father receiving the award from President Georges Pompidou.
The event was televised, and Dad even made a short speech in
French. My brother and I just clapped when everyone else did,
and marvelled at how shiny the VIPs' shoes were. We had to

clean our own shoes each day at boarding school, but we'd never seen such incredible shine.

It was a great occasion, although quite boring for a seven and ten-year-old, so my brother and I we keen to get up to mischief as soon as we could. Our greatest prank, which almost ended in disaster, was climbing over the safety rail at the top of the Arc de Triomphe, and dangling our legs over the side. We were promptly grabbed by a furious gendarme, who dragged us to his office and ranted to us in broken English. We cried when we heard the world 'jail', before our mother eventually came and rescued us.

From Paris we went to London, which was equally beautiful. I saw the Horse Guards ride past our hotel, and they made an impression. We then went back to mainland Europe and drove south through West Germany, Switzerland and finally on to Italy. On the way we met some Americans holidaying in France who were wonderful, and another rich family in Rome who appalled my mother by the amount of food they ordered and then left on the table untouched.

Europe in the summer of 1971 made a big impression on me. I had seen it at its best: the birthplace of democracy and human rights, prosperous and fair, and it valued scholarship and good works, or so it appeared to me. We went home via the USA, and saw the sights there as well: the Empire State Building and Disneyland. We finished with a week in Hawaii, where we tried surfing at Waikiki.

It had been an incredible six weeks that would change my life, or at least shape my perspective on the world. The West was something good that was worth protecting, and I hoped one day I might be able to play my part in doing so.

Back in Australia and back at school, life was pretty drab in comparison. I spent endless hours staring up at the large world map that hung above the teacher's desk: that was my classroom, and I couldn't wait to get back.

The final major piece of my personality sprung up in the endless church services we had to attend at school. I began to nurture a belief in a child-like warrior god who could be called upon in times of great fear to give you courage and strength. The combination of the idea of a childlike Jesus, and the stories of David and Goliath, and others, had an effect which has stayed with me all my life.

The tiny chapel seemed bright and uplifting to my seven-year-old eyes. I was always drawn to the three stained-glass windows near the lectern. The window on the right depicted a rugby player in Tudor House colours of red, white and blue, leaping for the ball; the one on the far left, St George slaying the dragon. It seemed like a good story to me, not because of any grandiose ideas of my own, but because here was a man who'd used his faith in God to fight something that was considered invincible. He even married the princess in the end, or that could have been my own wishful thinking.

Having been to Sunday school before I came to boarding school, I already had a concept of Jesus. I had no problem praying to him; not so much that I might be good, but that I might be strong and one day slay a dragon.

The window in the middle featured an image of Jesus Christ being crucified. I wasn't interested in that, though: suffering for the sake of suffering wasn't very appealing. But rugby and St George seemed to make sense.

CHAPTER 5

The Pebble, the Bible and the Book

In some ways, I was a paradox as a kid. I was strong for my age, and liked to test myself with feats of endurance or fear. At home in Blakehurst I practised underwater swimming and could do over twenty yards even as a six-year-old, far more than my older brothers and sisters. When I was a little older, at night at boarding school, I often couldn't sleep, so to relieve the boredom I'd climb out the windows of the old first-floor building, which to us looked like a haunted house or castle, and onto the steel fire-escape ladders that led up, as well as downwards.

The steel rungs felt cold on my hands and feet, and the moonlight a beautiful silver. I would just be in my pyjamas, because a dressing-gown would have hindered my movement as I shimmied up the drainpipes, and then on all fours up the final ladder to the siren box, a wooden pigeon-coop-type structure at the very pinnacle of the building's steep, sloping slate roofs. I'd do this alone as no-one else seemed interested in trading sleep for adventure, and it meant a definite 'sandshoe' – being bent over and hit on the backside with a sandshoe, a junior version of a caning – if

I got caught. I didn't do anything in particular while I was up on the roof, just sat and enjoyed the guilty pleasure of a successful 'escape'.

At the same time, however, I could be emotional and, at times, scared. If the teacher asked a question and I put up my hand and got it wrong, I felt ashamed. I worked hard in class and being publicly wrong was like poison to me.

Despite being quite comfortable on the highest rooftops at night, there were certain parts of the school I didn't like being alone in at all, as if I could feel the presence of ghosts. We were taught in chapel that the Angel of Death was real, killing the eldest son of all Egyptian families in a single night, and that Jesus rose from the grave after three days, so it seemed illogical to me that vampires couldn't exist. I wasn't about to hang around in dark parts of the school on my own to find out. One such dark night led to the 'Pebble Incident'.

Dad, like most middle-class parents of the day, wanted all his children to play an instrument, and I was 'given' the piano. It was a good choice for me as I enjoyed it. Our family all went to see *The Sting*. Dad and I loved the Scott Joplin music from the movie, and I practised till I could play a simplified version of it. My music career was to be short lived, however, ruined by a combination of Miss Sherwood and the *Phantom of the Opera*.

My piano teacher at boarding school was Miss Sherwood. She was about as tall as me, as an eight-year-old, and she wore knitted gloves, with the tips of her fingers exposed. Both my brother and I were colour blind, and while I had a good ear for music, I also seemed somehow to be 'music blind' – in that I couldn't look at sheet music and translate it to the placement of my fingers on the keys. While I was able to rote learn a tune by the movements and beat alone, I found deciphering the quavers and semi-quavers on the lines on the page was near impossible. Perhaps thinking I was doing it on purpose, Miss Sherwood would hit my fingers with a steel-edged ruler that she kept in her purse for just this purpose. While it caused me no lasting trauma and was probably a good way to get through to me, it made our lessons together a comical mix of scales and yelps. But worse was yet to come.

Although music lessons were scheduled during the lunch-hour, practice was at night, while all the other students were eating their dinner on the other side of the school. There were three pianos on the premises, all at the outer extremities, but the particular one I had to use was furthest away and tucked into a dark room at the back of the stage section of the school hall.

The school hall seemed like a concert hall at our age, and had a professional set of curtains, and rigging above the stage, which only the senior students were able to operate. Boys being boys, there was a lot of talk of a dead kid up in the attic. It was only a discarded mannequin, but I didn't like being in its vicinity on my own at night. I'd seen *Phantom of the Opera*, and I could never be quite sure whether someone was creeping up on me from behind as I played in the dark expanse. While I was brave enough on the school roofs, something about having my back turned to the danger unnerved me, especially with the echoing sounds and the wind in the tall pine trees outside. There was a lot of looking over my shoulder, and not that much practising of Miss Sherwood's set scales.

Having successfully avoided being attacked by whatever evil stalked the hall after dark, I made my way back through the trees to the other side of the school to snatch a hurried dinner that would be laid out waiting for me, as the rest of the students were finishing theirs. Making it back into the relative safety of lights and away from the 'living dead' of the concert hall, my mood changed to one of mischief. I'd just had a very boring thirty minutes of piano practice, followed by a narrow escape from a possible vampire attack, and now it was time for some pre-dinner fun.

This particular evening, I knew that my friend Rupert, one of the naughtiest boys in school, was in the sick bay - likely malingering, I figured. After failing to get him to come to the window by whispering his name a few times, I thought I'd attract his attention and maybe get him to climb out the window, or some such prank. I picked up one of the many tiny pebbles that made up the huge gravel driveway that encircled the school building, and pitched it up through the open window to see if I could rouse him.

The pebble hit the polished wood floors and made an awful racket. The next thing I knew, the scary hospital matron – with a look that could turn you to stone – was at the window, her 'flying nun' style bonnet flapping around in the breeze as she shouted angrily 'Who threw that? Who's out there?'

I knew better than to hang around and was off like a saboteur escaping into the shadows of the central school buildings, and down the ancient row of bricks that sagged in the middle from decades of boys trudging to the dining hall, speckled by years of pigeon poop. Pleased with myself for my escape-and-evasion abilities, I entered the dining hall, a little flushed but relieved. Here was food and shelter. I sat down at the far table with the boys who were just finishing and began to eat.

The dining hall was like everything else at school: small and unremarkable for adults, but huge and imposing for children. There was a high table at one end where the teachers sat, in their suits and sports jackets, and the students sat far below on a number of long wooden tables, with senior boys at the head to control the behaviour of the juniors like myself. I must have looked pale because a boy a few years older than me asked why I looked so breathless. I said something like 'I just had a lucky escape', and as soon as I'd got the words out, the much-feared headmaster stood up from the high table and the whole hall fell silent.

'School, I just had a very disturbing report from the Matron,' he said severely, 'that a boy threw a rock into the hospital. I want to know who it was. Stand up immediately.'

The school stayed silent, and while most were simply confused as to what he was talking about, the senior boy I'd been talking to looked straight at me as if to say, 'Well, that's obviously you.'

I looked down and fidgeted, terrified. There was no way I was going to stand up. Not in front of the whole school. Eventually, the headmaster sat down and the crisis passed, but my conscience had been pricked. I knew even then I should have admitted to it, and taken the caning that would undoubtedly have followed. It would have been a brave thing for an eight-year-old to do, but it was clearly the right thing to do. Bravery under fire was easy in theory, harder in practice.

Some things about the school were brilliant, although unlikely to be continued today. Laying steel traps for rabbits on the extensive school property was allowed. While this seems cruel, the alternative was poisoning by the local council, which was probably a slower death. Dad bought me ten new steel traps, which, unlike the older ones in circulation, closed with a tenacity that could take a boy's finger off.

I used to sneak out of the boarding house before dawn to check the traps, and to set them before dusk each night, carefully sprinkling dirt and leaves on top of the jaws to disguise the sharp silver teeth. I enjoyed doing this, as I'd enjoyed trapping possums in a wooden-crate-style trap in our rented house at Palm Beach.

Each possum I trapped I was given seven dollars pocket money, which seemed like a fortune. My friends and I had visions of making money from the cured rabbit skins, and bought the chemicals for tanning, but must have got the mixture wrong, because usually the skins were turned to hard hides, with large holes, to boot. Still, it was a useful lesson, and the sort of thing we would never have been able to do in a normal school.

Rugby was my first love, and I excelled at it at Tudor House, although athletics and cricket, not so much. My desire to emulate my heroes Dennis Lillee and Jeff Thomson, putting fear in the hearts of batsmen, came to nothing. I loved sports in which, if you gave your all, it was rewarded. For that there was nothing like judo, which I discovered in my third year, and soon became my new obsession.

Each Thursday was judo night, and I felt a thrill every time I put my uniform on. We met in the school hall, laid out the mats and then commenced a rigorous routine of sit-ups, push-ups and forward rolls. There was lots of chanting and slapping of the mats.

We were lucky to have an internationally renowned coach, Bill Broadhead, a huge, bearded man who spoke quietly but commanded huge respect. He was a man I wanted to emulate. By the time I was in my final year, I was the strongest in the class and he'd demonstrate moves using me as his partner. He was constantly reminding me to use skill to take my opponents off balance, and that this – not winning – was the essence of good judo. I didn't listen, of course, and continued doing what I had always done, because up until now it had worked.

At the end of each year there was a carol service, which the parents all attended, and the night before there was a judo exhibition. This was the highlight of the school year for me, particularly as it preceded the summer holidays. Two teams lined up either side of the sea of mats in the centre of the hall. The bright lights shone down on us, and the parents and brothers and sisters all sat in hushed silence on either side. The teams were ordered from the youngest to the oldest, and the match began with the first two junior kids facing off and bowing to each other before commencing their contest.

The winner stayed on the mat and then matched up against the next boy in the line on the other team. One by one the contests progressed, until it came to me, the last in the line on my side. The opposing team still had three boys left, meaning I had to successfully defeat all three if my team was to win. It was a chance for glory, and I relished it.

I won the first fight, and while I stumbled on the second, won that as well. Finally, I had to go up against a friend, who was about my size. He wasn't as strong as me when we were fresh, but immediately after two fights it was an even contest. We grappled in front of the hushed parents, who probably didn't know whether to be excited or appalled, as there was no doubt this was combat for twelve-year-olds, their sons fighting each other to the 'death', at least in their own minds.

I struggled as if my life depended on it, and to me it did, but to no avail. I was counted out and my friend was declared the winner. I was angry at myself, and felt a sense of shame in losing. To add insult to injury, my father didn't congratulate me, and even as many as thirty years later he continued to bring it up as the night I lost in front of so many people. Dad wasn't a mean person; in fact, he was a very kind one most of the time. However, his attitude to that night was not that of a good parent, and I vowed never to be the same for my own children.

As for learning the lesson Bill Broadhead wanted me to learn, it probably did eventually sink in, and perhaps using a larger opponent's weight against them is something I'm finally managing to do now. He died in the early 2000s, and while he had many thousands of students over the years, if he did remember me, his ghost would be smiling, probably laughing a huge belly laugh at me finally having learnt the lesson he was trying to teach me all those years ago.

There were more lessons to come, not all of them to do with my actions. Most teachers at the school were nice enough, and even the headmaster would smile when he saw you – if he wasn't about to 'sandshoe' you. But the deputy head was different. He was always sombre, and was at his most earnest when quoting the Bible. I don't remember ever seeing him not wearing a brown jacket, white shirt and tie, even when supervising the boys' shower time. He was a humourless character and the temperature seemed to drop whenever he was around. He always carried that

Bible, and I remember the red hair of his hairy knuckles poking out over his gold signet ring, when he rolled up his sleeves to hit you with the sandshoe. Not everybody who carries a Bible acts like Jesus.

The final lesson was a private, thoughtful one. While we had church services at boarding school every day except Saturday, there was also a weekly assembly, before lunch on Friday. In these assemblies, the students would be seated in neat rows of steel stackable chairs, and the headmaster would walk from the back of the hall in a dramatic fashion, holding a book.

Usually, this tome lived on its own in a glass case, with a single white glove next to it. The only person with the key was the headmaster and, each week, while we all waited for him in the hall, he'd open the case, put on the white glove and turn the page of the book. Each page contained a single name in gold letters. Then, at the assembly, he would commence by reading out that name, followed by a moment's silence. Each name was an old boy of the school who had died in one of the two world wars. We didn't know how or where they'd been killed; just that perhaps ten years earlier they'd been climbing trees, carrying out pranks on each other and catching rabbits, just like we did now: except that they'd gone off to fight in a foreign war and never returned.

It stayed with me, however, as I knew that whatever jokes we played, and whatever carefree lives we lived, we only did so because of the sacrifice of those people in that book. Boys just like us: no better, no worse. But they'd stood up when the country asked. Good things in life were largely procured by sacrifice, and privileged kids like us, who had reaped the benefits of this country more than anyone, were the people to do it if it ever became necessary.

CHAPTER 6

Kings, Princesses and Prince's Gate

Most of us at Tudor House went on to the senior school. King's School in Parramatta was a strange blend of English public school and some of the best and worst things about Australia. In 1976, for a twelve-year-old, it was largely a place to survive. However, the facilities were good and there were some excellent teachers for those who were willing to learn, although the cane swung like a sword for those who weren't.

Again, it was exactly the right school for me. It taught resilience and discipline and made us into good young men in the best sense of that word, even though I didn't necessarily understand it at the time. Forty years later I continue to be impressed by the strength of character of my fellow schoolmates. Some of that character might be genetic, some from family, but undoubtedly a lot is from the influence of King's. While education may not be an exact science, and for some it wasn't the right school, there is no doubt that I would neither be where I am today, nor have survived, without the tools and values supplied to me by the two schools I attended.

While King's is known for its archaic military-style uniform – referred to as the dress uniform – most of the time we wore practical blue shirts and baggy, patched trousers. In the 1970s and eighties the school was still dominated by tough kids from the larger farms in New South Wales, who could shoot, drive and ride to a high standard before they were twelve. While there was a certain *Lord of the Flies* flavour about it, it wasn't all negative. I think if the school had had to drive a mob of cattle from Sydney to Darwin, they would have achieved it, with all of the cattle surviving, and most of the boys.

In retrospect, the fact that the school hat was the trademark of both the ANZACs and – in the 1970s, anyway – a notorious bikie gang said a lot. No matter how shabby or small we were, we King's students were soldiers – boy soldiers, no doubt, but soldiers nonetheless. Not many people from my school joined the army. In fact, I'm the only one I know of, and I joined the British Army. Perhaps it was because they felt they had already done their time.

Ironically, this was a period of my life when I thought less about the military than any before or after. I focused on study, with the inspiration coming from some very clever, slightly eccentric teachers who didn't let the strict religious code that pervaded the upper echelons of the school make their lessons boring.

Again, I was lucky in all sorts of ways. As with Tudor House, boys' schools, at that time, were not entirely safe environments. While the chances of you becoming a victim weren't high, you still had to keep your wits about you.

The biggest threat was straight-out bullying, and the late seventies was not a time to be different from your peers. The harsh reality was that many of the boys carried mental scars from their time at King's for the rest of their life. Some ended their lives eventually, their feelings of isolation and hopelessness exacerbated by the treatment they received from their fellow students. I'd like to say I was a defender of the weak against the strong, but the reality was that, while I was one of those who felt pangs of guilt at the treatment of others, I didn't feel I could stand up against it, lest the unwanted attention turn to me. I wish I had made a stand, and my conscience has never quite let me forget that I didn't. Forty years have passed since I left King's, yet I still remember the things I did right, and the things I failed to do. One more than the other.

One thing I did do right was to learn that, if I committed to something, I could surprise even myself. When I was about fifteen, students from our whole year were lined up in the huge gymnasium and, one by one, we had to do chin-ups in front of the other students. The number we achieved was recorded. I'd grown quite lean and, as I approached the bar with everyone watching, I was full of fear. I jumped up, caught the bar and strained for a few seconds . . . but couldn't even do one.

While I wasn't the only one who couldn't, I felt a burning shame, and was desperate to improve. In the boarding house I found a strong bar that was used to hold up the dress uniforms after they'd been drycleaned, and each night, while the other kids were probably smoking or looking at *Penthouse*, I practised. I also did a hundred push-ups. Later in the year we had to redo the same test, again in front of the whole school year. This time, the combination of practice, determination and a little bit of fear produced a different result: thirteen, one of the highest numbers of anyone.

I did pretty well at school at history, debating, drama and English literature. I didn't particularly excel at sport, which was frustrating at the time, because it was the talented sportsmen who got most of the acclaim at King's. In retrospect, I was probably fortunate, though, because with my hunger for success, if I'd been in the first team in any sport, I would likely have pursued it to extreme lengths, at the expense of all else.

As it was, an unseen hand seemed to ensure I was allowed to achieve just enough not to be disheartened, but not so much that I was sure of the path ahead. My Higher School Certificate result was a case in point. I got a slightly lower mark than I expected, but it was just enough to get me into Law. Had I done Arts/Law, which was more fashionable and harder to get into, I would have been on the main campus for the first few years – rather than at the city-based Law School. I might have been too distracted there to complete the degree.

If, on the other hand, I'd had a dream result in my exams, and got a high enough mark to get into Medicine, I may well have taken that path. While some parts of me would have enjoyed that course, the fact that I joined the army as soon as it was offered to me suggests that life in a hospital would have been too 'political' for me, and I would have consequently got into trouble.

Years later I met doctors who wanted to be soldiers, wanting to go into battle with the SAS teams, but it seemed they should have just been soldiers, or doctors, but not tried to be both at once. A soldier can treat a gunshot wound. A doctor can't bayonet someone. As for me, I wanted to fight, not heal, even if the decision was a close one.

Some of the highlights of the King's years were the summer holidays at Palm Beach, where my best friend and I became 'fresher' lifesavers, which meant we'd passed our basic proficiency. It opened up a world of parties, dancing, kissing and pranks. I'll never forget the feeling of surfing before the sun came fully up, sometimes even at night after a few cans of beer.

Palm Beach had a multitude of tropical flowers – including hibiscus and frangipani – that would provide an unmistakable fragrance. It was the smell of freedom. Tantalising, and only a few years away as I approached the HSC. I learnt to drive and after a few failed attempts got my licence and the use of the family 'learner' car – a nondescript but much-loved white Toyota Corolla.

Around that time, I was also nurturing an interest in the birth of democracy, the development of rights, and leadership. The history I loved the most was the story of the Spanish Armada, its preparation and defeat in 1588, both by Sir Francis Drake and the almost divine intervention of weather. Good seemed to prevail when it needed to. In a different era, I thought that the medieval persecution of the Jews, and the later persecution of the Huguenots, was an extreme failure of fair and just principles – and the extremes of Christianity at the time seemed no better than extreme political ideologies of later years. It's probably not fashionable to think this way today, but it was the 1970s and that was what we learnt about.

We had some enlightened teachers who prescribed books that would likely not be allowed in our present world. One was John Reed's *Ten Days That Shook the World*, a positive and empathetic first-hand account of the Bolshevik revolution in Russia in 1917 (by an American, no less), at a time when the Cold War was still raging. It was an inspired choice, as was the study of the Andrew Lloyd Webber musical *Evita*. Not only was the music an evocative change in an otherwise boring classroom, it was a piece of history that otherwise we wouldn't have known anything about. Books like *Sons and Lovers*, *Wuthering Heights*, *Far from the Madding Crowd* and *The Mayor of Casterbridge* set me up for a love of the English landscapes of oak trees, stone fences and harsh season changes. Adventures like *Prester John* inspired bravery and adventure in exotic locations.

Although I'd given up my immediate desire to do anything military related, two events did make a big impression. In 1980, the SAS had stormed the Iranian Embassy in London, abseiling off the roof – using their brains, brawn and quick thinking to save the lives of innocent hostages. The following year, I was impressed by the wedding of Prince Charles and Lady Diana, in particular the soldiers riding beside the carriage. It wasn't so much the spectacle that I wanted to be a part of, but I knew that at both events there were military people who were the real thing; the best of the best to keep democracy safe. They weren't in a school room and they weren't talking a lot of hot air in parliament. They were at the coalface: saving lives and risking their own in the process. It looked more interesting than being a lawyer, but it also felt a long way away.

When final exams came around, I put in a fair bit of effort. Actually, I overstudied on the subjects I liked, like modern history, and understudied on those I was less excited about, such as maths, physics and chemistry. The exams were pretty stressful, but it was a good challenge to face. I neither excelled nor had any great disasters. I was happy they were over. We did the usual trip up the coast, with the same few friends who'd surfed together at Palm Beach. This consisted of jumping off cliffs into the lagoon in Yamba, burnt barbecued sausages and the usual heavy drinking for eighteen-year-olds, which was about four cans and vomiting in the bushes, but we were pretty happy.

This wasn't where I wanted to be, though. Europe, and particularly England, was such a focal point in my life. All the music I listened to – the punks, the New Romantics – and most of the history I was interested in had emerged from there. As soon as we got back to Sydney, I was on a flight, heading to see my older sister, Catherine, in Paris.

On the plane journey to the northern hemisphere, I reflected upon something that had been on my mind a lot lately. I didn't make it obvious to others – that wasn't the King's way – but now that my schooldays were over, I knew what I wanted to be in a perfect world, and I didn't see any reason why I shouldn't succeed at it. My father had gone a long way from Canterbury Boys High, without showing any great promise at school. It may seem arrogant, or entitled, but when a sports person has self-belief we call it a winning attitude, so why should others have to be embarrassed for having dreams as big?

CHAPTER 7

Grads and Undergrads and Fellows

Catherine had been living in Paris for the past year, working as a model. She was a flatmate of a stylish French couple in a central arrondissement on the Right Bank, while I stayed in a tiny cheap hotel on the Left. We went to lunch and dinner, and shopped, and watched old movies in tiny cinemas. I coaxed her to come skiing with me and we went to Courchevel in the French Alps for a week. Later, I took the train to Saint Anton, in the Alps in Austria, where I met some Australian boys, Tony, Geoff and Dave, who were also from Sydney and had just done their HSC.

We were all enrolled to study Law, although none of the four of us had any intention of becoming lawyers. They were set on business careers, and in many ways we could not have been more different, but that was probably the attraction.

When I got back to start Law School after two months in Europe, it was reassuring to know that I already had three friends there. They all lived near us and we did a lot of things together, which made the whole first-year experience more enjoyable.

The two mainstays of those years were the Law School and the rugby club, not necessarily in that order. I'd excelled at rugby at Tudor House, not so much at King's. That was probably because I grew late, and then very fast, and was still growing even after I left school.

At Sydney University, or University of Sydney as it rather pompously called itself, my ability at rugby was restored. I realise in retrospect that the rugby club was like a military unit. There was lots of hard work, camaraderie, singing and drinking. I was not a big drinker at this stage, but I soon learnt the lesson: no matter how badly you lost a game, three schooners of beer and you didn't care that much.

Rugby is basically combat without weapons. The only purpose of the ball is to indicate where that violence should be directed at any one time. It's good practice for facing fear, because you get graded according to your ability at the time, which means that however good you are you will generally be up against someone who is either just as good or better, depending on who is more motivated, both before (in training), and on the day.

My rugby career might have been slightly hindered by my social life - or, more precisely, girls. Even as a four-year-old, I'd been fascinated by a blonde nanny from New Zealand changing her clothes in front of me. Likewise, the icons of the late sixties, such as Jane Fonda and Raquel Welch had created vague images in my mind of the sort of people I wanted in my life. I liked women, and some liked me back, and as the years progressed, I was increasingly late or hungover when I arrived at games on a Saturday morning.

Apart from the shaking of heads from team-mates, it was pretty much accepted. There was one of every type in our group, from the eccentric biologist, to the student politician, to the dour, future orthopaedic surgeon, so my particular brand of eccentricity was simply part of the liquorice all-sorts that made up our club. At the end of the day, we put the team above whatever other interests we had, at least on Tuesday, Thursday and Saturday, and that was all that mattered.

At the end of my third year with the rugby club, it was decided that we would go on a tour of the USA and Canada. In January, we set off for San Francisco in our team blue blazers and rather ugly grey trousers. Actually, when I say 'tour', once we'd arrived in the US it was a sort of three-week 'spring break' with some rugby in between. We all bought as much duty-free alcohol as we were entitled to on the way over, and then proceeded to consume it as rapidly as possible.

I was probably the first to find an American girlfriend, and definitely the first to get dropped from the team for being late to training, having woken up in San Jose, a fair drive from San Francisco. The fact that I was dropped off at training, late, but in a red Corvette with a blonde at the wheel, produced cries of derision and respect in equal measure. Our coach, Peter King, was forced to drop me from the team, to set an example (although he seemed to quite enjoy his role of long-suffering 'parent' to his crew of ratbags).

Kingie, who worked as a barrister, was an educated eccentric who could quote Greek philosophers, but was also highly likely to lose his car keys. He was a mild-mannered professor off the field, but possessed an unexplained capacity for aggression and tenacity, once on the park. We all genuinely liked him, although we were confused by him at times, largely because, like us, he was '100 per cent Uni'. My path would cross significantly with Kingie's some years later, in a very different world.

Despite the distractions, I did complete my Law degree. However, while I managed to pass each subject, I wasn't the scholar I had been at King's. My father despaired a little of me, although my mother was very sweet, bringing Berocca and orange juice to my bedside on Saturday mornings when she knew I'd be likely to need them.

After that trip to North America, I decided on a change of academic direction. I'd always been passionate about movies (from *Patton* to *The Sting* to the obscure French arthouse productions), so I applied for entry into film school at the University of Southern California: the (George) Lucas School of Film Production. It was an area I found more interesting than law, and there was a chance to make the sort of epic movies that had influenced me growing up. I applied but didn't get in. Although I was disappointed, I was encouraged by the university to try again the next year.

My father, though, said I should apply for Oxford instead. As it happened, King's offered a scholarship to Oxford or Cambridge. So I applied, but didn't get that either. However, the person who'd won the scholarship, and whose university results had been much better than mine, couldn't get a place at Cambridge. The school came back to me with the fateful words: 'You were runner-up. Would you like to try to use it?'

CHAPTER 8

The Antipodean Argument

I contacted Oxford and said it would be a shame if the scholarship went to waste. Dad vaguely knew the provost of Oriel College, Sir Zelman Cowen, the former Australian governorgeneral and a distinguished professor of Law. I'm not sure how their paths had crossed, but Dad had received a number of awards, such as Commander of the British Empire (CBE), Order of Australia, Father of the Year, and was also on the University of Sydney 'Senate', of which he was most proud. I assume they must have met each other somewhere along the way, although they weren't close.

When your star is rising, everyone wants to know you, and when it's falling, no-one does. Again, I was lucky. This was before Dad's world came crashing down, and perhaps even a few years later they wouldn't have been 'friends'; although Sir Zelman struck me as someone slightly more compassionate and wise to the ways of the world than many of his successors.

I was only accepted for a one-year diploma, in the undergraduate faculty, so really it was just a foot in the door. I still didn't particularly want to be a lawyer, but I went anyway. It was a bit instinctive, in the same way that I'd completed my original Law degree without wanting to be a lawyer – or at least not being sure.

I knew I wouldn't be back in Australia for a while, so before I left I threw a party with all the friends I'd met through Sydney University. I got some invitations printed with a line from the Cold Chisel Vietnam anthem 'Khe Sanh', 'The last plane out of Sydney,' written in black in *Apocalypse Now* font. An interesting choice in retrospect. Underneath, there was a photo of Dad sitting at his desk in his doctor's rooms, looking at the camera, and saying something.

I added the caption, 'With good behaviour, you'll be home in one,' as if it was a prison sentence. It would have been slightly self-indulgent if I was coming home in twelve months, but as it turned out to be twelve years it was entirely appropriate. I knew my future lay overseas, at least at that point.

When I arrived in London I stayed with the family of Phillip Knightley, the *Sunday Times* journalist who'd been instrumental in turning Dad's findings about thalidomide into an international scandal. Phillip had married Yvonne, who was from Goa, and they had three children – two girls who were about my age and a younger boy. They lived in Notting Hill at a time when it was evolving from a 'bad address' to a posh suburb. Yvonne fussed over me, cooking me dish after dish, so I could be 'strong for the Boat Race' between Oxford and Cambridge, she'd say with a wink – in those days there was still an intense interest in the event. I was beginning to see how lucky I was to be going to Oxford.

Mum joined me in London a week later, and we hired a car and drove up to Oxford together. We found the roads highly confusing, and it took me a few years to realise that the 'A4 to Oxford' was a very different thing to the 'M4 to Oxford', even though at times you went from one to another.

We took the scenic route, making three stops. The first was at Runnymede, where the Magna Carta had been signed – what many people believe to be the beginnings of parliamentary democracy and the rule of law. We then visited the Royal Air Force memorial to the pilots who died in the Battle of Britain. This included many Australians, one of whom, Gordon McKay, who'd survived the war, had been a mentor for Dad. The memorial is on a high point that allows you to look back east over the city and imagine the sound of guns and engines in the sky in the summer of 1940, and to picture the individual pilots either surviving or dying. Looking out over the airspace where so many of them willingly went to their deaths, I had great respect for their sacrifice, and said a short prayer for what they had done.

I had got my pilot's licence a few years before, and even my aerobatic qualification, with a hope of one day perhaps becoming an air force pilot. My colour blindness made it impossible, but to be honest I didn't truly love it. While my friends and I had been thrilled by *Top Gun*, and loved all the corny lines, I was able to see the reality of flying. It didn't matter whether it was a fighter jet or a Cessna: you were in charge of machinery, rather than men, more like a racing car driver than a soldier.

The last stop was Maidenhead, a beautiful market town on the Thames. The exchange rate was good and while the prices for a Devonshire tea affronted Mum's frugal sensibility, she would never dream of being rude to staff – although we were both beginning to struggle to understand what the local people were saying, even an hour outside London. They didn't speak like they did on TV.

I didn't move into the college until the next day, so we spent the first night in Oxford in a hotel. There was a charm to the local area, and I was struck by how polite everyone was. I noticed even the police seemed incredibly friendly. Their first question was usually, 'What seems to be the problem?', and they called you 'Sir' as if they meant it. They were more than happy to give directions, which I couldn't imagine ever asking an Australian policeman.

It seemed like a place you could walk around late at night in safety. By and large, it appeared to be as benign as a film set, which in many ways it was. Not everyone was a student or a 'don', but a good percentage seemed to be, and it gave the place a great atmosphere.

The colleges at Oxford are all institutions in their own right, and each is like its own Hogwarts. The one I was going to, Oriel, had been founded in 1324. While the history seems complex, they adopted the coat of arms of a romantic figure, the Black Prince, who had won a major battle as a teenager, and whose symbol was three ostrich feathers with the motto, 'Ich Dein.' I serve. He was a great warrior with an element of tragedy about him, in that he died before he could succeed as king, leaving his young son to take the throne.

There were other things about Oriel's history I liked, including the fact that Walter Raleigh had been an undergraduate. In the early 1400s, the college had been a centre of rebellion against the excesses of the Roman Catholic Church, some of its scholars violently defending their right to pray directly to God, rather than purely through the Church hierarchy and saints. King Charles I had occupied the college buildings during the civil war in the mid-1600s, purloining some of its treasures for his cause. And in the modern era it was academia with a pulse, exemplified by the fact they not only routinely won the rowing regattas, they didn't mind celebrating with rowdy pagan-style burning of the boats ceremonies, where whole crews leapt through the flames with arms linked.

As well, in 1954, on the running track where we trained, Roger Bannister had achieved the first four-minute mile. Running a mile in less than four minutes had seemed impossible, but Bannister, an undergraduate medical student, achieved a feat that thrilled my father's generation. What I loved about this was the fact that Bannister was pursuing his studies at the time, rather than being a professional athlete. The track and its grandstand were largely unchanged from that day when it had been the centre of the world.

The college was right in the middle of town, and therefore always felt in the thick of whatever was going on. It was truly like a castle – part-boarding school, part-fortress. The premises were locked at night and if you were out later than 10 pm, you had to ring the doorbell to wake up the ancient porter. He was a lovely old boy who was a World War II veteran and had a strong West Country accent, which I could barely understand; nor could he understand me.

I was the only Australian at Oriel, although, as I've mentioned, the provost of the college was Sir Zelman Cowen. There were also some Americans, who were graduates from the Ivy League or Annapolis Naval Academy. Although I was studying Law, it was called Jurisprudence here, and my professor was a former Glaswegian truck driver. He'd studied Law part-time, and afterwards excelled as both a student and teacher. He was a good guy, and very clever. His appointment, probably like my own admission, showed there was nothing overly stuffy about the character of Oxford. Each person had much more to them than first appeared on the surface.

The whole place was filled with the unexpected. I worked hard in that first term – known as the Michaelmas term – which ran from October until Christmas, but it was fairly hard going. You had to neatly handwrite your essays with fountain pen, and as with any Law course there was a lot of reading and writing. They were subjects I'd done before – not that it helped much, as I hadn't worked very hard at Sydney University. My earlier studies probably did allow me to keep up with the very clever students around me, though, which was good for my confidence.

I met some amazing and inspiring young people, future leaders of the UK in whatever field they would choose. They were not all from private schools, by any means. Some had thick accents. One even wore a uniform already, and had been sponsored by the Royal Air Force (he would eventually go on to be chief of the RAF).

They were good people, better people than me, and I was lucky to be around them. They made me become a better person at a time in my life where I could have conceivably gone the other way. They say that one of the purposes of life is to meet people better than yourself and make them your friends, and this was pretty much my Oxford experience.

The atmosphere was inclusive, before that became a buzzword, and there were no real cliques. You knew everybody and had a smile for everybody, and vice-versa, whether you shared classes or not. While I was lucky to be there, and had arrived as an outlier academically, once I was at Oriel I generally lifted myself to their level. Although I knew Oxford was simply a railway junction before my next destination, it was an experience that would shape the way I acted from that point on. I wanted to ensure that I lived up to the privilege I had been given, which involved not just doing good things after I left, but making the most of the experience while I was there.

Among the many activities available was sport. Before I left Australia, but after I heard I'd been accepted at Oxford, I was at rugby training and got talking to our team captain, who happened to be Tony Abbott. He'd come back from Oxford a few years before, and advised me that if, like him, I didn't make the varsity rugby team, I should box.

He'd won a boxing Blue and he was very tough. He was earnest, driven by a fire within that I could relate to, and he didn't seem to mind what others thought of him. When he spoke of Oxford, he did so with a look of wistfulness and emotion that he couldn't quite put into words, particularly in relation to the friendships he made there. It was a look I would come to fully understand many years later.

Although I played well in the trials in rugby when I got to Oxford, I wasn't even put in the squad for the reserves. As it turned out this was lucky, because it meant I had no distractions when I tried out at the Oxford boxing club on a chilly, dark October evening. I was ready to commit, and a little bit pissed off about the rugby.

I still played rugby for Oriel, but if I had to make a choice between rugby and boxing, from that moment on it was no contest. In the same way judo had grabbed me as kid, I loved the one-on-one combat element. Rugby was a team game, and while there were occasional moments of individual play, basically it was working (and bickering) together as a group.

In boxing, however, you were completely on your own, and half the crowd wanted to see you get knocked senseless. It was the difference between playing in an orchestra and being a solo pianist. Funnily enough, my housemaster at school had said, disparagingly, that I had the temperament for a concert violinist. I guess he meant 'flashes of brilliance but overly dramatic and emotional', and he was probably right.

When I did a Myers-Briggs personality test many years later, I was amused at its one-word description of my type: the 'virtuoso'. It suggested I was a master of one particular skill, to a greater degree than most, but who had no desire to be in charge of others, because that would involve responsibility they didn't want, as they prefer to work alone.

Much to my children's amusement, an archetypal 'virtuoso' is Katniss Everdeen, the protagonist from the *Hunger Games* – originally a series of novels, of course, and one of the family movies we watch together. Typical of the way in which it's the people who are most like us who most annoy us, I'm always the most critical of Katniss's choices and actions. My father annoyed me much more than my mother, long before I realised we were in many ways, good and bad, almost the same person.

Over the dark winter months of 1986/87 I saw a side of England I hadn't noticed as a tourist years before. I was freezing and the local newspapers carried stories of the number of people who had simply died of the cold. It was so cold that training for the Boat Race had to be cancelled because the Thames froze over. It seemed to confirm that this place was more extreme than the Britain I'd seen before.

Margaret Thatcher was prime minister and there was a lot of division in the country; certainly, more anger than I had ever seen in Australia. However, in regional England I encountered 'the stayers': the descendants of those who didn't seek out greener pastures and greater opportunity like my ancestors. I saw them in long orderly queues for buses in the wind and the rain, grim-faced, not talking to one another as they waited their turn to get on the bus home. It was simply a phenomenon of a city centre and people all leaving work at the same time, but I'd never seen such long queues for essential services. It was the sort of thing we were told to expect in Moscow under the Soviet system.

I'd never seen such a flinty hardness in older people. Anyone over sixty in 1986 would remember the war – the bombing of London, Coventry and elsewhere, air raids, the food rationing, evacuations. A little bit of queuing for the bus in the cold and rain was nothing to them.

I was not in Sydney anymore, and while living in this strange place was sometimes maddening, I was also falling in love with the richness of British culture.

Just before Michaelmas ended, I went to a wine and cheese night advertising the Oxbridge ski week in Val-d'Isère in the French Alps. I decided to go on the excursion, as I wasn't heading home for Christmas and didn't particularly want to be alone in London in dark December. As a student-organised venture it was pretty budget priced. There was a charter flight there and back, and we were all staying in the same place – it was almost like a school trip. I knew one of the organisers from Oriel, so I wasn't completely alone. I'd always enjoyed skiing and had been on similar excursions at Sydney University.

On the trip I met Kit, whose real name was Christopher Rogers, a first-year biology student from Christ Church College who was to become my best friend. At first I gravitated towards those people I slightly knew from boxing, but I recognised in Kit someone who wasn't interested in acting in a conventional way. Perhaps we had some other similarities. I didn't know it at the time, but his father had had a sort of rise-and-fall story, involving negative media, and he seemed to take advantage of each day. Likewise, Kit noticed me, he told me later, because there was an enterprising Frenchman who was offering tandem rides on his hang-glider from the top of the mountain, down into the village, and I had tried it – which he'd thought was quite brave on my part.

As it was a package tour we all ate together. On one of the first nights, I was sitting with the boys I knew from rugby circles, and they were looking at Kit talking to everyone and laughing, and they said something disparaging to each other about him looking too young to be at university. Really, though, it was because he was the centre of attention.

Men, myself included, can be like that. We evaluate a threat to our own status, and either try to put the person down, or join them. In a split second, I made a decision. 'Who do I want to be? The person squeezing every ounce of fun from life, or someone who sits and sniggers at other people?' So I went and introduced myself to Kit and we were firm friends from that moment.

I later discovered that his family were yacht builders and had been around competition sailing all their lives, and they knew many Australians. I went to visit him and his family after the holiday ended and fitted in like an old friend. It seemed as if those who lived on and by the sea were a little more relaxed than their compatriots. Their home, on the coast of Hampshire in Lymington, 'The Mill' as it was called, was a converted mill house that had been operational until quite recently – for about a thousand years. It was the sort of history that I could not quite fathom, but simply had to marvel at.

Chariots of Fire had been a big family movie for us growing up. As a teenager, I watched it with Dad and we both loved it. The old-world morals and the bond between the members of the British athletics team had really appealed to us, along with the beautiful Maurice Jarre soundtrack. *Gallipoli* was another big film of my youth, and the main theme from that film (coincidentally written by Maurice's son Jean-Michel) was the sort of thing I listened to on my Walkman – especially while I was training for a boxing final against Cambridge.

Because I hadn't boxed before, I'd only had five months to get up to speed before I was placed in that square ring under the bright lights, in front of those screaming people. One thing that surprises you learning to box is how much it hurts to get hit hard in the head, and how it can cause you to lose consciousness. Also how enjoyable it is. The team met at the running track each morning before dawn, and raced each other around as the sun came up. During the evening we did more training, this time with skipping ropes and weights, and then sparred with each other in the makeshift ring.

I wasn't a natural boxer: I had a hard and fast punch, but none of the dancing skill and co-ordination that many of my teammates had. What I did possess was a determination that I wasn't leaving Oxford without something to show for it.

Our coach, Percy Lewis, was the most polite and gentlemanly person I had perhaps ever met. Whatever reason you might come to boxing training, you stayed because of Percy Lewis, someone you simply didn't want to let down. As a young man, he had emigrated to the UK from Trinidad after World War II without a penny in his pocket. He had served in the RAF where he began boxing, and soon he was the Commonwealth champion in his weight division. He became a professional and earned a decent living from it, before retiring and becoming a bookmaker.

For many, though, he'll be remembered as the Oxford University boxing coach, a job he did for about thirty years, for little or no money. He gave me many sayings that I never forgot; in particular, 'When you get tired, go faster.' It was maddening, especially when he said it when you were exhausted, but we knew what he meant.

The thing he liked about me was that I never missed training. I'd learnt my lessons from my past experiences, good and bad, from Tudor House, King's and uni: I could achieve anything if I worked at it, and followed instructions. As well as someone as headstrong as me could do, anyway. I was the only heavyweight in the team, and Percy went out of his way to make me spar against professional heavyweights, so I could see what it was like to be in the ring with someone my own size, and feel how hard they hit.

In early March we drove to Cambridge for the big match. The night before, we had a movie night and I was given the job of selecting the video. I chose *Gallipoli*, which I guess was indicative of where my mind was, even then. In the hours before the fight, after we had weighed in and there was nothing to do but wait and try to calm my nerves, I went alone to the main cathedral in Cambridge and prayed for strength.

It was a pressure fight, because by the time I stepped into the ring for the final bout of the evening, it was a 4–4 tie. I needed some divine intervention – and I got it. It quickly became clear that my opponent, who was also Australian, was a better boxer than me. It was a bit of a worry, but I tried not to panic. To my surprise – almost amazement – one of my lucky punches landed flush on his chin. In an instant, he was unconscious on the canvas.

The crowd (half of them, anyway) erupted. It was an incredible feeling. And while my opponent was strong enough to get up on his feet again, and put me under pressure, I managed to hold on. I was pronounced the winner, and Oxford had won the night.

It was a sliding doors moment for me. If my opponent had been half-an-inch closer with any of his punches, the result would have been the other way around. And while being the Oxbridge heavyweight boxing champion maybe wasn't a huge thing, it was enough to give me an edge, and perhaps subconsciously push me towards my next step. I didn't know what that was, but I had a feeling it wouldn't be the courts. Not yet, anyway.

We had an official dinner at a beautiful Cambridge college in our blazers and ties, and then got back in the minibus and returned home, singing Oxford songs loudly and badly all the way home. The next morning there was a story in the local newspaper gushing about our victory. My fight was described as an 'Antipodean Argument'.

As the summer approached and the evenings got longer, I began to see the beauty in England which I hadn't really noticed before. While autumn had seemed humourless and the winter hard, the spring and summer were times when there seemed to be a holiday atmosphere in the air. It affected everyone and everything.

Having done pretty much all I could do in the student boxing world, I figured that, rather than simply repeat the process next year, if I was lucky enough to be accepted by the college for the full bachelor's degree, and made it back to Oxford for a second year, I thought I'd try rowing. This, of course, was the king of sports at Oxbridge, especially at Oriel, who had won the college races for an unprecedented thirteen years in a row.

I was strong enough, and in tests on the ergometer, an indoor rowing machine that measured the strength and frequency of your strokes, I could pull enough to do well, although I had to master the skill. In retrospect I was fortunate I didn't, as I think elite rowing, as with elite rugby, would have taken me in a direction that I would ultimately have found disappointing. It would take another year of various false starts, but in the summer of 1988 I was to find that direction, in an unexpected place.

CHAPTER 9

Swing, Swing Together

There was some sort of selection process – the ergometer, I assume – for a development squad for the Oxford University crew, a sort of 'third eight' from which the university might choose rowers to go in the two top boats the following year. I went along for tryouts and got selected.

There were some really good people in the crew, both in character and rowing talent. One was a huge former Royal Marine. We rowed on the Thames – both in London where it was almost a harbour, and at Oxford where it was so narrow in places you could barely turn the boat around. I began to see how enjoyable it could be when the crew were completely in sync and the boat was moving fast along a smooth river. I wasn't a good oarsman, and while I was strong and fit enough, I struggled with the delicate, almost yoga-like movements that were required to keep us gliding smoothly at all times.

I wasn't going to give up mastering the skill of rowing without a fight, so in the summer holidays – they lasted from late July to the beginning of October – I flew to the US on a cheap Virgin

Airlines flight, and went to some of the US college campuses to row in their crews, or at least use their facilities over the summer months.

The Americans I met, often just in the street or on the river, turned out to be incredibly generous and hospitable. Once I got talking to people and explained who I was and what I was trying to do, I was greeted with offers to stay and train. They were only too happy to look after me and try to teach me what they knew. It was America at its best, and once again I was moved by their openness and infectious love of life, and kindness to strangers. I was ashamed to privately admit that they probably wouldn't have received the same treatment in Australia; nor the UK, where making friends, Kit and his family excepted, could take years.

At the end of summer, I was back in Oxford for the start of my second year. After working hard in my first term, my tutor had agreed to let me transfer to the two-year degree course from the diploma. I was excited by this, but to be honest not over the moon. I had always had a confidence that things would turn out, somehow, but also that more time in England simply meant more work. To go home meant comfort and ease; to stay, a certain amount of loneliness and hardship. I would let the gods decide, but once it was clear I was staying, more work towards my 'mission' began, whatever that was.

As autumn progressed, my rowing with the development eight was taking me to windswept artificial rowing lakes in the north of England. The company of the rest of the crew was good and we laughed a lot, especially me. And it was a great feeling when we got in unison and made the boat 'sing' along the water – as moving swiftly and smoothly in unison was called.

In Vermont during the summer, I'd met Jennifer. She lived in Long Island, and had invited me to stay with her and her mother. We remained in contact and over the Christmas break she offered an invitation to go skiing in upstate New York with her and her dad. I also had the option of staying with Kit's family who were holidaying in Switzerland at a place they used to go to when they were kids.

I got another cheap ticket to New York and made my way to the East Coast ski fields. After being there for a day I realised I'd made the wrong decision. I liked Jennifer's mother, but the father not so much – he smoked cigars and talked like a gangster. I missed the warmth of Kit's family, so I decided to return to Europe, and then head to Switzerland and surprise them on New Year's Eve.

I made an excuse and got a flight back to London, and on to Geneva. However, by the time I got there it was late in the afternoon on New Year's Eve. I got the train to Interlaken, which made me smile as I'd been there as a kid in 1971 and hadn't heard the name since. By this stage it was around 10 pm, which I wasn't concerned about, as I knew the party on top of the mountain wouldn't be in full swing until midnight.

To pass the time on the train, I asked some Swiss revellers – they were drinking wine and dressed for a party – whether they were going up the mountain. To my horror, they said it wasn't possible to do that as the cable car, as well as the funicular railway that took people from the valley floor to the resort, were both closed for the night. They were only going to this small town for New Year's Eve celebrations because the wine was cheaper than in Geneva.

Trying to find a solution to this disastrous development, I asked whether it was possible to climb up the mountain to get to the resort. They looked at me as if I was mad. 'Definitely not,' they said. Apparently, it was dangerous and would take four hours, but I was welcome to spend the night with them. I thought about it, and declined their offer. I'd come a long way to get to this party and I wasn't going to give up now.

Once the train stopped, I followed the signs to the cable car through the frosted village, carrying my huge duffel bag, with all my ski gear in it, on my back. I was fortunate that it was a moonlit night, so I was able to see the steep tracks of the funicular heading pretty much vertically up the mountain. I knew I wouldn't make it with my bag, so I carried it to the closest group of pine trees and buried it under the snow at the base of one of the trees.

It was a still night and I was wearing chinos, blue blazer and boat shoes. This was my travelling uniform, but I knew I was about to get warm. Luckily, the fastidious Swiss had beautifully maintained railway sleepers beneath the rails of the funicular, which made for sturdy, if large, steps. I started the ascent: one, two, three, four. In groups of ten. It was a private joke I often had with myself. No matter how tired or down you are, just put one foot in front of the other and run another ten steps. Then repeat. Then repeat.

I was fit and was making good progress. My main enemy was the mental element of wavering or second-guessing myself. I reassured myself I was going to make it, and it was all going to be so good when I did. I hadn't really thought about it, but I began to see it was pretty lonely and desolate on the mountains of ski resorts at night. The funicular track had stopped going straight up, and now snaked its way through a dark pine forest.

After an hour or so, I stopped to take my bearings. I couldn't see the village I was heading to, but I could see the lights of the 'sister' resorts on the mountains on the other side of the steep valley, far in the distance.

I'd never really been a smoker, even at school, although I liked the forbidden nature of it, and was happy to sit with the smokers as they puffed their illegal delights in the thick trees at the back of King's. I'd taken it up after the boxing match, though, as a sort of meditation. I liked the smell of cigars, but they made me cough up green phlegm. Instead, I'd have an occasional thoughtful cigarette, usually unfiltered. It also helped with the loneliness. You were never alone with a packet of Camels, I told myself, and to a certain extent it was true. Standing on this lonely mountain, it certainly felt true.

Eventually, I heard fireworks going off on the other side of the mountain. Midnight. I had missed it, but that didn't really matter. I'd get there by 1 am, I hoped. I had no idea how far I still had to go to get to the village, but as the track through the forest had flattened out into a gentle slope, I decided to start running. It would both quicken the journey, and keep me warm.

After about half an hour, signs started appearing on the side of the railway tracks, and while I didn't understand them it was clear I was approaching the station. Then, I saw the lights of the village reflected in the dark sky above the forest. I was here, or soon would be.

There was no time to lose, so I raced through the village, and up to the door of the main hotel, where I assumed the New Year's Eve party was being held. I arrived at 12.45 to be greeted by Kit and his amazed family. They suspected I might try to make a surprise appearance, but not after the funicular railway line closed for the evening.

The party was being thrown by the Kandahar Ski Club, the original group of English travellers who'd actually invented Alpine skiing. (Strangely, the idea of walking up a steep slope, then hurtling down and crashing at the bottom was not appealing to the Swiss.) The members were impressed that I'd walked up the mountain so as not to miss their party. As they were all English, and proud of it, they declined to celebrate European New Year's Eve, but rather Greenwich Mean Time New Year's Eve, which was 1 am. So I hadn't failed at all in my New Year's mission; in fact, I'd probably arrived at just the right time.

The Kandahar Ski Club had different grades of members, which followed the Olympic system. My story so took people's imagination that the committee elected me to membership of the rather distinguished club – whose origins dated back to the early 1900s – not only as a Bronze K, which was reserved for some sort of distinction, but as a Silver K, which generally denoted a feat such as representing the country at the Olympics. Kit was impressed and slightly bemused, as while he and his brother had been in the national squad as kids, they hadn't been awarded

Silver Ks. They were such beautiful people, though, they only celebrated it all the more, as I was part of their 'family'.

After New Year's we travelled to Turin to race in their Head of the River. It was a festival race of sorts, although taken seriously. The Italians were gracious hosts. Perhaps they were a little too gracious at times, as we were left with the nagging feeling that some of the endless degustation menus, and meeting with 'people wanting to practise their English', was to distract us from training. It was an enjoyable trip, anyway. Maybe the fact we weren't trying so hard, and were a little bit more relaxed, made us actually row better.

I got back to Oriel just in time to sit the post-holiday exams. They were designed to ensure you had done some work over the break, and they weren't particularly arduous. In normal circumstances, even if you only had a single night to cram you could have got through, but fresh from the airport I was completely stumped. My tutor put me on some sort of report where I had to see the Provost, and promise to do better next time. Otherwise, I wouldn't be allowed to graduate. I'd got the message – lesson learnt.

CHAPTER 10

Back to Oxford

In the wake of my boxing achievements, I was approached – discreetly, as was their way – by a second-year student from Oriel, who invited me to join a club. His family owned a banking house, and he'd been to Eton, but he was polite, and I liked him. The Bullingdon was a dining club, and one of its membership requirements was to get a tailcoat made, based on the hunting jacket of the Beaufort Hunt. Eventually, Kit would join too, after I left a year later.

The Bullingdon only met once a term for dinner. This event was organised by the president, who at this time was future prime minister David Cameron. A lot of fuss has been made of the club, with tabloid scandals, including Cameron allegedly snorting cocaine while a member. However, I believe Oxford would be worse off if everything like it was removed. There was certainly no human sacrifice or initiation ritual at Bullingdon; not on the nights I was there, anyway.

While the pair had just left the university, everyone was still talking about the exchange of invective between two former

Bullingdon members, Darius Guppy and Boris Johnson. Cameron was charming, and managed to get a First in PPE – philosophy, politics and economics – so he obviously worked pretty hard. I was amused to see him on TV standing behind the prime minister, John Major, in some sort of official capacity, only about a year after he graduated. I guess he would have been amused to see where I was a year after I graduated.

In the summer term of 1987, I attended a ball at Christ Church, which was the biggest and grandest college. The balls were expensive, about a hundred pounds a ticket even then, so when I say attended, a friend and I 'crashed'. That is, we got dressed up in black tie, or Bullingdon tails in my case, then scaled the stone walls of the college, and dropped down in a dark place – and joined the fun. Once we got drinks we were watching the goings on from a distance, when something caught my eye: three young men, in bright red tunics, tight trousers with red stripes, and spurs. They seemed very self-assured, yet still having a good time. I asked my friend who they were and he said, 'Guards Officers. Tossers!'

For me, this was not unlike the moment when I considered those criticising Kit. I looked at the young men and knew exactly where I wanted to be next. And it wasn't in an Oxford college, or wearing a suit on the Tube in the City of London.

The next week I found a little building on its own on the other side of the university, with a sign outside saying 'Oxford University Recruiting Office'. Inside, I met a Major Bulford, who had been a cavalry officer, and these days volunteered to speak to people like me. He charmed me and checked me out at the same time. He seemed to be a good person, and clearly he'd loved his time in the cavalry, so he was the perfect person for me to meet. He was now retired and a gentleman farmer in Hampshire.

I wondered whether my non-British status might be an impediment, but Major Bulford didn't discourage me. He said I *could* join as an Australian, as we were part of the Commonwealth, but that I'd have to do a 'year in the ranks' first. I nodded, without fully realising what this meant. I took the papers from the major, and he finished by saying he'd had other Australians come to enquire about signing up, but none of them had followed through. He thought I could be the exception to the rule.

While I was mulling this over during summer term, my father came to visit me. I knew he was coming, but because of favourable winds he arrived an hour earlier than I expected. I'd planned to stay in and have an early night; however, my friends had brought a party back to my room, as they were so amused by my attempts to fool Dad about my work habits.

So, despite my good intentions there was both a girl in my bed, and empty bottles strewn about the floor. It was still only about 8 am, and my flatmates tried valiantly to hold him at the front door of our shared house with the offer of a cup of tea, but he was never one for small talk. He was grateful for the offer, but full of beans, as he always was when visiting academics in England. He proceeded upstairs to my room, where I was trying to get dressed.

My father and I had butted heads a bit while I was at Sydney University and just scraping through my subjects – trying to be the 'social lion', as he said disparagingly. But since I'd been away at Oxford we'd got on much better. In his imagination I was studying all day, and networking, as he would have done, so when he saw the state of my bedroom, including 'guest' peeking out from under the covers, it must have been a shock. Once he took the scene in, he turned around and went back downstairs, calmly waiting for me to join him. He didn't even mention what he'd seen, as if it shattered his illusions so completely, it was wiped from his memory.

He insisted on driving me to my lectures, but this was a problem. From the start, I hadn't actually attended lectures. I'd simply done the reading in the college library – enough to get by. I knew from Sydney Uni that, if you'd done the reading, the lectures rarely left you any better off. In short, I was too busy with essential activities to go to lectures. As a result, the Law School was unknown territory for me.

So, after getting close to the buildings, I jumped out of the car, and went into the first lecture hall I could find. I thought I was less likely to be noticed if I chose the largest one. Of course, everybody stared at me as if to say, 'He's not even in this class.'

I met up with Dad afterwards and we had lunch. Then he returned me to my student digs before he set off for whatever he was in England to do. During our brief chat at the door of my room, he'd noticed the army recruiting papers on my desk, and was horrified. In his mind, my destiny was to become a respectable barrister in one of the Inns of Court. Being a fairly old-school Aussie, to him the British Army were the 'chinless wonders' who had sipped tea on the beach while the ANZACs were mown down at Gallipoli. This was not where he wanted me to be. I assured him that the papers were just junk mail that all the sportsmen of the university got sent.

My first experience with the British Army did not go smoothly. A month or so after our brief meeting, Major Bulford arranged for me to attend officer selection week in Yorkshire. 'Nothing to worry about,' he quipped in his jolly way.

I got the train up there and four of us, none of whom I knew, were picked up by a sergeant in a green, troop-carrying Land Rover. He took us to the local cavalry barracks at an ugly wind-swept town called Catterick. I'd never seen an army base up close before and it was pretty depressing.

We were shown to our rooms and given army overalls, along with a big number that we had to wear, so the examiners could grade our performance at all times. Over the course of a weekend, we were subjected to a number of tests, which ranged from 'crossing the imaginary river' by means of ropes, pulleys and planks, to speaking in a group on a number of subjects.

I had no idea what to expect, and it didn't come naturally for me to interject in conversations even if I knew what was being said was rubbish.

At the end of the weekend the officer in charge, a po-faced cavalry captain, pronounced that I had failed, and that he thought I was simply an 'Australian wide boy' – 'wide boy' meaning 'larrikin', more or less. I'm not sure if he was trying to help me or not, but help me he did. While I was annoyed by his judgement, it made me more determined to pass the real Sandhurst entry test, in a few months' time, and it made me apply all my ingenuity over a period of months to working out exactly what they *were* looking for.

I had to decide which regiment I was going to apply to join. Major Bulford had been in a cavalry regiment called the Royal Hussars, and as he had taken a shine to me for my determination, he said I should consider them. I learnt that his regiment had been at the Charge of the Light Brigade during the Crimean War in 1854. This led me to a sympathetic biography of the regiment's commanding officer at the time, Lord Cardigan, which I greatly enjoyed. While history records him as a fool, it seems he was far more complex. He was a product of his time, and exceptionally brave.

I had to have a meeting with a serving army officer to discuss possible regiments to join – you got accepted by the regiment before the army. I met Major Rory McDonald, a serving cavalry officer, at the Cavalry and Guards Club in London. I was wearing my best suit, which was something cheap off the rack from Top Shop. Luckily, I was probably forgiven as being a 'colonial'.

There were about ten regiments to choose from, and Major McDonald gave me a summary of the sort of people I was likely to meet in each one. While I thought there would probably be some snobbery towards me, I knew from my experience at Oxford that those who really had something to be snobby about generally weren't, so I opted for the Blues and Royals.

I did have a few things going for me: I was an Oxford graduate without being 'bookish', I was a boxing champion, and my father was well known. None of these things were enough on their own, but they helped me get my foot in the door. The rest was up to me, and my ability to impress them, and get on. It was a bit like the Sydney Uni Rugby Club, and the Oxford Boxing Club – they wanted to see authenticity and heart, and I was confident I'd be able to contribute to their regimental life.

A series of lunches were arranged, again at the Cavalry and Guards Club. The first was with a retired general from the Royal Hussars. We drank a lot and talked about horses. I think I probably 'passed'. For the Blues and Royals, I first had to travel to Combermere Barracks, not far from Windsor Castle, joined by a few other aspiring young officers. We went for a six-kilometre run with one of the squadrons, and then chatted with a young officer who had a devilish look in his eye. While we talked, he had a croquet mallet in one hand and was hitting a croquet ball hard in the lounge room of the officers mess.

I then had to meet the Silver Stick. He was the head of both of the Household Cavalry Regiments – two other regiments I'd decided to speak to. Our meeting was to be in his office at Horse Guards, in Westminster, which had been the centre of the monarch's cavalry for three hundred and fifty years. The Duke of Wellington himself would have walked the halls.

First, I met the aide-de-camp, whose name was 'Wendy'. although he didn't look like a Wendy (they all seemed to have nicknames). He got me to wait a few minutes in the sparse waiting-room.

Eventually, we both went into the inner office of the Silver Stick, whose name was Colonel Andrew Parker-Bowles. He was easy to talk to, and while I can't remember what we talked about, he knew a little about me, my father, the boxing, and, with just the slightest hint of a smile, even mentioned something about a 'report' from my tutor at Oxford. He struck me as very professional. If someone was going to send me into a dangerous situation, I had confidence he knew exactly what he was doing, and a good sense of what mattered and what didn't.

Five minutes later, I was shaking hands with Colonel Parker-Bowles and gone, back into the London traffic. It wasn't till a few years later that I learned that my suitability report – from my Oxford legal tutor – had been quite scathing. The tutor had got his revenge for me failing to do much work after I'd been admitted for a second year, or so he thought. He had written something like: 'I can't see why the military would be interested in this man. I wouldn't follow him unless I was in search of a good time.' It was the best reference I ever got.

Earlier in my time at the university, I'd thought I might do a further degree, a Masters, at either Oxford or Cambridge, and had looked into applications. Now, though, I knew what I wanted. I felt that if I was accepted into the Blues and Royals, it would be better than an Oxford Blue for rowing, which had been my other main ambition. About one hundred times better. *This* was what I really wanted, and how I saw myself in an ideal world. Now I just had to pass basic training and the dreaded Officer Entry Test.

Exams at Oxford came and went, and I did the usual last-minute cramming. I did everything I could to stay interested, but the academic life now seemed very dreary. Ironically, it wasn't even open to me had I wanted it. I'd looked into the possibility of a barristers chambers or the Inns of Court, but they'd only accept someone with a first-class honours degree. I'd be lucky even to graduate; which I ultimately did, but only thanks to some kind examiners who upheld the finest traditions of the university and didn't see the need to fail me. Although they probably could have. As it turned out, all my dreams were about to come true, and then some.

CHAPTER 11

The Guards Depot

The Blues and Royals, which I had asked to join, were a Guards regiment; that is, they were one of the six regiments that form the monarch's personal guard. That didn't mean they simply guarded the palaces – although they did that. Rather, it was an ancient designation of them as the most senior of the regiments. While it all sounded very elitist (and it was), it dated from a time when that word was a positive, not a negative one. However, it was a status won largely with blood, and generally the most senior regiments had simply taken part in more battles, which translated to having more people from within their ranks killed and maimed.

They had fought with distinction in just about every major battle you would have heard of, from Waterloo to Arnhem to Northern Ireland to the Falklands. They had been a stone's throw from my grandfather Jack as he carried the wounded in the mud of France, and no doubt he would have been bemused by them.

Surprisingly, for all their pomp and history, the Blues and Royals, or the Royal Horse Guards to give them their formal name, had actually fought on the side of the parliamentary forces in the English Civil War, in the mid-seventeenth century, against those who supported the king's divine right to rule as he pleased. They had stood by while King Charles I was executed for treason. I would reflect on this many years later, when the modern equivalent in Australia of the king, the ministers of government, seemed to think they were above the law.

The Blues and Royals, with their blue tunics and red plumes, were a recognisable symbol of London: the soldiers with helmets and swords riding beside the royal carriage in lines of huge black horses. But while they maintained the traditional appearances and ceremonies, they were still very much operational at the forefront of their field, in this case soldiering.

The ceremonial duties were done by a handful of people on rotation, while the large majority were on operations in Northern Ireland, or in West Germany preparing to defend Europe against a possible Soviet invasion. It all seems very dated now, but in 1988 it was deadly serious. Despite being ruled by the progressive Mikhail Gorbachev, the Soviets were still considered a threat to the democracies of the Western world.

Although I didn't dwell too much on the history of the Blues and Royals before I chose them, what I knew about their reputation was undoubtedly a factor. However, ultimately, like a marriage, while you might be the first to express an interest, it's the regiment that chooses you – once they've tested you. The first of those tests was about to begin.

The first of these tests was something called Brigade Squad: an extra two months basic training over and above the normal year of officer training that occurred at the Sandhurst Royal Military Academy that Guards Officers had to complete. The Brigade of Guards, as the six regiments combined were called, wanted to take special care that those young men who came to command their soldiers deserved that privilege. The Guards Officers were treated with great deference by their soldiers – that is, the men they were in charge of and gave orders to, but as with the choosing of the regiment, it was a two-way street.

While the soldiers didn't actually have any input into who led them in battle, in effect they did, because it was the corporals and sergeants who ran Brigade Squad, and represented the interests of the soldiers – those who would suffer if idiotic officers escaped through the net. They had a full eight weeks to see whether you were made of the right stuff, even before you went to Sandhurst. Eight weeks is more than enough, if you know what you're doing. And they did know what they were doing. Many of them had recently returned from bloody warfare in the Falklands, where they'd bayoneted Argentine conscripts to death, or cleaned up after huge bombs in Northern Ireland. They knew about war, and they knew about leadership, and what makes good leaders.

It was the usual breaking down and build them up stuff shown in a thousand movies, and it was quite gruelling. More importantly, I learnt what leadership was and what it wasn't. The most important lesson they taught us was a simple one: 'Officers eat last.' And if there isn't enough food, they go hungry. That phrase encapsulated everything that leadership was truly about, in that while the respect you'd receive as the platoon commander was considerable and unwavering, it depended upon you understanding that you rode on the shoulders of those more capable than you in many ways, and that you took responsibility for them and their welfare.

The real question in Brigade Squad was whether you had at least the raw material for leadership. While all the other recruits were also would-be officers, there was still an element of leadership in everything you did. For each exercise or activity an individual recruit would be given command over their fellow recruits, and their performance would be observed. Just as important as the way you gave orders was the way people responded to them, because this indicated your ability to command respect from your peers. And this was a measure, not just of your confidence when in command, but of how much you contributed when not in command.

It's said that the hardest promotion in the army is from private (the lowest rank, who is in charge of nobody) to lance corporal (the next highest rank, who administers the privates), because you have to give orders to your friends. Whether they obey them or not depends a lot on whether they think you have credibility. During my three years in cadets at King's, I wasn't selected to be a platoon commander. This meant I had no leadership experience to draw on, so I had to observe those who did, and think about it deeply.

An important part of gaining the respect of those around you is the ability to stand up and be counted when things go wrong. Another is to be able to inspire those around you when they feel they can't go on. I found I had the ability to do this, drawing on lessons of my past.

Towards the end of the eight weeks, when we'd been marching for a number of days and digging trenches in the hard, chalky ground of Salisbury Plain, we had a simulated gas attack and had to swim out to a small wooden dinghy moored in the middle of a dam. Once in the boat we had to huddle there for an hour or so until the instructors decided we'd had enough.

There was no requirement to stay silent, so myself and a few of the others led our crew in belting out some old songs from my Sydney Uni rugby days – which most of us knew, at least the tunes that is – in defiance of the cold and to show that our morale could not be broken. It's amazing how singing can lift your spirits at times when you're close to breaking point. Ever since then, whenever I'm getting that sinking feeling of defeat, I've found myself belting out our bastardised version of 'Men of Harlech'. I can imagine soldiers in tough situations down through the centuries doing the same.

It was like Percy Lewis's old saying, 'If you're tired, go faster.' If I am jailed, I can imagine myself belting out the 'Sydney Uni song', calling on the same reserves of courage and defiance in the face of adversity. I also remember Brigade Squad giving rise to another saying, shouted by the recruits as we trotted along with packs on our backs, mile after mile, 'If you're going to be a bear, be a grizzly!'

While it was only pretend enemies – as well as cold, hunger and exhaustion – that we were fighting on Brigade Squad, it didn't matter. The trainers knew what they were doing, largely because they were working from the templates developed from thousands of hours of training officers, and because they themselves were the descendants of some of the most proud and efficient soldiers the world has seen: those who by the time they had defeated Napoleon's soldiers that had conquered Europe, already had more battle honours than all Australian units combined, to date their total is almost ninety, for a single guards regiment. The 'offspring' of those soldiers had been to every major European battle since.

These were the sort of men I aspired to be. They had standards and they were uncompromising in their pursuit of them, and it permeated not just the way they led their troops but the way they lived their lives. It will likely seem dated to many, but to me the Guards were the real 'Chariots of Fire' and I didn't think what they stood for was antiquated.

After those eight weeks, I was thrilled when I was told that I'd passed. These corporals and sergeants who had served on the blood-stained hills of the Falklands, and endured the terror of Northern Ireland, had certified that I was up to the job of being their leader in battle.

I was one step closer to my dreams. And you can see, in photos of me taken only a few months apart, that I felt somehow I'd now become a man. In my Oxford graduation photos, I was a boxing champion with two law degrees, but I was still a boy, because

I'd never been a leader. While it was only the very early stages, something had shifted in the way I saw life, and my place in it. All I had to do was live up to it.

There were two more hurdles in my way. The first of these was the Sandhurst entrance exams, the trial of which I had failed badly only six months before. A week or two after Brigade Squad, four of us who'd passed journeyed together in a battered old Citroen 2CV to the exam, which took place over a weekend at what had once been a grand home in the country. None of us, including me, were nervous. We now knew who we were, and I'd had time to reflect on what it was they wanted to see.

I managed to blitz both the assault course and the leadership tests, which included an imaginary poison river. When asked 'Why do you want to join the army, and what do you have to offer?' I replied confidently and genuinely, 'I want to fight for democracy and the law, and I can best contribute by being a leader.' I meant it, and maintain that belief to this day.

The final test was a question of planning and character. You had about twenty minutes to come up with a strategy to deal with the following problem: you're in charge of a platoon with a badly injured soldier, who'll die if he can't get to a hospital within four hours. There are three possible routes to the hospital: the motorway, which is fast, but a longer distance, and possibly affected by traffic; a secondary road, which is safer but which requires slower travel; and by foot over a mountain, carrying the man.

After measuring the three distances and calculating the different speeds of travel that were given to me, I could see that neither of the two road routes would get him to the hospital in time. The mountain route would obviously be difficult, and involve hardship and discipline from my men. It was night, and the weather might be bad. The wording of the problem was designed to make you think that this route was out of the question, but in fact the drawbacks were mainly cosmetic, rather than substantial. However hard and uncomfortable it might be, this was the only way to complete the mission. I chose the mountain route. As an analogy for life, I've often thought about that problem – and that solution – in the years since.

All four of us from Brigade Squad passed the entrance exams, which we were all excited about. We squashed back into the old Citroen and headed for London, with its bright lights, pretty girls, cigarettes and beer. We were on our way.

The second hurdle was twofold. Firstly, I had to do a year as a soldier. That meant being a private, living with other kids straight from the housing estates of Liverpool, Glasgow and London's East End, who spoke with accents I hardly understood. I would have to take orders from someone not much older than those I'd been on Brigade Squad with. In terms of popular fiction, it would be like the Oxford toff ending up living with the family from *Shameless* or *East Enders*.

I'd agreed to without giving it a moment's thought, and not having any real idea what lay in store. It was decided that while I'd learn to do a soldier's job – being a crewman on a Chieftain tank – at night I'd stay with the officers in the officers' mess, and wear little white stripes on my epaulettes to denote 'potential officer', which wasn't really a thing; however, the Blues and Royals decided it *was* a thing, so it was.

The whole thing made sense, because they also wanted to see if I could fit in with my fellow Blues and Royals officers. Good morale and camaraderie mattered in a regiment, and without a smooth collegiate atmosphere that combined professionalism with a sense of humour, you wouldn't get far in a war situation, which was what we were preparing for, after all.

So, I worked by day in overalls as a tank crewman, specifically a gun loader, deep inside the bowels of a tank. I simply kept the ammunition flowing to the cannon and the machine-gun, while also writing down the coded messages that came over the radio, making tea and the dinner for the crew, and lighting the sergeant's cigarettes and handing them to him.

Sometimes I'd narrowly avoid catastrophic crushing when the tank gun fired and recoiled, I'd inhale poisonous smoke, there was the stress of trying to copy vital code with a texta while the tank bounced around like a ship in a storm, and I'd regularly be abused for some small failure of duty. In short, it was one of the happiest times of life.

I was finally a soldier and we were preparing to defend the Western world from those who would destroy it, with our lives if necessary. At the time, the list of European countries under Soviet rule was lengthy: East Germany, Poland, Hungary, Romania, Czechoslovakia, Yugoslavia, Ukraine, Latvia, Lithuania, Estonia and Belarus. Our intelligence suggested that a Soviet invasion of Western Europe, in the same way they'd invaded Afghanistan, was possible.

Best-selling novels like Tom Clancy's *Red Storm Rising* and *The Hunt for Red October* described the way a war between the Soviets and NATO would unfold, and spies from both sides were regularly being caught and imprisoned. The so-called Cold War was still very cold, with borders lined with tanks, missiles fuelled and ready to fire. All it took, we believed, was a single incident and we would be at nuclear war.

In 1962, the year before I was born, it had almost come to that, and President Ronald Reagan had spent billions preparing the US for nuclear war. While we assumed our forces were superior in both technology and training, the Soviet armies were numerically superior, and had defeated Hitler's similarly more advanced armies.

If the Soviet tank forces rolled west en masse from their bases, supported by attack helicopters and jet fighters, with tactical nuclear and ballistic missiles used by both nations, the time it would take for NATO tank units stationed in West Germany, like us, to be vaporised was said to be three minutes. It was a grim figure that was the basis of much black humour by us, and probably gave rise to our innate sense of squeezing the most out of each life experience.

CHAPTER 12

West Germany

In West Germany in the winter of 1988/89 there wasn't much for me to do in Sennelager. I'd become friendly with the 2IC – the second-in-command of the Blues and Royals – who was a charming man named Major Gordon Birdwood. A handsome, sandy-haired forty-year-old, he was only ever called 'Fluffy'. The nickname might seem ridiculous, but all the officers who had joined in the 1970s seemed to have them. I was simply 'McBride'. I don't think they felt that 'David' suited a rough giant from Australia.

Fluffy's great-uncle had been General William Birdwood, who had commanded Australian units in World War I. He was one of the few British officers who'd won the affection of the diggers and subsequently had many streets in Australia named after him, including one in Bexley. Dad was impressed to hear that my boss was a Birdwood, and when he eventually met him they became firm friends. My father often dropped in on Fluffy and Bella when he and Mum moved to London in later years.

I still had another nine months or so before my year in the ranks would be completed and I could start Sandhurst. However, they had plenty of soldiers at Sennelager, and after I'd done a few major exercises, mastered the art of being a loader on a tank, and generally got to grips with what went on in the unit, they tried to be a bit more imaginative with how I spent my time.

They may have been slightly embarrassed that the British Army was forcing an Oxford graduate who'd passed his Sandhurst exams to be a soldier for a year, simply because he was a 'colonial', although I wasn't bothered. A deal was a deal, and it was a great way to get to know my fellow officers in a way I never would when we were based back in the UK, and everyone went to their homes each free weekend.

Perhaps Fluffy wanted to ensure I had enough in common with my fellow junior officers that I could 'survive' later on; or it might simply have been that he loved flouting the rules. Just because I was in the ranks for a year didn't mean I couldn't have a bit of fun, he reasoned. Fluffy was a typical cavalry officer of that generation in that he went skiing, waterskiing and had done the Cresta Run – a toboggan challenge in Switzerland – all to a high standard. He decided I should go to St Moritz and do the Cresta, for a month, as part of my 'training'.

So I arrived in Switzerland around Christmas, then introduced myself to Fluffy's friends. They were all very well to do and quite idiosyncratic. He seemed to know more people in the European royalty than the British military, and it was a bit like stepping onto an Italian movie set, with dubious dukes and fur-clad starlets calling you 'darlink' and examining you between deep puffs of gold-tipped cigarettes.

They were all extremely polite, and being a friend of Fluffy's seemed to be all they needed to know. They were perhaps slightly bemused by me, especially when I explained to them that I was here as part of my duty, and that I was not to return until I had 'gone from the top'.

The Cresta had a two-tier system. You could either start from the middle of the run, level with the clubhouse, or from the top, which involved a few minutes' walk further up the mountain. If you started at the top, by the time you reached the second starting point you were travelling at about 50 kilometres per hour, with your face only a few centimetres above the ice. This meant you'd be doing double that twenty seconds later in the final stretch to the finish point at the bottom of the valley. Fluffy had set me the task of qualifying to go from the top, as though it was a genuine military objective. Not many people managed it on their very first trip – although not many people stayed for four continuous weeks.

The longer toboggan run was truly dangerous, and they'd had the odd fatality over the years, so it made sense that before you were allowed to go from the top, you needed to qualify by recording three fast times from the middle station. Because there was a single lazy 'S' bend without any high protective side walls, if you didn't know what you were doing, you'd get flung off the track into the generous piles of straw, which were newly laid each day.

The main issue at 'Shuttlecock', as the corner was called, was to avoid getting hit by your toboggan. These had sharp blades to cut through the ice, and were made of steel, weighted by lead, for a total of about 20 kilos. I crashed badly after my second week, as my jumper had ridden up, exposing my bare skin to the sharp edge of the corner while I slid sideways for a few metres. I went to the local Swiss doctor, who put four stitches in it, muttering about what a silly thing the Cresta was, and telling me not to do it again until he took out the stitches a week later.

There was no chance of that, and I got straight back on the course the next day. As predicted, the stitches immediately split. At least I didn't have to return to have them removed, I reasoned. I still have a fat scar on my hip to this day.

Being at St Moritz wasn't just about tobogganing, though. There was a clubhouse with three floors, including a bar and a viewing deck, and the popular drink was something called a Bullshot. This was a shot of Bloody Mary in a shot glass, which was regularly drunk as an alternative to coffee by riders and spectators alike. As the run closed each day at 12pm sharp, it seemed rude not to celebrate another session without injury with a lunch in the sun on the terrace at Sunny Bar.

As for the Cresta, it was pretty hard at first. I kept crashing out at Shuttlecock. The only way to avoid doing that, while still maintaining sufficient speed, was not to brake at all for the first ten seconds, as you gathered speed down the first straight after the start, but then brake hard for two seconds before the first corner of the S bend – pushing the spikes on your special boots into the ice – so you had enough control to steer a good line around the big left-hand corner.

The correct line was counterintuitive and required a certain amount of courage. Rather than give in to your fear and try to stay as far away from the dreaded side as possible, you had to embrace it and get as close to the edge as you could at the beginning of the circle – so much so that you could actually see the abyss out of one eye – and then rely on gravity and faith to pull you back down into the safe part of the track by the end of the corner. Start dangerous, finish safe. This was more easily said than done, of course, and if you were going too fast all that theory counted for nothing. You'd end up in the straw, making sure all your body parts were accounted for.

Eventually, sometime in my third week, I managed three of the required times in a row, and qualified for the 'top'. I had plenty of second thoughts while I stood waiting my turn, but I wasn't about to back down: this challenge felt somehow linked to me following my dream. I jumped on the toboggan, and I was off. I didn't break any records, but I didn't break any bones either. I was smiling from ear to ear for the rest of the week.

My month in St Moritz came to an end and I returned to the base in West Germany. The Christmas stand-down period was coming to an end, so it was back to work. Apart from the tank-loading drills, we did a lot of running each day, and cards at night. I played rugby for the regiment and cricket in summer, although we never went off the base and into the German cities – apart from Berlin, where we were manning the Soviet borders.

The German population had no love for the British troops, and I could understand why. The huge NATO exercises not only disrupted their lives, but frequently caused fatalities. Not long after I arrived, a US fighter jet crashed into a German suburb killing about ten people. Such tragedies were regular occurrences. While we were ostensibly there to protect the West Germans from a Soviet invasion, since we'd occupied them continuously since the Second World War this was clearly not the only reason.

Our barracks had housed the Wehrmacht during the war, and the rumour was that it had been the dreaded Waffen SS, although I never confirmed that. I enjoyed the historical aspects of the place, and I noted that when we drove back to the barracks after a rare weekend off in London, we basically retraced the steps of the Allied armies in 1944/45: from Normandy, through Belgium, Holland, across the Rhine at Aachen and into the heart of West Germany.

I didn't yet know that much about the Eastern Front, where the Russians had destroyed the bulk of the German Army, so for me this advance through Western Europe was the greatest military achievement I knew of. As far as I was concerned, they'd fought for everything that mattered, for democracy against tyranny, and at great personal cost. Every time we passed through a city or crossed a river that had been a scene of one of those terrible WWII battles, I felt a silent respect for those who'd died liberating Europe.

During this time, Dad visited me at the base while he was on a trip to see some German scientists. It must have been a welcome break from his tribulations in Australia. Eighteen months earlier, a reporter on the ABC *Science Show*, Norman Swan, had done a story about him, which suggested serious lapses in his scientific work in a paper he'd written in 1982 on the anti-nausea drug Debendox. My father was now fighting for both his reputation and his career.

After thalidomide had been permanently withdrawn from sale, Dad had set up an organisation in the early 1970s called Foundation 41, based in a building next to his beloved Crown Street Hospital. The purpose of the foundation was to study the effects of other drugs on the development of the unborn baby during the first forty-one weeks – hence its name.

When Dad had conducted his thalidomide experiments in the early 1960s, his methods were quite amateurish. Unfortunately – and indisputably – his professional standards slipped with the Debendox experiment.

Concerns had been expressed internationally about the drug, concerns shared by my father. He was unable to access Debendox, but, with a mindset I can now relate to, having had one door close on him he searched for new ways to prove his theory. He found a drug with similar chemical properties upon which to perform the experiment. If it seemed that this other drug might be damaging to the foetus, he could extrapolate from that.

This was always going to be a long shot, and cooler heads wouldn't have considered it. Cooler heads, though, mightn't have had the success he'd had with thalidomide. Dad was trusting his instinct.

Bill set to work experimenting with the drug, and with the facilities and team at Foundation 41 he put together a paper that suggested it was capable of causing deformities. However, he'd amended the results of the experiment to make it seem more conclusive; specifically, changing the total number of rabbits experimented upon and the number of deformities in the group.

Among the researchers who worked with my father was Phillip Vardy. I remember an awkward moment between my dad and Phillip – who was a paraplegic as a result of a motorcycle accident – at a Foundation 41 annual fundraising event. As he was introducing Vardy to the crowd, Bill said something like, 'And now we'll hear from Phillip Vardy, a man who got a first in biology at the University of Queensland, but who failed motorbike riding.'

As my father said this to a packed auditorium, I recall the look on Vardy's face, which said it all. I can't blame him. Phillip gave his presentation professionally, but it was certainly an instance of Dad not being a great people person. He had empathy and a genuine love for his patients, which probably drove him in the thalidomide days, but in relation to everyday things, sometimes his words were ill considered.

In any case, Dad's paper on Debendox listed Phillip as a co-author. The paper hadn't been published when Phillip saw that his name had been used on a fraudulent piece of research. Understandably, he was furious. Vardy then became a whistleblower.

My father, though, dug in his heels. As far as he was concerned, he was fighting a heroic fight. Because he wouldn't admit his mistake, he'd suffer death by a thousand cuts in the media. He sailed full steam ahead towards his own shipwreck.

Although Dad's life was unravelling, he seemed in good spirits when he came to visit. Of course, I knew about his problems; however, being so far away from Australia I don't think I quite realised at the time how much pressure he was under.

Dad had been keen for me to become a barrister and hadn't wanted me to join the army. However, his attitude changed after the visit. He came to dinner one evening. It was quite a formal occasion, with only one very long table that seated about fifty a side, with everyone in their dress uniform, including spurs.

The regimental band played throughout the meal, and Dad was amazed by the spectacle and sat with a smile on his face all night. He couldn't quite believe the quality of the band, which played many of his favourites. It must have reminded him of his own father and grandfather, with their brass-band pedigree.

The officers were extremely polite and deferential to Dad, which was reassuring for me. They could have easily been snobby towards an Australian doctor who was under a cloud, but as the father of a fellow officer – even one who wasn't fully in the regiment yet – they wouldn't dream of it. Words such as 'kindness' and 'manners', which can sound somehow dated and effete, don't do it justice. But instinctively knowing the right way to behave in any situation, whether fierce or friendly, was a skill that not many did as well as the officers in that mess. I learnt less about leadership in class-rooms than I did watching the actions of my contemporaries, and I was very proud to be a member of that unit that night.

I had a few days' leave after Dad's visit, so he and I went to Hamburg. On the way we stopped at a horse stud that had been recommended to me by a retired army major, because it was the cheapest place in Europe to buy polo ponies. I should probably give a bit of background. Years earlier, I'd tried polo on a country property with a friend from school, whose family played it. He was a natural; me not so much, but I'd loved it. The possibility of eventually playing polo well was definitely an attraction of the cavalry for me.

Dad was in his element talking to the owner and the grooms. He'd bought many Hereford bulls in England, along with hugely expensive tractors. I found two I liked, which were both small, not much bigger than donkeys, but they were well trained and could manoeuvre around in circles easily. They weren't expensive as far as horses go, about the same price as a carbon-fibre racing bike today. Understanding how little money I had, Dad bought them for me, which was extremely generous of him. He had the same look on his face as when he used to watch me driving the miniature racing car he'd bought me.

We arranged for them to be transported to England, so they'd be ready for next year's season, when I'd be based at Windsor.

I was determined to play in the Blues and Royals team at the All England Polo Club, at Smith's Lawn. To me, it was one of the most exhilarating experiences that the country had to offer. I had one opportunity to do it, and I wanted to give it my best shot.

The All England Polo Club was usually only open to princes, millionaires or Argentine professionals; however, the one exception were Household Cavalry officers. They had stables nearby and instead of having to rent them at an exorbitant price, as civilians did, it was simply a matter of using one of the many empty stables, built when every soldier had their own horse, and then you'd simply ride your pony across the road and through the park to the field each afternoon after work. Once you had a horse at the barracks, the only expense was hay and shoeing, when the farrier came each week.

It was a long way from the southern suburbs of Sydney to Smith's Lawn, and while I wasn't there yet, if I didn't prepare this year it wouldn't happen at all. Of course, Dad's journey – from Dungog – had been even further, and he probably got some sort of vicarious pleasure out of it as any parent would. Polo is obviously considered to be elitist, but I was always aware of where I'd come from and how fleeting my opportunities in this amazing world were.

Regarding Dad's hopes for my career, I think he knew I was academic, and probably thought I was being wasted in the army. But I knew that many of the people he most admired had been military officers, and while he might have preferred me to be a lawyer, at least during his visit to Sennelager his eyes were opened to the reality of what I was doing. I felt that he respected my decision.

Interestingly, many years later, a friend from school suggested that my joining the British Army was a method of escape from my father's issues, but I don't agree with that. It was me pursuing my dream, and Dad – despite his initial doubts – was only too happy to help.

CHAPTER 13

Serve to Lead

Having completed my year in the ranks around October 1989, I left West Germany and started my official officer training at the Royal Military Academy. It was situated in leafy Surrey, about an hour south-west of London, in the town of Sandhurst. Like its American equivalent, West Point, the college is usually called simply by the town name.

While not as old as Oxford University (by a long stretch), it holds a similarly revered place in the national psyche – both Prince William and Prince Harry are graduates – and has some equally grand buildings. When I arrived, I was in no doubt I was in a special place.

During my time at Sandhurst, university graduates only did a six-month course, while non-graduates, who were the majority, did twelve. The assumption, which perhaps was a little optimistic, was that university graduates were more mature. The downside for us graduates was that it was a very intense course, and in order to compress the year-long course into six months, they seemed largely just to have cut out sleep from the curriculum.

Somewhat depressingly – soberingly, at least – the three graduate companies were named after great battles of the First World War, if you can call them battles: the Somme, Amiens and Marne. It was a grim, ever-present reminder of the realities of war, not that it put me off.

Each of the university graduates was already technically a second lieutenant when we arrived at Sandhurst. We just had to survive the various hurdles to the graduation parade in six months' time. Few of us wanted to excel: we'd passed the exam that mattered – the entrance exam, and been accepted by our regiments – and we knew the thing that really mattered after that was how you performed in real life.

Winning a 'Sword of Honour' at Sandhurst (that is, graduating at the very top of your class) was no guarantee of future success as a leader. If anything, it would likely make soldiers and officers alike distrust you as a 'try-hard'. So we sought to be neither the best nor the worst – and, as at boarding school, to have as much fun as possible in order to pass the time.

Each company was run by a major and a colour sergeant (a junior sergeant major). It was a great honour to get the posting, as only those who'd been earmarked for bigger and better things got to teach at Sandhurst. Our company commander was a Major Harvey, from the Duke of Wellington's Regiment (infantry), and Staff Sergeant Veivers of the Cameron and Gordon Highlanders, who got to wear a fancy tam o' shanter, and tartan trousers with white spats.

For those of us who had done Brigade Squad, it was nothing we hadn't seen before – except with even more marching. We marched ten minutes to breakfast, we marched to lunch and back, and also dinner. There was no going out at all for the first term, which from memory was about three months. We had night exercises, marching, cleaning, day exercises, marching and cleaning. You were never as thin again in your whole life as when you graduated from Sandhurst. This was actually a bit of a problem, because our dress uniforms were tailor made. Many a senior officer just about gave himself a heart attack, trying to squeeze back into the uniform for formal dinners, after their Sandhurst years had faded into distant memory.

Anybody who'd completed Sandhurst, whether the year before, or forty years before, would have given me the same piece of advice: 'Be the grey man.' But I was an Oxford graduate (to my knowledge, there were no others), I was going to the 'elite' Blues and Royals, I was six foot three and I was Australian. Needless to say, I was not successful at being the grey man.

Despite that, I made a pretty good start at Sandhurst. Brigade Squad had enabled me to excel at the fitness side of things, while I was also adept at other important skills, such as 'drill' technique, when Guards-trained officers came to attention we stamped our feet so hard the ground shook; polishing my boots so well that I could see my reflection; having the best ironed shirts, meticulously hung with exactly 30 millimetres space between them, held in place with invisible tape; and ensuring industrial grade 'hospital corners' on my bed (which, in fact, I'd been doing since I was seven years old).

I loved the army and its traditions, and I got on quite well with the major and colour sergeant. I also liked the bright lights, and didn't see them as mutually exclusive to being a good officer. My heroes, whether real or fictional, had seemed to feel the same. I'd seen so much of the Sandhurst training regime before at Brigade Squad that it was hard not to be tempted by the odd night on the town.

As a result, by the end of the first semester I was already in trouble for something to do with discipline – being back after the curfew. My instructors found that annoying, because as far as they were concerned I should have been taking the opportunity to lead and shine. However, I firmly believed that being a really good officer meant having a personality that was more than simply a regurgitation of the army field manual. There was only so far that soldiers would follow a robot, and those who inspired more than simple obedience usually had more to them than shiny boots and a nit-picking attitude.

Towards the end of the year, I made the academy rugby side. In early December 1989, at the beginning of the Christmas break, we went to Berlin to play one of the better Welsh regiment teams, who were one of the units based out there. Exactly what they were meant to do if the mass of Soviet armoury, which surrounded them, decided to close in on them was anyone's guess.

For thirty years Berlin had been a city divided by walls, where people got shot trying to escape. In those decades, a number of spies on both sides traded secrets for what were then large amounts of money. Some of my contemporaries from Oxford were involved in the spy game, moving around the world disguised as embassy staff. But as we arrived, people were now able to cross from East to West Berlin, and the wall itself was being chipped away. We were there as history was being made, and we didn't know quite what would happen next. It was an atmosphere of both excitement and confusion.

We played on a huge flat green field that had apparently been created for the 1936 Berlin Olympics. The Welsh Fusiliers, who were much older than us, probably relished the chance to punch a few 'Ruperts', as they called us, and not go to jail for it. Not expecting this extreme level of competition, I was surprised to get punched hard in the face in the first few minutes. I needed four or five stitches on the bridge of my nose, so I had to come off before I could exact my revenge. I was taken to a British military hospital where an army doctor stitched me up in about ten minutes in a pretty slapdash way. I'd joked that I wanted to go back to play the second half – he may have taken me seriously.

The stitches didn't stop me wanting to go out in Berlin, not only to see the wall but to see the city I'd read so much about. We went to the famous streets and monuments, and saw people massed near the wall. Some were hugging people who'd arrived from the East, who had a dazed look about them, some were smashing at sections of the wall with sledgehammers. I managed to stuff a plastic bag full of pieces of it, with bright graffiti on the outer edges.

I had always wanted to somehow be part of the liberation of Berlin. In my imagination it had been at the head of a column of tanks, which was not how it turned out. Instead, the Soviet Union had collapsed from within, and my part, if any, was simply being part of the larger NATO force. It was still nice to see your dreams happening before your eyes.

In May 1990, I made it to the end of training. Everyone at Sandhurst had been absolutely pushed to our limits. For myself, it was mainly because I was burning the candle at both ends, and involved in my first larger-than-life relationship. It wasn't a good time to do so, but we don't get to choose the time, and it's not something I regret, although it meant I was lucky to *just* slip through the heavy graduation doors without being crushed by them. I can only thank my instructors for having faith in me, and hope that they're not dissatisfied with the officer I eventually became. Kit, his brother and family and friends, and my then-girlfriend Louisa, all came up for the traditional graduation ball, held in the palace-like Old College building built in 1799, with its huge stone entrance steps and towering roman columns.

It was the first time we'd worn our full mess dress, complete with spurs, just as I'd seen the officers wearing at the Oxford ball three years before. I was now officially a subaltern in the Blues and Royals. I hadn't been an overnight success by any means, and even if the process had taken less than two years, it had involved a lot of jumping from log to log at just the right moment. I don't remember any great feeling of triumph, though. It was great to say farewell to curfews, rules and reports, but we all knew the real soldiering was yet to come.

CHAPTER 14

SAS Selection

After two years as a lieutenant in the cavalry based at Windsor, in command of a troop of armoured reconnaissance vehicles – small-tracked mini tanks that pushed up in front of the main battle tanks to observe the enemy position and report back – I applied to do SAS selection. It had been in the back of my mind since I'd seen them abseil off the Iranian Embassy roof in 1980. It was a little bit James Bond, or so it seemed. I'd thrilled to both the Bond movies and the books as a kid at boarding school, and why not be part of the best of the best if you could?

I knew it would be hard to get in. It was a serious place, only spoken about in hushed tones. The identities of the SAS were secret. Everyone knew someone who knew someone, though, which meant you could gradually put together a mythical idea of what life in the SAS would be like.

The failure rate for the admission process to the SAS was about 90 per cent for officers. Considering that only the most competent and self-assured would even apply, that was really quite off-putting. However, it made being successful in SAS selection seem like a major validation, which was also a factor, if I'm completely honest. But was I tough enough? A lot of me doubted that I was, but all of me knew I had to try.

Among the many significant hurdles to SAS selection was that you had to have completed a number of years as a platoon commander and be a captain. Fortunately, two years on from leaving Sandhurst, I'd achieved both of those goals. In retrospect, gaining a little more experience in the unit as a platoon commander wouldn't have been a bad thing, but you couldn't tell me that at the time.

You couldn't just apply for the SAS. Your application had to be approved, which meant you first had to convince your own unit that you were capable. My unit begrudgingly agreed, as I was beginning to get into trouble – although for minor things. It definitely felt like time to get out of Windsor, though. The castle precinct was beautiful but increasingly stifling for a twenty-eight-year-old with big plans for the future.

Once the SAS had approved my application, I was given three months' leave to train in Wales. I loved spending time in probably my favourite part of the world, the Welsh–English border. It was a place of magic and history, where you never knew if that huge oak tree you were having lunch under had once hidden a prince, or maybe an outlaw. It was summer and I can remember marvelling at the green of the trees. While those who've grown up in the UK maybe don't appreciate it – as we Australians probably don't appreciate the colours of the beach and the desert quite as much as we should – the green of Britain's mature trees on a summer evening is more than just a colour. It has an almost mesmerising quality, at least for me.

Before I even had my application approved, though, I faced the most unforgiving test of all: one of medical fitness, namely colour blindness. In my particular case, I have no problem with traffic lights, but can confuse a light pink shirt with simply a dirty white, and struggle with recognising different coloured stars in the sky. And if you show me those ingenious Ishihara dot tests, I see different numbers to non-colour-blind people.

There are six grades of colour perception – CP 1 being normal vision, and CP 6 being the most affected. I'm CP 3/4, but in order to be allowed to do SAS selection I needed to be CP 2. This meant I needed to get all the dot tests right, which, for me, was easier said than done. So I got to work. I went to Harley Street, London's traditional medical heartland, and bought myself an Ishihara test booklet. There was a deluxe model, so I thought I'd better get that. These were the days before the internet made anonymous buying so much easier. Luckily, no-one asked if I was a doctor, or whether I was someone trying to cheat on an exam; however, I wore a suit and was very friendly, just in case.

Once I'd purchased the test, I was horrified. I managed okay with the first plate, but after that, with pretty much every plate I saw one number and the correct answer was another. Happily, Professor Ishihara had kindly made a list of the right answers. So I memorised the numbers, and could recollect them even if you changed the order. For instance, I knew if I saw a '2', I need to say '7', while '42', for me, was actually '26'.

There were thirty-eight plates and I practised and practised until I couldn't be tricked, even if I jumbled the order, which they sometimes did. The only problem was that there were some where I wasn't able to see any number at all, in which case I had to memorise the dot patterns. Tricky.

On the day of the test, I was nervous as I walked in to see the eye specialist. I was thrilled when I passed the Ishihara test. The specialist did note some irregularities, however, so he decided to give me something called the lantern test, just to be sure. This test now stood between me and my dream. The slide projector was like a sentry barring my way to the SAS.

In the lantern test I was shown pinpoints of green, white and red light, of ever-diminishing brightness, and their positions changed each time the slide was replaced. Early on, I knew I'd fail the lantern test. I could pick the red asterisks in the black distance, but the tiny pin pricks of pale green and white were indistinguishable to me. I was clearly just guessing.

'Hmmm, that's curious,' said the doctor, as he realised I could do the dot tests perfectly, but the lantern test not so much. 'I've never seen such a case,' he added, with a hint of a smile, 'but I'll certify you CP 2.'

I wonder whether he'd concluded that anyone who'd spent hours memorising thirty-odd clusters of dots probably had the ingenuity and determination to work around his colour-perception problems. I could have kissed him. Second hurdle complete.

The next test was a big one. Pass the mountain phase of selection. I trained every day of that summer of 1992. 'No days off' was my motto. As with the boxing beforehand, I knew I'd have to dig deep, and I had no idea whether it would be enough. I didn't fool myself about the fitness standards required: I trained until I was able to do it.

I knew the routes I'd have to run and climb, and I knew the weights I'd have to carry on my back, so there was simply no excuse not to master them. Except that it was very challenging. You didn't need to be an Olympic athlete, but you did need to be one very determined soldier, who really, *really* wanted it. And I did.

It was tough, though. After long days on the mountain alone, there was a lot of frustration and even tears. The smallest miscalculation on the map might mean I got lost. It might only be for ten minutes, but that would mean I wouldn't 'make the time', and I'd be left wondering how anyone ever could.

There was also the vegetation: baby heads, as they were called in the soldiers' irreverent way. These were small tussocks of grass, each about as big as their name suggests, and because they were unevenly spaced, it meant walking on them was treacherous. To start with, yomping fast seemed absolutely impossible (yomping being running with a pack on my back; in this case, full of sand bags, bricks and rocks). Everything about SAS selection seemed impossible to start with. But once I practised it, and practised it, I slowly began to realise I might be able to manage it. I still needed to bring out everything I had, and be lucky.

I had one particularly mystical experience during my Pen y Fan training. While most of the time I was walking on remote hiking tracks where I didn't see a soul all day, occasionally I either started or finished next to a main thoroughfare. One day I was walking alone with my pack and 'rifle' (actually a thick wooden fence post with an iron bar taped to it, so it weighed the same as a real rifle), crossing a small road. It was misty and there were no cars to be seen.

There was a white van, though, Kombi-like but slightly bigger, parked nearby. It had a sign in the window: tarot readings. The chance of them getting any trade out here was slim. It was possible they were simply travelling the country and making the occasional reading. I smiled to myself at first, but as I'd finished for the day and had achieved my target, I thought, 'Why not?'

I knocked on the door and was greeted by a well-dressed, polite man who looked more like a bookkeeper than a fortune teller. I left my pack and rifle outside and sat at his kitchen table as he read my cards. He said it was going to be a hard road and he didn't mean just a year. He turned over three cards with female characters on them and commented on them. They were all key people in my life. It was eerily accurate; more so as the years pass. Forty years later, I'm still not sure what the final outcome of his words will be, or even if I imagined the entire unlikely event. If he was simply a magician, though, it was still definitely worth ten quid.

CHAPTER 15

The First Day

It was day one of the two-week SAS selection process. We set out from the barracks to the base of Pen y Fan in open-backed trucks, each holding about twenty silent, unsmiling soldiers. One hundred and sixty of the British Army's most determined and fit men – some officers (like me), but mainly regular soldiers. We all had 20-kilogram packs and rifles; thankfully no helmets.

I felt sick as I jumped out of the truck. Three months earlier, when I'd come to Pen y Fan and seen how big a challenge it would be, I had despaired of climbing it at all. I'd done so much training since then. But would it be enough against the 'best of the best'?

All of us were queued up at a wooden gate as if at the start of a marathon, and we began individually at thirty-second intervals. We had four hours to get up to the top of Pen y Fan, down the other side to the road, back up to the top, then back down to the start. The first hundred soldiers to make it back would stay to take on the next challenge. The others would be 'RTU' – 'Returned to Unit'. This would involve both a sense of shame, and your dreams evaporating.

I wasn't going to let it be me. All the work I'd done over the previous three months came to the fore. I dug deep and was so fired up I even managed to run ten steps at a time up the hill, then walk ten steps, followed by running ten steps. This must have been demoralising for those who started out five minutes before me. I caught a few people up in a relatively short space of time. If they were wheezing as I jogged past them, their confidence would be broken, I reasoned, fairly ruthlessly. We weren't here to make friends – not on day one, at least.

At the end of the first four hours, I was staying and dozens of the best of the best were going home: RTU. It felt incredibly satisfying to have made it this far. But it was still only the first day.

There were about eight marches over the two-week period, which got progressively harder and tested different things. Some of the routes were a bit tricky, and if your navigation was weak you'd get lost and fail. One day was heavy-pack day. It was a shorter march, but you had to carry a pack that weighed about 40 kilos. It was so heavy that when you first put it on your back, you couldn't believe you were going to make it. But you did, because you felt your life depended on it.

One of the hardest was a night march. It was almost no distance at all, but in the pitch black it was highly confusing. We had to cross a number of barbed-wire fences and sometimes retrace our steps. For some reason, the whole night left me feeling demoralised. I have flashbacks about it to this day.

Every day people would drop out – they were either 'cut', injured or voluntarily gave up. As the numbers were whittled down, the banter among us became more friendly. After we'd shed the majority of wannabes, there was a shared sense of camaraderie. We began to acknowledge that if someone had made it this far, they'd done pretty well. However, the fact remained: whether you failed on day one, or on day fourteen, you still failed.

The scariest moments came on day eight. I'd been walking with a 20-kilo pack on my back for about eight hours, up the steep mountain and down the other side. I was slightly behind schedule and only had an hour or so to go. I was going to have to sprint to the finish if I was going to make the cut. There was a small stream at the bottom of the valley, flowing slightly faster than usual, because it had been raining steadily all day. The rain was affecting my visibility and had made it harder to see the mountain tops and to make sure I was on track.

I waded into the stream, which I'd crossed many times before in training, but when it was a little lower and slower, and I was a little less tired. One downside of being six foot three is that you're top heavy. I placed my foot on a rock, counterbalancing pack and rifle, and as my boot slipped, I toppled into the stream. I was carried along by the surprisingly strong current, my head hitting the bottom – smooth river rocks, thankfully – and bouncing up again.

In normal circumstances, it wasn't a dangerous situation. However, with a 20-kilo pack on my back, and a rifle in my hands, if I sank I'd be at the mercy of the currents. I couldn't just drop the rifle, as I knew that would be the end of my selection dreams. It would start to flow away downstream, and I'd waste too much time looking for it. I had to hold onto it with both hands, gripping that fucking rifle like my life depended on it, hoping that eventually I'd get washed to a shallow section where I could stand. I held my breath and prayed.

As I bounced off the bottom of the stream, the events of the last few months flashed through my mind. It wasn't hard for me to pray in such a situation, as I'd been living the life of a warrior monk ever since I'd been given permission to try out for SAS selection. To my extreme relief, I somehow managed to hold onto the rifle, get my footing, balance myself and make my way to the far side of the stream.

Having dealt with that tricky situation, and a few others besides, I eventually got to the final day of the fourteen. It was time for the 'long march'. One hundred and sixty of the British Army's toughest soldiers had begun the SAS selection process.

Like a *Hunger Games* or *Gladiators*, that hundred and sixty had
turned into a hundred the next day. Still not very good odds.
Then a hundred turned into eighty. We were now down to forty-
five – five officers and forty regular soldiers.

The long march was approximately twenty-four hours of
solid marching without breaks. We'd stop to drink water every
few hours, but the only food we'd eat would be chocolate bars
snatched as we walked. It was the usual 20-kilo packs. I sneaked
in my Walkman – I wasn't going to do it without music. I was
prepared to be military to pass, but not *that* military. We set off
some time in the afternoon and planned to walk 65 kilometres or
so, finishing in the afternoon of the next day.

The night route snaked down a high ridgeline. Because 65 kilometres is such a long way, it was sometimes necessary to retrace
the same path. I was at the front, making good time, occasionally
seeing other shapes in the distance but basically on my own in
countryside that looked like *Lord of the Rings*.

It was a dark night, but I was enjoying myself listening to one
of my favourite dance tracks, Felix's 'Don't You Want Me'. The
chorus was blasting at full volume when in the distance I saw a
pin-prick of red light that disappeared after a second. 'Someone is
using a torch,' I thought. 'Naughty, naughty.'

Then it appeared again and died. Finally, I realised what it
was, and in my exhaustion, I laughed out loud. On this incredibly arduous, incredibly serious, route march over dangerous
crags and cliffs, someone was strolling along having a cigarette.
Whoever it was, I wanted to give them a high five. That was style.

Eventually we met each other alone on the path. It was a 'Flash
Harry' sergeant who spent as much time on the town in London
as in the mud. I smiled and said hello, and kept on smiling for a
few hours. Light up a smoke? Why not? I went back to my music,
buoyed that in the midst of all this seriousness, there was still
some style and some humour. Only ten hours to go. Luckily, I had
fresh batteries.

Coming down the final few kilometres I stumbled across a bonus. In the forest there was an ancient disused railway track. The rails and sleepers were long gone, but where they had been laid was a relatively flat and smooth trail leading all the way to the final destination. Funnily enough, as I was trotting on down it, exhausted and elated at the same time, I ran into my only real friend on the course.

We were opposites in almost every way, except for our desire to pass this course. He was from the Parachute Regiment, tough and dour. I was limping with a twisted ankle, heavily strapped up with tape, with the pain suppressed by an overdose of Nurofen. However, I wasn't the only one with an injury. Probably most people had one by now, and I was bigger and stronger than most. We were both making good time, but as the cut was made by sending home the slower half of the group, you still couldn't be sure whether you'd make it or miss out by a single minute.

Marching for twenty-four hours on your own tested your ability to put mind over matter for long periods, to be able to fool yourself that all you had to do was one more hill and the rest would be gravy. It was the motto that had driven me for the previous four years as I did course after course in the army, getting qualifications that would take me to the next step. At times, it was a bit like digging out of prison with a spoon. But I had to tell myself freedom was just one brick away. 'Ten more steps and then I'll quit'; 'Just one more course, and then life will be easy'.

After twenty-four endless hours, I completed the course. I had made it. Better still, I was told I'd passed. It's hard to describe the feeling. I was tough enough; I was smart enough. I had pushed myself to my absolute limits and I had survived.

However, although I'd passed this test, there were still major hurdles left to overcome: 'The Jungle' and officers' week. The Jungle was four weeks' training 10,000 kilometres away from Pen Y Fan, in one of the hardest places to soldier on earth: the jungles of Borneo. We did a few days' preparation in the SAS barracks in England, and then made the long-haul flight together, before a day in Brunei city, all of which was pretty tense – a bit like the first journey in the trucks on day one.

We had a hard run on the beach together to acclimatise and the psychological pressure on the weakest men started to be applied. I was quite fit, but at 95 kilos or so, I wasn't much of a middle-distance runner, so I was one of the ones who got a bit of the 'stink eye' and abuse. I hadn't seen anything yet, though, and the next day we jumped up into trucks and drove out to the prehistoric jungle area.

It was a few hours' drive, but our uniforms were soaked in sweat within a few minutes. The mud road came to a dead end in an ugly patch of jungle that marked the end of civilisation. We were told to get out, and we started walking off in single file for a few hours, up and down the steepest and most miserable tracks I'd ever seen. We slipped and slid our way in the mud, tripping on roots, and a few people had nasty falls.

We were issued ArmaLite M16s, the US rifle best used in the jungle because of its lack of small parts that could get lost in the mud, unlike most of the overcomplicated weaponry used by other Western armies. In the jungle you couldn't see the enemy unless they were right in front of you, so you didn't need a telescopic sight, but you did need a weapon that fired pretty much every time you pulled the trigger – whether it was covered in mud, or soaked by a deluge.

We did a lot of fire and manoeuvre training with blank rounds. It was basically a military-style dance of death where your small team of six people are fanned out in a line and three of you move in unison, while the other three kneel and give covering fire through the gaps between you. Then your team kneel down and fire while the others move forward and past you. It's simple in theory, but quite difficult in practice, and very hard in the jungle that was undulating, and covered with vines, roots, rocks and tree stumps. If you've seen the movie *Heat*, with Al Pacino and Robert De Niro, you'll know what I mean, and apparently an SAS operator worked on the film.

It was very tiring, and involved magazine changes on the run, and frequent running into trees, or face planting into rocks. And at all times you were watched by the instructors who looked at you disdainfully, and only ever gave you negative feedback. It was all part of the psychological game, of course. There was a saying, 'The instructors don't fail you, you fail yourself,' and there was a lot of truth in that.

Each day people got sick of the constant stream of negativity, or got injured, or both, and one or two more would ask to go home. This meant you'd be more or less instantly flown out of the jungle to warm showers, decent food, sleep, and instructors back at the base who treated you as soldiers, not rats to be experimented on. Having said that, I had no problem with any of the instructors. They were obviously just doing their job.

There were some things about the jungle that were hard to believe when you arrived. Firstly, how humid it was. From dawn to dusk your uniforms were soaking wet with perspiration, as if you'd swum in them. You had a spare uniform in your pack, but that was only worn when you were sleeping in your hammock at night.

When you got up each morning, you needed to put the wet ones back on again in the dark. You'd also cram everything into your pack – all your food and water, as well as your hammock and your 'hootchee' (the rain sheet that hung above it and protected you from the nightly deluge). Then, before the first rays of sunlight had come up, you'd lie down in the mud, stock still with your weapon as if you were about to be ambushed.

You lay motionless for a full thirty minutes while your instructor sat comfortably about five metres away, watching you like a hawk to see how often you twitched or took your eyes off your 'arcs', an area of trees thirty degrees to your left and right where, if the mythical enemy came charging at you, it was your job to shoot them. At night you did the same thing, in position before the light faded, again lying motionless in your wet clothes for thirty minutes before you were allowed to put up your hootchee, string your hammock just below it, get out of your wet clothes, into the dry ones, eat a can of cold food – no fires were allowed – and get into the hammock.

One thing you did sometimes get was good sleep, although at other times you were 'attacked' by the enemy at night and needed to get out of the hammock, grab your rifle and ammunition 'webbing' (the chest pouches that held your magazines of ammunition, medical kit and water) which, hopefully, was directly underneath you, get your boots on, and start returning fire as you retreated from whatever direction the enemy were firing their blanks from. Once you'd gone a few hundred metres in this chaos, amid the absolute pitch black of the moonless jungle, the instructors called you back and shamed you for any pieces of equipment that you didn't manage to take with you because you weren't properly packed away.

Each day there were more and more challenges, and the psychological pressure of not measuring up and being singled out by the instructors grew. It gradually – depressingly – became clear to me that I wasn't going to succeed at my ultimate goal. In comparison to the others on the course, I was not in any way good enough. I still made a decent go of it, and managed to get through each day not being so bad that I was forced off. One thing I wasn't going to do was quit. They'd have to fail me, and if they did, I'd improve and come back.

I was the worst of the 'remainers', but at least I was a remainer. That was no mean feat for someone whose preparation for the jungle was going to Vietnam-themed cocktail bars in West London. In many ways, being put upon by instructors, and to slowly see your dream fade away in front of your eyes because you weren't good enough, was the sort of life training you could pay a million pounds for.

*

After four weeks of pretty much being the most derided candidate in the 'trees', as the jungle was called, we still had a hellish final march out through secondary jungle, which is jungle that has been burnt and grown back even thicker. It was basically like walking through a giant lantana growing over a stinking swamp. They starved us at the end, mimicking hard operational conditions, and when we got to the barracks we had our first meal in three days, and our first shower in four weeks. However, the main relief for me was that the constant berating of the instructors had stopped.

The next day we were called into a little office, one by one. The chief instructor, who had spent a working lifetime in the SAS, and seemed a decent guy, gave it to me straight, but without any malice: 'You failed.' It was no surprise.

We got back on the plane to fly back to England for still one last test, or at least the five officers did. The rest had a week off. I was told to attend 'officers' week'; I guess to keep the numbers up. It was really only a few days, and the finale was delivering a military plan you'd devised to a lecture hall full of serving SAS soldiers.

The five of us were put in a little classroom and told to prepare two things: a speech about 'Who you are and what you have to offer', and a plan based on a problem they'd given us.

I had nothing to lose, so I decided to come out all guns blazing in the speech, harnessing my anger about everything falling apart for me in the jungle. 'I've come a long way to get here,' I told them, 'and I couldn't have done it unless I had a fair bit to offer you, and I'm not about to quit just yet.' It went pretty well, and these intimidating blokes seemed quite impressed that a 'Rupert' wasn't afraid to take it to them, and had a bit of fire in his belly.

Having salvaged a little pride, I went to the schoolroom, and turned to the plan. The 'mission' was to disable an unmanned electronic installation that was crucial in launching Scud missiles – from a country that sounded like Iraq into a country that resembled Israel, in a war that looked like the recent Gulf War of 1990. After reading the problem a few times and trying to calm my nerves, I looked over my shoulder at the other officers scribbling away, furiously looking up statistics in military manuals. Then I took a deep breath and began.

In the same way that some things were deceptively simple, this was deceptively complex. Amongst the pages and pages of topographical, weather and weapons data, the key words were 'unmanned' and 'air superiority'. I kept thinking I must have missed something, but in the end I decided to back myself. I was called back in.

'Candidate Five, deliver your plan,' said the chief instructor.

I paused in the awkward silence, took a sip of water and tried not to let them see my legs shaking. I had notes but didn't need to look at them.

'We'll fly in a single helicopter,' I said, 'break the equipment with a spanner, and fly out.'

I was half-expecting to be laughed out of there, but it became apparent that this was pretty much the right answer. And it seemed that the answers offered by the others had been overcomplicated, simply because they couldn't shake their years of conventional military thinking.

I'd still failed, though, so I went back to the accommodation block to pack my stuff. However, as I was leaving, I was told that the commanding officer, who'd been there in the session, wanted to have a word.

The CO's office was neat and welcoming and he asked me to take a seat. Although I was intimidated by him, he was friendly – a former Welsh Guards officer, with no false hard exterior. He said he thought I *might* have something the regiment needed: a good brain, and a fresh approach. He told me the SAS would sponsor me through the infantry officer's course, and arrange for me to be deployed to Northern Ireland afterwards so I could get the infantry experience I was lacking. I would then come back to the jungle in a year's time, to try again for the SAS, without the need to repeat the 'Brecon Beacons' – the mountain stage.

It was an extraordinary offer and I don't know if anyone had ever been made it before – or since, for that matter. I'd gone from being devastated to having a glimmer of hope. I wasn't returning to the Blues and Royals. I was off to do preparation training for operations in Northern Ireland.

CHAPTER 16

Snakes and Ladders

The Barrett M82 0.5 calibre rifle was titled an anti-materiel weapon – that is, it looked like an oversized sniper rifle, but its purpose was not to shoot people but 'soft-skinned' vehicles such as Land Rovers. In essence, it was a cannon disguised as a rifle.

As it had a large telescopic sight, it could be aimed accurately from about two kilometres. This meant that if it was firing at you, you had no chance of being able to see the firer, and your only option was to seek cover until the danger had passed. It needed considerable skill and training to operate properly, and no-one expected it to be used against professional troops in Northern Ireland – any more than we expected to see the IRA piloting a helicopter. However, once the dreaded '50 Cal', as it was known, made an appearance in the Northern Ireland Troubles, nothing felt quite the same again.

It was a regular patrolling day and when the British soldiers first heard the *bang* of the 50 Cal going off, they thought there'd been a bomb blast. Looking around, however, they couldn't see the usual smoke cloud, nor were there any obvious casualties.

While the exact details of what had happened were subsequently suppressed by the army brass to avoid panic in the troops, the rumour grapevine was impossible to stop.

According to the grapevine, the force of the 50 Cal had not only sounded like an explosion, but a soldier who had been hit by the round had been stuck to the wall he was standing in front of by the heat of the explosion. No-one even realised he was dead for a few minutes, as he appeared simply to be frozen. When he failed to answer the shouts of his team-mates, they approached only to find he was very dead indeed. We didn't know it at the time, but it seems that the weapon had been deployed not from a far-off hilltop, but a relatively close delivery van with a hole cut in the back doors, which could be resealed after the shot had been fired.

The IRA's use of the 50 Cal had the desired effect and soon all British Army infantry units patrolling the streets of Northern Ireland lived in fear of being torn in two by this fearsome weapon – without even knowing what hit them, or where the enemy were. It was into this tense atmosphere that I arrived in Northern Ireland in the winter of 1992, as a platoon commander of the second battalion, Royal Regiment of Fusiliers.

I was reminded I was lucky in Armagh. We would patrol the city in platoon groups, and I was given one section, while a fellow officer and his team were allocated the neighbouring streets. One day, after my platoon and I had returned to base, I was falling asleep when *bang*, the buildings shook. I leaped out of bed, got dressed, and ran outside to see what needed to be done. The whole platoon was out the gate in a business-like fashion barely five minutes after we'd been in bed, getting ready to start dreaming.

We filed out and patrolled towards the blast site. That entailed walking, spaced out, with rifles on our shoulders ready to fire, while slowly turning and moving backwards for a few steps every ten metres to check behind us, and covering each other around corners. Five minutes down the road, our radio operator got the signal: 'One NVS ['no vital signs', which meant 'dead, but we aren't admitting it yet'], three seriously injured, enemy unknown, prepare for a second ambush as you approach the position.'

I acknowledged the message and spread the troops out. They didn't need any micromanaging. They were a professional bunch, with a good sergeant. The nuts and bolts were taken care of and all I had to do was make the big decisions.

Ten minutes later, we arrived at the area of the blast. Ambulances and the police were there. They were used to this by now. We cordoned off the area, having seen no signs of enemy anywhere. As the officer on the spot, I gave a statement to the local TV crew, but simply confirmed the blast and the number of casualties.

The rumour grapevine, which was always the quickest of all communications, confirmed that a corporal, a well-liked and athletic young guy, had died on the way to hospital. In a ruthless kind of way, we were relieved, as apparently he was in bits, and whatever life awaited him probably wasn't worth living – not for someone who lived for sport, adventure and doing something for their country. The concern was now for two things: other casualties who were fighting for their lives, and catching the perpetrators.

My brother officer, the platoon commander, had also been badly hurt, his foot blown off. It was a sophisticated attack, the result of twenty years of bombs and countermeasures that had resulted in both sides being experts in their craft: one killing soldiers, one defending them.

Not only were the soldiers attuned to the nuances of Northern Ireland after two decades, but we had the best possible intelligence service: half the population supported us, and hated those who didn't. On the other hand, the other half, even if they weren't actively fighting us, were certainly never going to lift a finger to help us. It was a bitter, prolonged war, as only they can be when people who live a stone's throw from each other, and are alike in so many respects, are at the same time involved in a titanic struggle against each other.

We buried the corporal a week after he died. It was a small sad occasion, with only his company of soldiers there, as well as his parents and girlfriend. We gathered in a little churchyard on the base, with a flag-draped coffin and his fellow soldiers in their uniforms. A piper played, and then walked off into the distance, while still playing the mournful tune, giving the impression of a spirit leaving this earth forever.

I can only imagine what effect the corporal's violent death had on his girlfriend. She might get over this, but the knowledge that someone she'd been intimate with, and likely hoped to share a life with, had been blown to pieces must have scarred her deeply. At least they didn't have children.

This funeral summed up for me why integrity in military leadership mattered. Whatever the politics of the girlfriend, death made things personal. It was the same with any death of a soldier in operations. She would have been asking herself: did my partner die in the pursuit of something worthwhile, or was his life wasted because of some sort of short-term political pantomime?

Later in my life, I'd have serious reservations about another war in which I found myself entrenched. In Northern Ireland, though, I genuinely felt we were serving a good cause in protecting the people.

CHAPTER 17

The Age of Love

After my deployment in Northern Ireland finished, I was posted back to the mainland. I now had my first medal for operations, a fairly nondescript purple ribbon with green edges. My next posting had been arranged for me by the SAS to enable me to return to their selection course with the necessary infantry skills that I lacked.

As the evenings were growing longer in the English summer of 1993, I was doing another course. Warminster was a pretty town, near Salisbury Plain. The base was one of the more attractive ones, and the space reminded me of King's School.

There were about sixty of us on the course, formally called the Platoon Commanders Battle Course. I was the only captain on it. The rest were lieutenants; that is, junior to me. I had also just done a deployment to Northern Ireland as a platoon commander, which no-one else had, and was from a cavalry unit, which people could tell by my cap badge, the little black insignia in the top of my beret.

I got on with the job of learning as much as I could about being an infantry officer. I applied myself and the course went well.

I would have been better off learning how to be an infantry soldier – someone who's used to taking orders, not giving them – but that's getting ahead of the story.

It was summer in a beautiful part of the world. That always spelt trouble for me. The ancient Greeks said you couldn't be favoured by the gods of war and love at the same time, but what would they know? The big fat bees were buzzing slowly around the overflowing bunches of wildflowers on every country lane, and as soon as I had time off, and sometimes when I didn't, I was off to Oxford, where my girlfriend at the time, JoJo, was studying Politics, Philosophy and Economics.

I'd bought a Harley-Davidson motorbike with the money I'd saved in Northern Ireland. From memory, we got paid slightly more for being in a heightened state of danger. It had a custom cowhide passenger seat, so it took a few months to arrive. As with Australia, to get a motorcycle licence in most of the UK was quite onerous. But in Northern Ireland, I'd heard that it just involved riding around the block.

So the week before I was due to pick up my 1344cc Harley, with an engine bigger than many small cars, I dutifully turned up to the test centre with a borrowed bike, expecting to get my licence rubber-stamped. No such luck. The examiner wouldn't even let me sit the test, because the registration on the bike had expired the day before. It seemed a little nit-picky of him, and, as I'd just been patrolling his streets as a soldier for the past three months, a little lacking in gratitude.

I decided simply to dispense with the licence. I knew how to ride a motorbike, and while this was a little bigger than the 80cc postie bike we had at Dungog, I could learn on the job. JoJo said she always suspected I didn't have a licence, because every time it came up I'd smile and change the subject.

The two of us had fun criss-crossing the country on this big black and chrome machine that sounded like a broken truck and looked like a Meat Loaf cover photo. She wore her shortest skirt and I had leather trousers, so it was fair to say she was probably the coolest PPE student at Christ Church.

The dance-party phase was hitting England. It was something we sampled, along with all our friends. Perhaps the highlight of the summer was arriving at the annual Oxford University May Day Ball with JoJo and Kit and his girlfriend. It was held on a beautiful sloping piece of countryside just outside the city, and, unlike the college balls, not only had a number of big marquees for bands to play, but also fairground attractions, so it was a bit like a temporary Luna Park. It was black tie, although less formal than the college balls and more fun, being open to anyone who could stump up the fifty-odd pounds for a ticket.

The gates opened about six in the evening but we were fashionably late, having had a few cocktails at a friend's place a few streets away, before making our way into the ball. As we entered the park and were issued our fluorescent wristbands, our excitement grew. We were laughing a little at some joke and then turned to see the sunset quickly fading, revealing the spinning bright lights of the fairground rides. It was rare that we felt so good, four close friends in the perfect setting on the perfect night, in the perfect city.

I went to other parties as well that summer, although I probably should have been taking things a little more seriously – for instance, doing the Parachute Regiment basic training course. In my mind, I was focusing on what really mattered. In the thirty years since, I've often wondered whether, if I had that time again, I'd do the same things.

Over the summer I was contacted by a few people who tried to give me tips on passing 'The Jungle'. I was heading to Borneo again in September. One of these was a former SAS regimental sergeant major, named Billy. He'd seen me at officers' week and thought I had something to offer. We met up at a motorway service centre and he told me as much as he could in a couple of hours – some of it fascinating, some hilarious.

We sat in my slightly dishevelled old station wagon and Billy tried to explain what the really important things were. He said that, ridiculous as it might seem, appearances were everything in the SAS. As he said this he looked down, and was appalled to see that there were paper scraps on the floor of the car from my various road-trips. He couldn't stop himself cleaning it up for me, muttering something about 'bloody messy officers'. I didn't tell him that I'd already tried to clean it prior to him getting in. In retrospect, that might have been a bad omen.

Billy added that the Regiment, as the SAS was called by members, could be extremely unforgiving of any minor infraction. Some people had been denied promotion on fairly ridiculous grounds, such as the tiniest failure to prepare their gear properly on a long-forgotten mission in the Middle East years earlier. After a long chat he wished me well, and said he hoped I'd pass this time.

I said goodbye to JoJo, getting her to promise she'd say a prayer for me in Christ Church Cathedral – against her better judgement, as she was an avowed atheist. I travelled to Hereford to join the other candidates, and got my bedspace in amongst those who'd just passed the mountain stage of selection.

We had a few days pre-training, which was pretty unremarkable. Then we headed to the jungle. After we arrived in Borneo, we had a run on the beach to acclimatise and the usual berating by the instructors began. Again, while I was fit, I was no middle-distance runner. I kept up, but was at the back with the bigger guys. I was already feeling the pressure.

Even thirty years later, my second experience in the jungle is difficult to write about. At one point early in the course, when the chief instructor spoke to me, he treated me as if I was already badged – that is, part of the unit. In some ways that put me under extra pressure, in that he and the other instructors expected me to be at an even higher standard than those who were on their first trip. It meant that the slightest deviation from the letter of the law resulted in the most scathing judgements.

Just a few days in, the pressure was continuing to build. Lots of little things went wrong. It's hard not to conclude that sometimes things are meant to be, and we're successful at things we don't deserve to be, and sometimes they're not, and no amount of effort will change that. Certainly, neither JoJo's prayers nor mine seemed to do much good. It was clear by the end of the third of the four weeks that I was going to fail again.

Almost the only smile I had was in the midst of yet another hour of torrential rain. We'd been lying in the mud for hours, supposedly waiting for the enemy to attack, when some wag got the idea that the rain was so heavy he could get away with a sneaky morale-boosting lung-buster – a cigarette – if he put up a rain poncho and crawled underneath it. Within a few minutes, three of us were puffing away and giggling like fifteen-year-olds while the storm raged outside. There was a limit to how much fear of a pretend enemy we could keep up, day after day, and a little bit of humour was like water in the desert.

It didn't last long, and sheet rain can block out most things, but not the smell of cigarettes. When we next saw the instructor, he asked who'd been smoking. There was no point dropping anyone else in it, so we all immediately owned up. It was the usual death by stare, but I'd given up caring by then.

I didn't have time to think too much about failure as I went from one miserable task to another: climbing cliffs, navigating difficult terrain, attacks on enemy positions, carrying 'casualties' on stretchers. It wasn't until I was in a group briefing on the top of a hill in the trees, when for the first time in a few weeks there was nothing for me to do but sit and listen to an instructor explain the final move out of the jungle, that the full realisation set in.

I was struck by the contrast of the beauty of the golden light of sunset – dappled as it came through trees – and the black feeling of defeat in my heart. I'd given everything, but it wasn't enough. I was as low as I had ever been.

If that wasn't bad enough, I ended up having an argument with the chief instructor, who wanted me to quit, but I refused. I wasn't going to give them the satisfaction. I would finish the course, and at least retain some pride. However, unlike the previous year, and it seemed a bit petty to me, they didn't let those who had already failed complete the final walk. The four of us were told to get on a small helicopter to be taken back to base.

There was no room inside, though. You had to stand on the outside with your boots on the landing rails, hanging onto a chain to stop you falling off. As we climbed up over the trees, I felt like just letting go. But while I didn't know what was ahead, I knew I'd survive and that somehow my mission wasn't over, even if this wasn't it.

To see the dreams that I'd hoped for, and worked for, crumble in front of my eyes, and with only myself to blame, was really hard. Ultimately, though, I came to feel toughened by the experience. I didn't know where I was going next, but wherever it was they had better be ready.

CHAPTER 18

Rwanda

'I know there is a God, because in Rwanda I shook hands with the Devil.'

Lieutenant General Romeo Dallaire, United Nations
Peacekeeping force, Rwanda, 1994

After failing SAS selection the second time, I left the British Army and got a job as a security consultant for a firm that largely employed ex-Special Forces people. What was good was that this was 'real'. You could see the effect of your actions. And, much as I'd desperately wanted the SAS badge, I didn't really want to take orders. Nor did I want to give detailed orders to a large group of people about every tiny detail of the way an operation should run – from the location of the toilets and the smoking area to 'actions' on every single possible event (trivial or serious, likely or highly improbable) – as the army required you to do.

The good thing about being a security consultant in Rwanda, or any dangerous place, was that you were a one-man army who lived on your instincts, and your ability to bluff. That appealed to me more than being an army team leader. This was poker, rather than rugby, and while it required a bit of madness, ironically my last couple of years engaged in the SAS selection process had given me that, if not the formal qualification.

A few weeks before, I'd been celebrating 1994 May Day in Oxford. I had already got this job after a few brief interviews with a couple of former Guards and SAS officers. People in the army had vouched for me being a good operator, and that's all that was needed. Initially, I was meant to be going to Zaire to do security for the diamond mines, but when I heard about the situation over the border in Rwanda, my spider sense told me I'd likely end up there instead.

I flew first to Zaire and then by military plane into Kigali, Rwanda's capital. My first indication that things were done differently here was the huge book that each traveller's details were entered into on arrival. It was like a Domesday Book. They weren't quite using quills, but this was pretty medieval. It seemed that this was what the world looked like after the apocalypse: passport details being handwritten in a big book after you arrived at the airport.

I was picked up by a driver and taken to my house, which was just a suburban home, sort of a 1970s bungalow, the kind of place you'd expect to see in nicer areas of Los Angeles. Until recently, it had probably been occupied by a well-to-do Tutsi or expat. I didn't think too much about what had happened to them.

The job my firm had set up for me was security officer for UNICEF. The organisation was re-establishing itself in Rwanda after withdrawing during the massacres that had occurred four months before, in which reportedly half a million members of the Tutsi minority ethnic group, as well as others, had been killed by armed Hutu militias. I didn't know what had happened to the previous security officer, but he hadn't wanted to come back.

I moved into the house with a number of UNICEF personnel. Unfortunately, I took an instant dislike to them, and they to me.

To them I seemed like a soldier who didn't care for their rules, which was true, and to me they appeared to care only about their own careers, and showing off to each other, rather than helping the Rwanda people.

My job description was pretty loose, but I decided that being the security officer meant making sensible decisions to keep as many people alive as possible. That involved an evacuation plan should the civil war take off again, which was quite possible. The Tutsi army under Paul Kagame – the Rwandan Patriotic Front – had taken hold of the country, but it was still volatile and there was talk of a counterattack by the Hutus massed on the Zaire border, which was only about an hour away by car.

The Hutu militias were largely being sheltered by the sympathetic Congolese in Zaire, and the only thing stopping any attempt to retake their country was their attitude. I wasn't sure whether they still had the energy for the fight. I wanted to see that for myself, rather than waiting in Kigali listening to rumours and waiting for the Hutus to suddenly appear. It would be too late by then, as ten Belgian soldiers killed by the invading forces under Kagame had found out. Reconnaissance and intelligence were worth a thousand men, as Sun Tzu probably said.

I had a Land Cruiser and a driver, who was one of the few surviving Tutsi civilian men. His wife and family had been killed. He was called Gabriel or Celestine – something biblical – as most of them were. The city itself was surprisingly green and hilly, a little like Edgecliff in Sydney, or even Beverly Hills. There were a number of large houses lining wide roads, with beautiful big trees shading them. Most had gates and some even had swimming pools.

The highlight of my day was buying from the 'cigarette boy'. He was this little kid who couldn't have been more than six years old, and may have been as young as four. He still had that pudginess that toddlers have in their face and body. The boy had almost certainly been orphaned and, while I was in Kigali, he came each day with cartons of cigarettes, which I bought and sometimes used as currency. I paid him more than necessary but not so much as to put his life in danger.

I knew he had enough to eat and that he'd be back the next day. He epitomised the survivor spirit, and while he never smiled he didn't cry either. I would have liked to have employed him full-time, but he was safer doing what he was doing. I wonder what he's doing now. If he is alive, he'd be around thirty-five.

A few streets from where I was living there was a church. In the midst of the massacres, Tutsis and moderate Hutus had sought refuge in them – only to find the doors barred shut behind them and grenades and gunfire raining in on them through the windows. The church had been cleaned of bodies but there was still plenty of blood, and it wasn't hard to imagine the screams and the terror of a few months before.

The most poignant reminder of the massacre was when I ventured out of Kigali one day into the green valleys and mountains surrounding the city. Because I didn't want my driver to have to revisit sites that might be traumatic for him, I dropped him off at his home. I came to one of the many village sites where people had been herded and kept in the open in a field for a few days before being killed. Reports indicated that the guards had been drunk and beyond the point of no return that comes when soldiers lose all discipline. They'd selected captives on a whim, and tortured or dismembered them, laughing about it together.

There was a slight slope with a dirt track on it, and apparently the soldiers had said to a captive, 'You're free to go.' Then they'd chopped off their feet, and said 'Go on, run away home,' and watched while the person slowly attempted to crawl up the slope away from them, bleeding out before they reached the top of the hill.

Here, there were still individual bones lying around as the clean-up was nowhere near finished. But it wasn't the bones that moved me; rather, the little pile of identity cards that lay like a pile of leaves next to a guard post. Staring up at me were the photos of the dead and disappeared. What struck me was how hopeful and happy they looked in the photos. A father of two; a university worker; a trainee nurse; a university student. All smiling. Proud of their country and their place in it.

It was useful for me to have a place to make phone calls and otherwise get myself organised, which pretty much meant taking whatever space I could find in the empty buildings evacuated by the fleeing population, and making it my own. In some sort of exercise in black humour, I commandeered the offices of the World Bank. It was pretty trashed but the windows were intact, and it had a nice mahogany desk and big leather chair, in which I could swivel around and put my big boots up on the desk. The UN did do some things right and they had IT technicians trying to get the phones and fax machines up and running. From memory, there were computers but it was the pre-internet days, and I think they largely acted simply as word processors.

Rwanda was a new beginning for me and I was beginning to enjoy it. Despite the huge numbers killed in the civil war, there was something about the appearance of the first shoots of life emerging through the fires and the rubble that was life affirming. Markets were beginning to get bigger and more lively, and people smiled a little if you smiled at them or made a joke. We couldn't change the past, but the best way to approach the future was by looking ahead.

UNICEF – the UN's children's emergency fund, of course – was largely concentrating on their well-established programs of delivering blackboards to schools etc. To me, this seemed a little pointless. The schools weren't yet operational and the biggest danger for children was stepping on anti-personnel mines that were littered throughout the countryside.

I decided that this was the priority and sought to get clearance from the British military commander to start a de-mining program. In so doing, I met a Belgian who was doing communications for Médicins Sans Frontières in Europe. I was impressed with her coolness and matter-of-fact attitude. The NGOs, like MSF and Red Cross, impressed me. They did tough work and had stayed in Rwanda right through the massacres. They weren't pushing a pro-Western political agenda like the UN, and didn't show any favouritism to either side.

The Irishmen who ran the Red Cross amused me by saying that, while the massacres were taking place, they'd refused to give up their house to the invading forces, despite threats of violence. Eventually, it was the soldiers who gave in. They were my type of people: bloody-mindedly and doggedly committed to saving lives, without fear and without wasting any effort on appearance. They'd also refused to leave the country and the people they were meant to help, supplying medical services and food, in the face of the most dire danger to themselves. At the same time they seemed to drink heavily, and see nothing wrong with letting off steam in the local nightclub, which continued to operate during the heaviest fighting. The people from UNICEF were the exact opposite – teetotal and serious – but they had fled at the first sign of trouble.

The Belgian MSF woman introduced me to an English television producer. He was in the country trying to organise an interview with a senior Hutu general, for a 60 Minutes-type show. They wanted to get across the border to Zaire, to a place called Goma, and needed someone to take them. I was keen to see the state of the Hutu army for myself, so after deciding I liked the producer (who had some sort of a British Army connection), I agreed to take them with me.

My UNICEF co-workers were more concerned with ensuring their cocktail party for the international director – or whoever he was – went off successfully than with what was going on over the border, and wanted me to generally act as the VIP's bodyguard. I didn't bother trying to convince them that a Hutu army was more dangerous to them than a gatecrasher, but I wasn't interested in acting as a chaperone for the international director. I'd done enough polishing of doorknobs for 'big-wig' visits in the army.

I couldn't take the Tutsi driver as it would be too dangerous for him (and us). I also needed a very reliable car, which ours wasn't. UNICEF had just taken delivery of a number of brand new Toyota Land Cruisers – with V8 engines and leather seats, no less – and I decided I'd borrow one. It wasn't particularly hard, as all I had to do was stride up to the motor-pool clerk and confidently ask for the keys to the number my chosen car had on the side – and drive off before he had a chance to think twice about it.

Being an army officer at least equipped me with the skills of looking as if I had authority to do things. During my army days, I'd frequently found myself taking charge in situations in which I had no real authority. And I mused that since my mother, soft-hearted as she was, always gave generously to UNICEF when the envelopes with heartbreaking pictures of developing-world kids came around each year, I had as much claim to the vehicle as anyone. It was being used for a better reason than ferrying VIPs around, anyway – that's for sure.

We didn't have detailed topographic maps, only lines on a page, not unlike a pirate map of old. I decided to take a mountain route, which was a lot shorter than the main road. I also knew the main thoroughfare would have a lot of roadblocks on it, and I wasn't sure we'd be allowed through them all. Of course, I expected the mountain path to be undulating, but it was actually much steeper than I expected, and it was lined with gravel. It was very beautiful, but so high at the top that I wouldn't have been surprised to see snow. I was beginning to regret the decision. We tried to stay calm by listening to the one cassette we'd brought along: Éric Serra's soundtrack to the film The Big Blue. It still reminds me of Rwanda to this day.

Nearing the crest in a remote area, we got a puncture. I wasn't bothered at first, because we had a spare. One thing I didn't have was the key to the lock nut. As I contemplated what to do – without revealing any concern to my passengers – the previously deserted mountain road started filling up with curious villagers, or refugees. They surrounded the car and looked at us with silent thousand-yard stares.

Rwanda was densely populated, and even the mountainous forested precincts were teeming with people, usually out of sight. I didn't know whether we'd suddenly get mobbed by people who were starving – or simply angry – and I knew I had to change that tyre pretty damn quick. I simply bashed the lock off, which also showed onlookers that I wasn't someone to be messed with. Within five minutes, we were watching the still silently staring crowd shrink in the rear-view mirror.

It was downhill all the way into Zaire now. We still had a few more hurdles to cross – the ubiquitous militia roadblocks that spring up in any civil war, as much a way to shake travellers down for food and money as to control the country. Nothing says 'I'm in charge' like stopping cars and taking whatever it is you want.

When you're approaching a roadblock in a country in the midst of a war, there are a few dos and don'ts. Firstly, have the right car. Today we were lucky and the one I'd borrowed from the UNICEF motor pool was just right, with its V8 engine, mag wheels and tinted windows. Even the stereo can help, because if you're playing loud music when you wind down the window, it's at least unnerving for the guards. It shows that you're treating them with the same disdain that you might cattle on the road.

Then there's the attitude. This has to be in the middle: half-smiling because, like them, you're a pirate, not a civilian. Equally, you need to be a little serious, as if you're on a mission for the 'big boss' and you are not to be fucked with. Your speed is also crucial. If you go too fast, it'll look like you're going to try to run it and they'll open fire; too slow and it will suggest you have a guilty conscience – that you believe you don't deserve to get through.

So you slow down just enough that when you wind down the window you can look the guards in the eye with your best 'I'm more dangerous than you' stare. Then you shout at them to move the barrier – after flashing whatever official-looking pass you have; just briefly, as if it's something powerful. You then drive off, swiftly but not *too* fast. As if you're a busy businessman entering your regular parking station.

This was about the third roadblock we'd come to that day, and probably the most dangerous. The soldier on the makeshift boom gate of rope and oil drums had the usual mix of uniform and broken mirrored sunglasses, perhaps stolen from someone he'd gunned down in the massacres, or a fellow soldier he'd killed for them. He had an AK-47 in relatively good condition, and at least he didn't have a wig on – the sure sign that things were going to be bad.

We stopped the Land Cruiser and he and I had a brief conversation. While he was pausing to think about whether to let us through, I offered him a packet of cigarettes. He motioned for two, which I handed to him, in exchange for us driving out immediately. We were both happy. Smoking might be bad for your health, but cigarettes had saved a lot of lives over the years. We crossed the border into Zaire about five minutes later, and soon Goma came into view. We'd made it, and I was as surprised as anyone.

I'd only been in Rwanda for a few weeks, but felt very much at home. There were no rules as such; you just made things up as you went along, which suited me fine. As long as you believed what you were doing was right, and would save lives, you did it. I was now going to see the huge refugee camps, and to help decide how likely an invasion by the defeated Hutu army might be. If the 100,000-odd refugees – civilians and militia members alike – decided to move back into Rwanda, it was going to cause some serious logistical and military problems.

The Goma refugee camp was like nothing I'd ever seen. It was a bit like a battlefield, except there were small blue plastic sheets made into shelters, and people were huddled underneath.

There had recently been heavy rains, and the civilian refugees and the militias were living side by side in the mud. It seemed that the NGOs were overwhelmed and were treading water – almost literally. You could see the desperation of the local people, as well as the lack of support they had received from the world community.

Death and disaster in Africa no longer seemed to have much of an effect on the West. Even with half a million killed and many more displaced, there hadn't been much of a response. We couldn't do much to help here, but maybe the television story could bring more attention to the situation.

The crew had arranged for an initial meeting with a former Hutu general to explain himself and their side of the story. The interview was conducted on the veranda of a large suburban house. The general had a number of guards standing around, as well as on the road beyond the house. They were wearing neat civilian clothes, as if they were playing golf. They had guns, though, and looked quite professional – if not exactly the Guards Division.

It was a tense situation, because I felt that anything could happen. A commercial TV investigative interviewer might ask some silly questions in order to get that 'wow' factor for the trailer, or for the show itself. There was a possibility these soldiers might seize the camera, or us. I stood and watched from the garden, ready to get the crew into the car, if necessary. There were only four of us, so we were heavily outnumbered, and we had to bluff the soldiers into believing there'd be big trouble if anything happened to us.

The general explained himself to the interviewer, who asked questions like: 'What do you say to those people who say you are a war criminal?' He looked pretty calm and nondescript, not that I was surprised. It's usually only in movies that villains look evil. This was a chance for the general to appear civilised and reasonable and I didn't think he'd blow it. He didn't and we packed the equipment into the Land Cruiser and prepared to leave. Leaving was the tensest part. If they were going to do anything it was then, or following us after we left, when the camera was packed away and we couldn't prove it was them who'd attacked us.

In the car I spoke to the producer, who was the brains behind the show. He said that the general they'd spoken to wasn't actually the senior general he'd been hoping to interview. It seemed that the other general was staying in a nearby hotel, but had declined to speak to us.

We decided to see if we could find him, anyway. We went to the hotel, outside which all the journalists were camped, a sort of sprawling mass of tents and generators. They were struggling with the technology. In those days, the only way to get stories back to their headquarters in the UK, US and elsewhere was to fax them via satellite phones powered by the generators. The problem was that both were unreliable, and if the power or signal was lost halfway through the delivery process, it failed and the story had to be sent again.

All the major international journalists seemed to be here. However, I kept hearing that getting the pieces published wasn't easy. There was a saturation in the West about atrocities in Africa, and simply reporting on tens – or even hundreds – of deaths didn't appear to justify page space. Apparently, it needed to be thousands, and it seemed that journalists were sometimes resubmitting rejected stories, with double the number of deaths. They didn't see it as dishonest; rather, a desperate attempt to get the world to care about something they could see was significant. There was an echo of my father's story to it.

That night, in the remote hope we might run into the Hutu general in exile, we crashed a wedding at the Sheraton Lake

Side hotel. It was pretty funny, and like a lot of things in central Africa, the truth was almost stranger than fiction. Less than three kilometres away were 100,000 desperate and dying refugees, but here was a wedding with two hundred guests, all dressed to the nines, with white taffeta, black ties, shiny shoes, white tablecloths and flowers on every table. There was even a Michael Jackson impersonator. We tried our hardest to blend in, but were the only ones not appropriately dressed. I hadn't thought to bring a dinner suit. It didn't matter, though; we just bluffed it as if we were at a roadblock. We were press covering the wedding for *Hello!* magazine, we said. No-one seemed to think that was unbelievable, I guess because it wasn't.

As the speeches wore on, we made the decision to give it up. I wasn't happy about the possibility of fighting with hotel security. We'd already recorded an interview with a senior military official, and it wasn't as if the general was likely to say anything apart from the fact that he was defending his country from a foreign invasion (both sides could, accurately, make that claim), and that he had nothing to do with the massacre of civilians.

We drove back into town and went to see if we could find out more about the overall situation in Goma from local sources. This meant going to a nightclub, where all the NGO staff were likely to be. When we got there, we came across another crazy scene: it was heaving with a raucous group of Westerners dancing and doing shots. I didn't blame them. They were living on the edge, confronted daily with overwhelming tragedy, and when given the chance to let off steam, they did. We didn't see any reason not to join in.

The next morning I woke up with a fearful hangover. We were returning to Kigali, and decided to go directly along the main road. There'd be fewer checks heading back to the city, as no-one wanted to escape into Rwanda. No sane person, anyway.

My world was expanding. I enjoyed this kind of work; even the heartbreak of lost causes, or at least making some small difference in the world. You had to act for your conscience whatever the orders were. Sometimes it was the rule-breakers who were happier with themselves than the prefects. Power structures could let you down.

CHAPTER 19

Il Cattivo

It was in 1997 – a couple of years after Rwanda – that I was approached by a friend who needed a favour, although not the kind of favour someone usually asked for. Isabella had been married to an Indonesian, but they were now estranged. He'd taken their five-year-old daughter with him, and she was desperate to get her back.

I guess I had some sort of reputation. She was Italian and she called me *Il Cattivo*. It meant something like the 'bad guy' or 'bandit'. Clearly, I seemed to her like the sort of person you approached if you wanted someone to help extract a child from another country. We met up in a bar in West London so she could better explain the situation. It was clear that we were discussing criminal activity, even it was for a good cause, and we wanted to be discreet. I agreed to it pretty much immediately.

Isabella had tried to retrieve her daughter before through legal channels and she detailed, showing me the paperwork, those many failed attempts. It was times like these that I despaired of the law: I could see how expensive and demoralising it was for everyday people. Sometimes, justice seemed only for the wealthy.

It wasn't so much that I thought the task would be easy, but it was something that had to be done, and I knew that I was a good person to do it. The security area was rife with fools and conmen, and if I didn't take the job I thought there was a good chance Isabella would get fleeced, or maybe double-crossed by someone who realised they could get more money from the father; perhaps they'd hire someone who'd stuff up the whole mission through overcomplication.

The pictures Isabella showed me of her little girl smiling, and the tension on her face then, were powerful. This, at least, was a decent use of my skills. I couldn't really *not* do it. I could say it was too risky, but what did that mean: too risky for me, or for them?

She would pay my expenses but nothing more, so that gave me the moral high ground which helped in these situations. Doing the same thing simply for money or reputation stacked the odds against you – karma-wise, at least. And as with the SAS officers' week, I knew a simple plan was a good plan. I also had the ability to bluff officials, and not to fear violence so much that it paralysed me.

I flew out to Indonesia to see the area and consider some possibilities. I planned to meet up with Isabella a few days later. Her daughter lived in a big compound in Java, with her father and lots of servants. He ran a successful export business and had the local officials on his side. No legal methods would be successful, as business owners in the region were too important to be crossed by a local judge. While our own systems of law in the Western world certainly favoured those who could afford good lawyers, I knew this was an entirely different proposition.

Looking at a map of Indonesia and its thousands of islands, I'd decided there were two main escape options once I'd located the girl: one long and grinding; the other short but requiring a bit of bravado and luck. The lengthier plan would involve an internal flight to Borneo, walking across the border into the Malaysian states, then flying to Singapore or Bangkok.

When I got to the Kalimantan–Brunei border in Borneo, however, I could see the border crossings were well guarded and the jungle reminded me of the secondary growth I'd walked through during my SAS jungle training. So I knew it was dangerous enough for adults – and impossible with a child. You'd struggle to move any faster than about three kilometres a day, and you'd get caught by an army patrol if you were lucky, and die if you weren't.

I flew back to Java and tried the 'idiot abroad' route. This involved going to one of the golf-course island resorts off the coast of Singapore, which were part of Indonesia, but used for golfing day trips by the rich based in Singapore. While Singapore had professional, computerised customs, with good communications with international law enforcement, I discovered that one area in which their immigration officials might be a bit more forgiving was rich people who'd had a few too many G&Ts on a trip to these resorts and lost their papers.

So, I decided to try my luck. I got on a ferry, without the correct ID and visa, but with lots of smiles and a $20 'gift' to the chief customs guy. My strategy was 'Not too little, not too much'; my transgression was, after all, just the result of losing my papers on a golf trip.

It was a lesson I'd learnt years earlier. If you're down on your luck and need a room for the night, go to an expensive hotel, not a cheap one, because they're used to millionaires arriving in bare feet and ripped clothes, and wouldn't take the risk that you weren't one. Having arrived safely in Singapore, I went straight to a cheap hotel, as that's all my budget stretched to, and opened a Bintang as I took in the heat and smells of the downtown area.

A good thing about having donated to the official was that next time – when, if everything went according to plan, I'd return with Isabella and her daughter – he'd be less likely to refuse another bribe. It was a typical con trick of those I generally despised, but this time it was for a good cause.

While I drank a second Bintang, I thought about the journey that had brought me here. From my time in Africa, I was beginning to see what I was happy to do and what I wasn't comfortable with. I was realising I wasn't suited to taking orders unless they were based on some sort of ethics. I was comfortable about this particular job. I trusted Isabella and believed I was doing the right thing. This was the sort of job for which I'd so wanted to join the SAS: using my brains, and bravado, to help people when they couldn't help themselves. I was Goldilocks trying the different beds.

The military didn't entirely suit me, but there were some things that were right about it – assuming you worked for an honest government, that you were genuinely trying to protect your country, preserve the rule of law and, if necessary, save lives, risking your own in the process.

The problem with being a private security consultant was that you simply did whatever you were paid to do. It looked like being a soldier, but it was not the same. Being a mercenary with a job to defend a particular country was workable morally, as long as you were defending a country. However, the problem with private security contractors like those I worked for in Africa was that they lacked that moral high ground.

It wasn't that I ever felt I was working for James Bond master-villains, but I wasn't employed by particularly good people either. You were just as likely to be perpetuating misery in the world as relieving it, considering that the only people who could afford you were the large corporations and institutions. Helping individuals with their challenges was satisfying, though. So I was quite happy out here in Singapore sipping the Bintang, and awaiting Isabella's arrival.

We arranged to meet back in Java in the city near where Isabella's ex-husband and daughter lived. Isabella was able to visit her child; however, she had tried and failed to take her back to Italy once before, and so comprehensive was the former husband's hold on the local authorities, he didn't seem fearful she would try again.

The daughter didn't have a passport, but, back then, very young children could still get away with being on their mother's passport. While I was waiting for Isabella I went to a local toystore and bought something to amuse the daughter during our lengthy trip. It was the most elaborate Barbie I could find – a Rapunzel, with a huge long plait of blonde hair, stretching all the way to her high heels, and a purple sparkling ballgown. It came in a large Perspex case, complete with stand and castle backdrop. It was bulky, but I decided it was worth the space in my bag.

The day came to make our escape and I met Isabella and her daughter outside the compound walls. I tried to act relaxed, as there was nothing to be gained by panicking. The plan would either work or it wouldn't. The three of us had a short picnic together in a park, and I pushed the little girl on the swings before giving her the Barbie. She seemed happy. We got an icecream and I asked her if she wanted to go to Disneyland. When she replied, 'Yes, of course,' we got a cab – all very normal – and took the short trip to the local airport. No passports were required there. We were in the air in about 30 minutes.

Isabella had sat rigid in the taxi. Her face was white as she smiled but she couldn't really talk as her jaw was stiff with fear. It was time for me to keep her daughter laughing and guessing, hoping my confidence would be infectious. We got off the first plane in Jakarta and quickly changed to another local flight to the golf resort. Again, no passports were required, and we acted like a Western family on holiday. By the time I suspect the husband realised we'd gone, we were landing at the resort.

I was beginning to get nervous, because I knew this was the tricky part. I had learnt some useful things from the military, including the value of rehearsals. Because I'd been to this exact exit gate only a week before, and crossed without a valid visa for a small bribe, I believed it was likely to work. *Likely*, but definitely not guaranteed.

I'd asked Isabella to wear her shortest dress and now smile her biggest smiles, as she berated me for once again losing our papers. I saw the chief customs guy I'd seen the week before and gave him a smile and high five. I explained the situation, and apologised via another $20. Then, it was *thunk, thunk*: the best sound in the world, the rubber stamps hitting the passports.

We were so close now, but still not quite home and hosed. There was an awful, endless, five-minute wait for the ferry. The boat seemed to be in slow motion as it docked, full of passengers, and everyone took an age to disembark. Finally, we got onboard, counting the seconds and minutes, *almost* free.

Thankfully, the little girl was still happy. For her, this had been the best day ever: seeing Mummy, getting a new doll, scoffing down an ice-cream, and with someone big to swing her around whenever she asked.

As the crew threw off the ropes and the engines revved up, the ferry began to move. Then there was shouting from the jetty and my heart almost stopped. Isabella looked like she was going to be sick again – she'd already vomited once this morning from the fear. I squinted to see what the shouting was about, half-expecting there to be policemen waving guns; instead, it was simply a middle-aged American couple, late for the ferry. I wanted to kill them and kiss them at the same time.

Then we finally set sail. An hour later we were in Singapore, and six hours later on a flight to Italy. I spent a couple of days in the mountain village where Isabella's friends lived and where we had gone to lie low for a few days. It was a remote, tiny place and very peaceful after the previous week's adrenaline rush. I didn't feel entirely comfortable, of course.

Although it was nice to relax for a while after the drama, I was no longer needed and it was time to leave mother, daughter and extended family to enjoy each other's company. It was a good feeling, although I knew I'd have to watch my back from the father. Pricked ego can be a big motivator. I realised that the best thing for me to do was to fade into the background, which is what I did.

After the job with Isabella, I had the idea that I could take on more of these jobs. I'd done some research and discovered that there were plenty of similar cases. However, generally the mothers (and they generally *were* mothers) were relatively impecunious and to do things properly required a bit of cash. I'd come up with an idea, though, that was a bit unconventional.

I knew that Isabella's story was compelling, so as we'd been organising – and then executing – her escape from Indonesia with her daughter, I'd been doing some filming. I thought we might be able to make it into a TV show, and with some help from a show-business agent, I made it into a TV pilot. I figured I might be able to do the same with other reunions, because they were likely to be equally tense and dramatic. I thought the cost of the rescues could be met by filming the stories and getting them aired.

There was some interest in the UK, which was great, but naturally there were legal difficulties with them sponsoring illegal activity. I was happy to argue the rights and wrongs; TV corporations weren't so keen. They said they could pay me through some sort of a trust account, but I didn't like the sound of it. I went home to Australia to see my parents and for a holiday.

Back in Australia, I had a meeting with Channel Nine and James Packer. We had dinner in a harbourside restaurant with a beautiful view of the bridge lit up as a backdrop. Kerry Packer was still alive, but James was getting more involved in the business. He impressed me when he said he thought that TV should be a force for good, which is why he seemed to like my show.

When I was in the Guards, I'd been a member of the polo club. James had also played there, although, having been a talented schoolboy cricketer he had a good eye for the ball, and he was much better than me. I remember watching him enviously from the sidelines one perfect summer's day at Smith's Lawn, after my team had been knocked out of the competition, and his team, Ellerston, with smart black and white shirts, played in the finals. After I'd played a single season at the Guards, the following year I had a choice of SAS selection or polo – and for me it wasn't really a choice. It all seemed a long time ago now.

Anyway, during the dinner, James tried to convince me to pursue Christopher Skase with a view to making a television program about the chase. Skase, of course, was the fugitive businessman who the Australian government had been attempting for years to extradite to Australia from Majorca to face his creditors. Channel Nine's lawyers kiboshed the idea, though – and I wasn't keen, anyway. My instinct said it wasn't quite right. Reuniting desperate mothers with unhappy and lonely young children seemed to me to be on the side of good, even though the line might be blurry. If something bad happened while you were trying to do something good, it was bearable. But chasing Skase was probably slightly over the line.

Through James, I met a friend of his and we got along well. She was amusing and intelligent company and a breath of fresh air. I went to a dinner party at her apartment and began to mix with her friends. It was a different crowd than I was used to in Sydney, as most of my contemporaries were doctors, lawyers or stockbrokers, who I now had little in common with.

James's friend didn't drink and noticed that I did. Even before I'd left England, my instincts had been telling me I should start doing something more productive than going to dance parties and pubs. Since my life was largely 'three months of danger, one month holiday', heavy drinking during that holiday didn't seem so unreasonable to me. However, I could see things needed to change and I wanted to spend more time doing something like martial arts or serious mountaineering, although the idea was still unformed. One thing I didn't want to be was sixty years old, and still in the same three pubs having the same three conversations, with the same three friends.

As usual my instincts took control, logical or not. So, one night I accompanied my new friend to a twelve-step AA meeting. At that stage, she hadn't drunk for several years and exuded an air of quiet confidence that I admired. And she hadn't lost her sense of fun.

While I didn't warm to AA immediately, there was something about the people there that I found appealing. It seemed worth a try. So I kept attending the meetings and began my first period of sobriety. I started on ANZAC Day 1998, which I'd chosen especially for its military connotations. It was to last ten years. My head cleared and I gradually felt I could tap into a power I'd not felt before through prayer.

As the fog was lifting, I remained optimistic about my television show. However, I also came to accept that most TV networks were like tabloid newspapers and would always sensationalise things, and that this would likely drive me to situations that would test my moral compass. On the other hand, I knew that it wouldn't be too expensive to finance further pilots, whose content would be more or less within my control. I decided that to raise the money, I'd try to get my first-ever job as a lawyer – about ten years after graduating in law from Oxford.

I secured a position with the commercial department of a major firm in mid-1998. Fortunately, I was able to front up and do a good job, without simply dismissing it as 'boring' – which I'm sure I would have done if I was still drinking. I was lucky to be mentored by one of Australia's very best commercial lawyers, Tony Coburn, who was also an absolute gentleman. Tony patiently taught me how to write legal letters, powerfully and succinctly. Much of my best work in years to come owed a lot to his mentoring.

But while I was open-minded about staying at the firm if I felt I was able to help people, I had a feeling I wouldn't be a commercial lawyer for long. The pursuit of money for its own sake simply didn't excite me enough. It seemed pointless to work for fifty weeks a year for unlikeable clients simply for a two-week holiday, no matter how good that holiday was. I'd lived like that as a security consultant and it twisted your soul in a way money couldn't fix.

While I was settling into my new role, my father, who had been barred from practising in 1993, was applying to be reinstated on the medical register. During his time in the wilderness he'd met another doctor who had been struck off and who'd gone to Western Samoa to work pro bono for a couple of years in order to rehabilitate his reputation. Dad had thought this was a good idea and he'd followed suit, taking with him – among other necessities – his beloved cameras (small and large), and his collection of novels by Somerset Maugham.

When Dad returned to Australia, he happened to meet a generous former QC, George Masterman, at a social function. George kindly offered to represent him in his application pro bono. My father invited me to come with him to meet with George, and as the QC was the perfect gentleman, he could only hint at what Bill needed to do. As a son, however, I could be more direct and tell Dad what he needed to hear, and what no-one seemed to have had the courage to tell him before.

His 'Debendox rabbits' story had been ridiculous, and, as far as I was concerned, he had to admit he'd made a mistake. It wasn't good enough simply to claim that a year in Samoa was sufficient to rehabilitate him. The magic words the medical tribunal wanted to hear were: 'I lied, and I'm sorry.' For someone as stubborn as Dad, it wasn't an easy sell, even when George Masterman joined me in trying to talk sense into him. Luckily, my father had none of his acolytes there – by now, they had all deserted him.

As it was, when he finally got to court, and even though it was clear the judge was trying to help him – and even though the prosecutor was largely on board, he struggled to take responsibility. But in the end, we got over the line, and Dad's licence was restored. It would be a turning point in our relationship in a number of different ways.

Under Jung's definition, I had become a man – because while my father wasn't dead, there'd been a shift, so that while I respected him, and knew that I owed him everything, I was now able to be honest with him about his mistakes and the course of action he needed to take. Likewise, probably because he had so much respect for tertiary education, he'd respected my opinion as a lawyer, and while it was painful for him to admit he had lied, he seemed to see that admitting it, even by implication, was the only right course of action. I think he also appreciated that, after my years in the army, I now had 'street smarts'. As well, perhaps he was aware that I was the most similar to him of all his children, in that I was by no means an angel, but I knew when to hold my ground, and when to make a tactical withdrawal.

As I suspected, his relisting was met with joy by the media: everyone loves a redemption story. We posed for photos with arms raised for victory on the steps of the tribunal. The next morning, he and I caught a taxi together to the Channel Nine studio at Willoughby to be interviewed on their morning show. We enjoyed each other's company and joked together about the events of the day in the back of the cab. Dad had been reminded how much affection the Australian public had for him, and I felt a valued part of his team. It was a good day for both of us.

CHAPTER 20

Toyota Taliban

I knew as soon as we crossed into the Khyber Pass that this was going to be more than just another trip for me. In recent months I'd been among the Tuaregs of the Sahara and ventured to Iran as well – both had been unforgettable – but Afghanistan was the place that really caught my imagination. This wasn't travel: this was history infused with genuine danger.

It was November 2000 and I was here as 'fixer/security' for a documentary series, *Journeys to the Ends of the Earth*. Unit manager was my official title. The places we were going were largely beyond the reach, or even interest, of the average person. The premise of the show was: 'If Marco Polo was alive today, where would he go?'

Although the child-rescue TV series that I'd planned hadn't made it into production, because of the legal issues, I was still interested in the power of popular documentaries – both to help people and to show the beauty of the developing world through stories and characters, rather than history lessons. So when a friend from school, David Adams, called me to say that The

Discovery Channel had commissioned a documentary series, and asked if I wanted to come to Afghanistan with him as security for the episode being shot there, I was tempted. *Really* tempted. However, it was probably out of the question to take eight weeks' leave from my job at the law firm.

Much as I enjoyed the detective work of the law, I had ambitions of doing something more satisfying than filling in 15-minute time sheets. I decided to take the leap into the unknown and left the firm. My plan was to work on as many episodes as possible, and from there hopefully move on to my own show. Thankfully, David had the clout to get me hired for the entire series, even though he had to argue it with the other producers.

After the first episode, which involved a trip to the Sahara, I no longer had to justify my role. My experience in trouble spots around the world allowed them to be free to concentrate simply on filming and having fun. During the series we went to Iran, Georgia, Azerbaijan and Russia, and they were all fascinating in their own way. But Afghanistan – and being offered the opportunity to compare the narrative in the Western media about the Taliban with the facts on the ground – had been the magic word that made me float out of the legal profession. Without it, I might have stayed a commercial lawyer.

Admittedly, the preparation in Sydney for the trip was mind-numbing, and even made commercial law seem interesting: visas, equipment checks, insurance, shooting logs. But as soon as the doors closed on the aircraft – business class, no less – I could breathe a sigh of relief. When the others were probably getting nervous, I was starting to feel a little more alive. Once we landed in Pakistan, the adventure would begin. Once we crossed over into Afghanistan, the adventure would *really* begin.

Initially, we filmed a separate episode in enigmatic Pakistan, where we saw many beautiful and colourful sights. Sadly, if war hadn't been raging in Afghanistan for the previous twenty years, this was what Afghanistan would probably have been like. Peshawar, the ancient city that marks the border between Afghanistan and Pakistan, was not much changed from the days of Kipling and the Raj. The city – which had been the base for the CIA-sponsored Afghan resistance fighters against the Russians in the 1980s – was a chaotic melting pot with an amazing covered bazaar. It seemed like Casablanca to me, or at least the way that mythical place was portrayed in the famous film.

The larger geopolitical forces that affected the region were of only passing interest to me at the time, like clouds in the sky to a shepherd. I was mainly concerned with how they would affect us. And fortunately, it seemed they wouldn't, as long as we continually made it clear that we were neither spies, investigative journalists or missionaries, and that we were here to promote Afghanistan with a positive, travel-based story.

From the relative safety of the local five-star hotel, the Serena, with its piano player in the lobby, and Fashion TV on cable in the bedrooms, we set off on day trips to the Federally Administered Tribal Areas (FATA), which were very different to Peshawar, and dangerous for locals and outsiders alike. On the hill above the road stood fortress-like compounds that housed the local landholders. They had their own private militias and spy services. The Pakistan Army had tried to subdue them on many occasions and always failed. The world largely left them alone, and I wasn't about to take any chances with them either.

As we drove around, we stuck strictly to the advised schedule and route. We'd taken to wearing the local clothes, complete with turban-style scarf, and started growing our beards as best we could. I kept my thick, army-style trousers and walking boots underneath, just in case. Wearing tribal garb wouldn't stop us being kidnapped, but it might keep us alive a little longer if it happened.

In Pakistan – or, more correctly, the FATA – we were invited to watch a game of polo. Actually, it was less like polo and more like the local sport, buzkashi, a kind of horseback rugby, armed with sticks. It was played on a dusty soccer field with small concrete grandstands on either side. The competitors were skilled and aggressive, and as the field was so small the horses were constantly jostling, whirling around, and then galloping headlong either towards each other or a concrete wall.

Soon, I was doing more than simply watching this unfold from the sidelines. The cameraman, English Peter, who spoke the language and had lived in Afghanistan for a decade, mischievously told the local guides that I'd played polo when I was in the British cavalry, and that I should play. They immediately offered me a horse. It was a big compliment and a big risk on their part. Their horses were their lives – worth more than their homes, and much more besides. Of course, I said yes.

It was the most incredible feeling being there amid the mayhem. It was a combination of fear, a determination not to fail, and the sheer adrenaline rush of galloping, competing, and the roar of the crowd, which had gathered by now to see the local heroes in action.

It was a fiery contest, but it told you everything about the people in this part of the world that they didn't hesitate in giving me their best pony, not their worst. I felt shamed by their generosity. They didn't ask me lengthy questions, or get me to sign a waiver. They'd looked at me in my Afghan garb, decided I knew what I was doing, and – despite the fact that the horse was tiny, and I was far heavier than any rider it was likely ever to have carried – they honoured me with their most prized possession.

This wasn't like Smith's Lawn, and I hardly hit the ball, which ricocheted off the concrete stands, but the crowd whooped and cheered from the sidelines every time I thundered my pony into my opponents, and my opponents did likewise to me. By the end, both my horse and I were exhausted, but I was smiling ear to ear. This is why I'd come to this part of the world.

Somehow, this match seemed like a parable of the West's relationship with South Asia. I suspected that they didn't hate us because we were Christian, they hated us because we claimed to be superior, but were actually phony and duplicitous. A few days later, we'd enter Afghanistan, and I'd see the full extent of that failure.

Everybody hated the Taliban, but to me they were simply the latest in a long line of those who'd taken control of Afghanistan by force. I knew that for over two hundred years Western nations had been meddling in Afghan politics, and we couldn't behave like shocked vicars if they eventually got rulers who rejected our Western values.

They hadn't massacred civilians like the Hutus had done, or been involved yet in any wanton destruction of the country, like the so-called warlords of the Afghan civil war. They smashed TVs, but only because nothing good came out of them: as far as they were concerned, it was all propaganda, smut and advertising. I wasn't entirely sure that a bit of TV smashing would do the West that much harm, but the Western media thought it was particularly barbaric.

While the double standards of the West were constantly on show to me, I didn't dwell on them. I was focused on ensuring we got to film what we wanted, and for us all to get out alive. It didn't make any sense for me to annoy or judge the Taliban: they were the reality we had to work with, whether we liked them or not. I needed them to like me, or at least tolerate me. If that was going to happen I needed to show them respect, and attempt to understand them a little. I had to be able to negotiate with them if things ever went tits up.

So, while I knew what the others on the *Journeys* crew thought about the Taliban – a mixture of fear and loathing – mostly, I felt a soldier's curiosity. Of course, I didn't know at the time that they would eventually become my enemy; my instincts were telling me simply not to miss this opportunity to find out more about them.

The first contact we had with a Taliban was in Pakistan, at the border before the Khyber Pass. He was about fifty years old, sitting cross-legged in a hut. He was wearing a black turban, but none of the dramatic black eyeliner for which they were infamous.

Our calm border official probably would not have described himself as Taliban, because, strictly speaking, that meant religious scholar, and had come to mean 'army of god'. But the Taliban were the government, and he worked for them, and seemingly not unwillingly. His hut was devoid of any shows of wealth or status, but while he wore no uniform of any sort, it became clear by the way other people scurried around him that he was the man in charge.

He served us tea in a small candle-lit room, which served as the border checkpoint for Western visitors entering Afghanistan, and was pleasant without being obsequious. As with Rwanda back in 1994, there weren't many people heading into the region, and those who did were receiving a personal greeting from the border guard. He watched our manners as we drank the tea, as if that was just as important to him as what we said, and asked us a few polite questions, the answers to which he didn't seem to care about. He simply smiled and nodded his head and poured some more tea, as if some divine force was telling him the truth about our purpose.

After drinking our tea, and with the crew not sure whether the meeting had ended or not, he took our passports and handwrote his signature on a page. We were free to go. As we left, I said the Arabic blessing 'Wa Aleikum-Salaam', which he seemed to appreciate and returned in kind, with a slight smile. I was glad I'd taken the time to visit a mosque in Sydney and received some instructions on how to pray, as well as a few basic phrases.

We then began our journey into probably the most dangerous part of the world, the eastern provinces of Afghanistan, armed only with our charm and wits. I was convinced that would be enough. One thing the Taliban had done effectively was disarm the population. If we were going to have trouble, it would be from the regime, and I was determined that wouldn't happen.

We spent the night in Jalalabad – about 60 kilometres from the border – and went on to Kabul the next day in our old Russian four-wheel-drive, arriving in the evening. The city was ruined after the civil war, although at night it wasn't so apparent as there were few streetlights left. Houses were lit either by candles or kerosene lamps. Soon, we came upon what the world regarded as the Taliban: a pick-up truck overflowing with lean young men in black turbans and thick black make-up under their eyes, brandishing weapons. If there was no room on the tray, they stood on the running boards. I made eye contact with one of them. He smiled at me and I admit it sent a bit of a chill down my spine. We didn't want to cross them.

They didn't bother us – assuming, correctly, that we must have had clearance to get this far into the country without being stopped. One amusing thing about this particular sight was that their vehicles were in such stark contrast to their attire. Although they were dressed in simple black robes, without any Western accessories, and could have come straight from the nineteenth century (apart from the Kalashnikovs, and rocket launchers), almost without exception they were driving brand new Toyota Hiluxes. Apparently, they'd been fitted for the US market with bright orange paintwork, spotlights, mag wheels and off-road tyres. They even had beach scenes custom-painted on the side, with curvaceous women and sunsets over Malibu. The image would have been gold for any photojournalist brave, or stupid, enough to snap it.

English Peter explained that they'd been a gift from Osama bin Laden in exchange for refuge. The Americans had been trying to kill Bin Laden for a number of years as a result of terrorist attacks for which he'd been responsible on their embassies in Africa. Now he was in Afghanistan, and was paying to be allowed to live there, when no others would take him, via food and vehicles.

We made our way to the once-grand Sheraton Hotel, where we were staying. There were bullet holes in the walls and the staff seemed to have dusted off their clothes simply to look after us. From memory, we were the only guests.

Our first meeting and opportunity to film was with the minister for health, who was a medical doctor. He lived in a well-guarded but unpretentious house on one of the Kabul hills. He explained that the country was in the grip of a terrible famine and he was devoted to saving people, especially children, from starvation. I detected no hypocrisy in his words, and, certainly, he didn't live grandly. As he talked to us, he was simply sitting on a carpet in a plain room, drinking tea.

We travelled around the ruined city, filming the bombed-out public buildings. Then we went to the zoo, which surprisingly was still functioning. It was said that one of the warlords had fed someone who had displeased him to a tiger. There were also stories of the escape of the wild animals during the war – some had been seen fleeing past soldiers engaged in fierce battles.

Among the animals still there was a pair of eagles. While I'm not scared of birds, these were four feet high, and I couldn't help but think that they were probably capable of killing a human – having huge beaks and hand-like claws with sharp nails. Scary as they were, though, they didn't deserve to be mistreated, and I was disappointed to see a couple of Taliban poking one with sticks through the chicken-wire cage. They didn't hurt the bird, but it was indicative that they weren't exactly model citizens.

In fairness, it probably wasn't any different to the way soldiers in the UK army might behave. I wanted to give them an order to stop, but my job wasn't to make trouble. Even if it meant watching them torment a bird, we weren't here to challenge the Taliban.

As the trip wore on, I began to feel more confident around them. It became plain that they were largely uneducated and rough soldiers: nothing more, nothing less. They might harass us momentarily, but they didn't have any master plan for world domination. They had taken control of the country for Islam and to end the tyranny by warlord, but exactly what that meant was still a work in progress.

The health minister had recommended we stop at a refugee camp outside of Kabul. While the government had wanted us to see it, I had no reason to suspect any bad faith on their part. It was on a bleak mountainside, and while nowhere near as big as the one in Zaire, it was still heart-wrenching. We were shown the tiny bodies of children who had died that day – small packages wrapped in white sheets. As the Islamic tradition requires burial on the same day as death, it seemed unlikely to be an attempt to mislead us.

I counted about eight; not a huge number, if it wasn't your child. We filmed a couple of fathers crying, asking us why the West wasn't doing more to help them. There didn't seem to be anger against us – just the pain of parents who had lost children. We had no answers.

There were three Taliban guards assigned to us. A short one with a round face and a prosthetic lower leg, who seemed to be the leader; a taller one who was younger and had a pock-marked face, and another who I hardly noticed as he was the most junior. It was a typical cross-section of any army: the good, bad and the ugly. 'Pockmark' looked a bit mean, but the man with the prosthetic leg was clearly an officer, and reminded me of a captain from the British Army.

While the rest of the crew were finishing their lunch, I asked the 'captain' to take me around the poppy fields. We spoke plainly, one soldier to another, through an interpreter and where possible in broken English. He recognised the soldier in me, and we didn't spend much time talking politics. He asked me why the Americans were placing sanctions on Afghanistan, because the sanctions were killing their children. I had no choice but to say it was largely political bullshit.

He told me he had fought in a battle in Bamiyan, the last major conflict of the civil war, which was where he had lost his foot. I was impressed with his prosthetic leg and I thought of my fellow officer who'd had his foot blown off in Northern Ireland.

I asked him about his weapon. He showed me and said it was good – not accurate but reliable. I asked about the Hiluxes and he smiled as if to say, 'They are the best.' 'Toyota and Honda [motorbikes being their other preferred mode of transport]. Reliable, not like Indian copy,' he said, and gave the thumbs up, followed by a thumbs down.

One day while the crew were filming elsewhere, the three Taliban and I went to view the former poppy fields that the Taliban had burnt. I was interested to see if they had just burnt some for show, or had really tried to eradicate them as claimed. Field after field seemed to have been destroyed. When I asked them about it, one of them said, 'Mullah Omar has decided it is un-Islamic to grow poppy that kills people.' Interestingly he didn't say 'Afghans'; rather, 'people'. The media in the West was happy to talk about how the Taliban had destroyed TVs and banned kite flying, but rarely mentioned that they'd also banned the destructive opium poppy, because they believed it was dangerous for everyone.

The Taliban 'captain' and I had a conversation in broken English about the preservation of Buddhist statues. He said that Mullah Omar, the leader of the Taliban, had decreed they would not destroy them, as they would attract tourism. He had no problem with idols of unbelievers, apparently (although that would change with the obliteration of the Buddhas of Bamiyan statues a few months later). However, he was increasingly frustrated that the West would give millions to protect monuments, but nothing to feed those dying of starvation in the refugee camps. The emergence of the camps was largely a result of the bad harvests of the previous two years, which had been exacerbated by the effects of the war against Russia, which the West had sponsored to the tune of many billions of dollars. I had no answer to that.

On one of the last days of the trip, we were sitting in the courtyard of a little private guesthouse in a more affluent suburb of Kabul – in other words, one of the least destroyed. An English expat had rented us the space for a few days. I was lying face down on a banana chair, trying to sleep. The crew were packing their equipment for the trip back to Pakistan. After eight weeks of being a fixer, both here and across the border in Pakistan, I was growing tired of the camp life and was making the most of simply resting for a few hours while we were in a safe place. The four-wheel-drives would be coming to pick us up in an hour. Then in walked an unexpected visitor.

The first thing I heard was the words 'Where is my neighbour?' I instantly went from dreaming of clean sheets in the hotel back in Pakistan to 'alert' mode. The second thing I noticed was the AK-47 the man was not just holding, but pointing at the crew. This guy wasn't Taliban, though. He had the appearance of a nervous bank robber confronting a teller, demanding the cash or else.

The man was wearing the traditional white headscarf with black headband of Saudi Arabia. Once again, he asked loudly, 'Where is my neighbour?' It's odd the things you notice. I immediately picked up that his English seemed fluent, but with a nasal American accent, as if he was from New Jersey.

This time, he said it with more urgency – the weapon pointed across the courtyard at the crew, then at me, then back at them. His eyes were wild and he was panicked. If we didn't give him an answer soon, he might shoot someone, or all of us. If someone had grabbed a pistol in response, he definitely would have shot them.

Whoever this guy was, he looked more scared than aggressive. He seemed to think we were there to harm him, but I gambled that he wouldn't just shoot us in cold blood as long as we stayed cool and calm. And I was in charge of security – I'd been employed for precisely a situation like this.

Lying on my stomach on this banana chair, I decided the best thing was to smile my way through the crisis. The neighbour he was referring to was the owner of the house. I told him she was shopping, trying to sound as much like a harmless, larrikin Aussie as I could. I guessed the reason he was so agitated was that there were four youngish, fit-looking men here, wearing local dress but clearly Westerners, and more likely to be soldiers than employees of an NGO. He might have thought we'd come to arrest or kill him and his family. His alarm was probably understandable.

This man was slightly overweight, unusual in Afghanistan at the time. He had a thick black beard and a better standard of dress than the Afghans. His Arabic scarf was pristine, which again was unusual in dry, dusty Kabul.

As his AK moved up and down a little, he was slightly unsure of himself – this was not good. It doesn't take much to pull a trigger. In this small space he was going to hit *someone*, and if the assault rifle was on 'auto' he was going to hit most of us. Rising up on my stomach as far as I dared, I knew that if he pulled the trigger I was going to have to leap at him. I was preparing myself to do so, while at the same time keeping my friendly Aussie smile fixed on my face. There was still plenty of opium smoking going on in Afghanistan, and it wasn't impossible that's what we'd been doing.

I stretched slowly to demonstrate to him that I was just waking up, and everything was totally cool. After I said, 'She's just shopping, man,' I added, 'She'll be back.' He gave me a wild-eyed stare. Then there was a long pause while he trained the weapon again from me to the others, then back to me. I tried to will the crew to stay cool.

Fortunately, he then calmed down. He seemed to realise that we were telling the truth. Then he muttered some sort of

insincere-sounding apology, saying, 'These are dangerous times.'
He left through the open gate of the courtyard, then disappeared
into the house across the road. The other crew members were
staring after him and were still a bit pale. No-one spoke for a few
seconds.

'He was harmless,' I joked, trying to diffuse the tension.

'Why was he so bothered?' the others asked.

'He thought we were soldiers,' I explained. 'And he couldn't
see the owner of the house and didn't understand what we were
doing here. He seemed to think we'd killed her.'

When English Peter, who had spent the night at his home
in Kabul, arrived at the house later that day, he told us who our
visitor had been.

'He was something called al-Qaeda,' he said. 'And he would
have shot you in a flash if he'd wanted to. What's more, the
Taliban would have simply accepted it, taken your bodies to
the edge of town and dumped them.'

Peter was one of the few Westerners who'd met Bin Laden
in recent years, filming him in a cave after having to travel
blindfolded for a few hours. He said he had a cold-fish hand-
shake. Peter went on to explain that al-Qaeda members, while
unmolested by the Taliban, were apparently jumpy because the
CIA were attempting to capture or kill their members, if possible.
A couple of years earlier, President Clinton had launched cruise
missiles into Afghanistan in an attempt to target their training
camps. Some of their operatives had also been captured and
interrogated in the Far East – Singapore and Bangkok. As Bin
Laden was clearly undeterred in his intention to attack the US
any way he could, it was possible that al-Qaeda assumed the
Americans would in turn try more attacks against them, perhaps
with a ground team. Hence our friend's panic when he saw us in
his neighbour's house.

Nine months after we departed Afghanistan, I was back in
Australia, and I'd just been out to dinner with my then girlfriend.

Neither of us watched much TV but for some reason it was on, and we saw the eerie image of the Twin Towers in New York, viewed from a great distance and in silence. We stood transfixed wondering what it meant, when one of the towers collapsed. We soon heard the reports that Osama bin Laden had taken responsibility.

After the Afghanistan expedition, the production crew did a few more trips. We went to Azerbaijan and Georgia; also to far-eastern Siberia, Kamchatka and Vladivostok. Finally, we journeyed to Cambodia where I was interested in hearing about Pol Pot. As fixer I did a fair bit of travelling on my own.

I was taken to the remote border camp where Pol Pot had spent the final years of his life under house arrest. He had been dead a few years now, and although the walls of the little cottage had been pulled down, his possessions still lay around in the ruin, including what appeared to be his heart medication. I thought it was interesting that it was still lying around, so I souvenired it. It was like having Mao Zedong's nail clipper. His guard had burnt his body after his death, and the little ash pile was still visible.

The highlight of the Cambodian trip was cruising down the Mekong River on a 'smugglers' boat, a large wooden motorised barge capable of holding a large amount of cargo. None of the crew spoke any English at all. They smoked their cheap cigarettes watching the swirling currents ahead, and occasionally gave me a yellow toothed smile. At night we would make camp at the little villages that emerged from the forests. They seemed only to be accessible by the river, apart from a few footpaths that led into the jungle.

One of my favourite memories was seeing the village kids diving into the water and screaming with joy as the sun went down. Even in this modern world, and after the devastation of the previous thirty years, it was great to see children enjoying the simple pleasures.

By this stage, though, my heart was no longer really in this type of travel documentary. However, I couldn't go back to my old job as a solicitor. I had come too far in life to be pushing papers around for corporate clients. Something was driving me in a new direction. But what next?

CHAPTER 21

Politics

I'd always been interested in politics and, when I arrived back in Australia in 1998, I'd joined the Labor Party. This was largely as a result of British Prime Minister Tony Blair who, at that time, had really impressed me. Through the 1998 Good Friday Agreement, with the help of the major players in the IRA, he had done the impossible: brought peace to Northern Ireland. This was politics at its best, the Labour Party solving the big problems in a collegiate way, rather than the Conservatives, who seemed to see every opportunity for war as an opportunity for votes. My English friends didn't agree with me and saw through Blair even then; perhaps I was more naïve. But after the misery I had witnessed around the world, anyone who achieved peace in a never-ending war seemed worth supporting.

I hadn't done much with the Labor Party except go to a few branch meetings, which I'd enjoyed. I found the people there to be good people. They seemed to want the best for the majority and were aware of the difficulties faced by the most marginalised, who weren't simply lazy, but often faced insurmountable problems not of their own making.

After *Journeys to the Ends of the Earth* came to an end in 2001, I needed a job. My former coach at Sydney University rugby club, Peter King, was now the local federal MP in Wentworth. I heard he was looking for an assistant for the upcoming election campaign and thought I might be good in the role. He represented the opposite party, of course, although when I explained this to him, he didn't seem to mind. I'd have to resign from the ALP, although I think I simply stopped paying the membership fees.

The prime minister was John Howard, perhaps the most divisive figure in Australian politics. He had fooled me into thinking he was something he wasn't on the basis of a single issue. After a mass shooting in Tasmania in 1996, he had used the resulting national horror to push through sensible, restrictive gun laws. It was the sort of thing that clearly needed to happen in the US, but likely never will. Even in Australia it was a contentious issue and it was quite an achievement on his part.

This was the sort of politics I admired, and I had no problem working in the engine room of a campaign for his party. As I saw it, as a staffer you were really just like a lawyer, arguing your client's case, and could just as easily work for one party as another – in the same way lawyers can switch from prosecutor to defence counsel. And Kingie, after all, was an old friend.

In August 2001, a Norwegian tanker ship, the MV *Tampa*, saved hundreds of refugees from drowning, about 140 kilometres north of Christmas Island. The ship's captain tried to deliver them to the next port, as was the custom of the sea. The next port was Australia. It soon became a heated political issue.

Up until then, Howard's chances of being re-elected PM appeared to be zero. His success with gun control seemed a long time ago, and nowadays he looked like an out-of-touch old man from a generation most of Australia had left behind. However, the way he dealt with this issue ultimately assured his victory. His strategy was to play to the fears of the electorate – a powerful force. While it seemed ridiculous to me at the time, Howard, with the help of the media, managed to paint these desperate people as a threat to the nation.

He dispatched the SAS to take control of the ship and its passengers. The major public exposure of the SAS in the UK had been of them ambushing and killing armed IRA terrorists, so this seemed an overreach from Howard, and a misuse of their skills. But it was clearly popular. The refugees were painted as queue jumpers, a slang term that implied they weren't playing by the rules; also, that they'd soon be stealing jobs from Australians. There seemed to be no basis for this accusation, and in many ways, everyone in Australia, apart from the Indigenous, was a queue jumper.

The *Tampa* drama played out during the weeks immediately before and after the 9/11 terrorist attacks in the US – and anyone not in Australia prior to that date was now a potential suicide bomber. It didn't make much sense for terrorists to come by boat without papers, necessarily spending months in detention, when they could come by plane with false documents (as the real 9/11 bombers did). That didn't seem to matter to voters. I recall thinking that if this was the sort of thing the Australian SAS did, I'm glad I didn't try to join them.

Anyway, Howard won the election, and despite my unease at the simplistic and one-sided way he spoke about geopolitical events, I went from being a campaign assistant, paid from donations, to having a part-time job as a political staffer. Being completely broke has a great way of making your belief systems more pragmatic, and I was pretty sure I wouldn't be asked to advise on diplomatic issues. I'd grown up with my parents being Liberal voters, if not party members, so I didn't expect I'd see anything too alarming.

My main role was to answer letters from residents wanting us to solve some problem they had with their neighbour or their council. People largely seemed to see their local MP as a last-chance genie who could swoop in and save them when everything else failed. In most cases we couldn't, so we applied the 'lottery principle': fix one or two cases and make a big display of that in our own publicity.

This was the reality of local politics. There weren't enough staff to do much except answer letters with vanilla responses such as 'Thank you for your letter'. That *was* the response. Not *solving* the issue. To my frustration, this didn't seem to be a job for anyone who actually wanted to change things. Orders came from the central office of the party, and the three years between elections would be spent gathering mailing lists, attending dog shows, and preparing for the next campaign, in which we'd promise whatever the polling people told us those who were thinking of changing their vote to the other guys wanted to hear us say.

It was a time of atypical behaviour for me. I wasn't partying, I wasn't risk taking. However, for all its faults, I found politics interesting, even if I was in a party whose values I was increasingly coming to question. After about six months, I was encouraged by the campaign manager from the previous election to stand for pre-selection for the state seat of Coogee in the election to be held in 2003.

This involved gathering support within the Liberal Party, and getting party powerbrokers to support me. The culmination of this was having to make a speech in front of party members, both local and from headquarters.

It was quite a nerve-racking experience. The highlight came after I gave the speech, when someone asked whether I felt guilty for oppressing Irish freedom fighters during my time in the British Army. I answered that I had no regrets for volunteering to fight for rule of law over the rule of the gun, or something equally catchy, which got resounding applause.

I felt elated afterwards, largely because putting my hat in the ring for pre-selection was a significant challenge. A bit like SAS selection, I knew I wanted to try it, and that not to do so would have seemed like a cop-out. I didn't know what would come of it if anything, but pre-selections could be extremely bitter battles, and, among other tasks, you were required to hold your nerve in public before an audience, half of which were actively working for your downfall.

I did have concerns about getting involved in state politics, though. Most of our donors were property developers, who wanted the candidate to improperly influence their prospective developments. I hated asking for money from anyone, let alone taking it from people who only wanted something I couldn't give them in return. On the positive side, the only way to fully understand politics was to get involved, and I did learn a lot about how things work. I met some wonderful volunteers who did the thankless leg work for the political parties. They couldn't do enough for me as the candidate, and only wanted some kindness and appreciation in return, which I was more than happy to give.

I had my doubts about the sincerity of the Liberal Party leadership, but figured the ALP were likely similarly compromised. And by and large it seemed the same sort of well-intentioned people operated at the base of both major parties: they were basically good people labouring under the misapprehension that the 'others' were somehow different. Unfortunately, they were able to be manipulated by the most cynical of people who, a bit like American TV evangelists, knew exactly which buttons to push to get them to respond. I suspended my cynicism as much as I could, and got to work as best I could, making public appearances, shaking hands and raising money, not sure where this path would lead but simply trusting that somehow it was where I needed to go.

It was gratifying to win pre-selection, and Dad was proud of me. Having said that, he did immediately add, 'It's not a seat you can win.' It was probably true as it had been a Labor seat for many years and the incumbent state Labor Government seemed unlikely to be troubled at the election by the Liberal opposition and its youthful leader John Brogden. Still, his attitude was a little deflating.

While he had grown to respect my choice of the British Army, my life afterwards had seemed quite lost to him, as the only careers he really valued involved offices, and houses in the suburbs, something which simply hadn't interested me in my twenties and thirties. Like most doctors he was conservative, and his father had been before him, but had little time for politics.

Dad was happy to come out door-knocking with me, though, which was a good bonding experience. We'd spend a couple of hours going from door to door around the steep streets of Coogee, and then adjourn to the Coogee Bay Hotel for a self-cooked steak and cheesecake in the beer garden.

One memory in particular stands out. We knocked on a door and an older woman answered. We introduced ourselves, and she said, 'I know exactly who you are, Doctor. I used to be the dispensary nurse in Crown Street Hospital. I remember when you came in and asked me to take thalidomide off the shelves. I think you've been very badly treated by this country.'

Dad's eyes had filled with tears and he was quietly sobbing. While he'd put on a brave face during all these years, it had taken a toll on him. It must have been so gratifying for him to be reminded that he had, in fact, given the order for thalidomide not to be used by the hospital.

I was standing on the promenade at Coogee Beach one day in mid-2002 – still a year before the election – when the phone rang. It was English Peter, the cameraman from our trip to Afghanistan. He said his sources told him there'd been a massacre of Taliban in Mazar-i-Sharif in the north of the country. They'd surrendered to US forces and had been kept in an underground fortress, which had been deliberately flooded, drowning them like rats.

While neither of us expressed any great disgust about this, it was the sort of crossing the line that both of us recognised.

English Peter could see that to ignore this alleged massacre simply because it was against the Taliban would make him as bad as those he despised. Even the Taliban did not condone the killing of prisoners.

It would be a dangerous story to cover, and Peter needed a wingman, someone who knew how to work both a camera and a gun, and who was able to recognise bullshit when he heard it. So he'd called to see if I'd fly over and join him in making a documentary about the incident. This was another turning point in my life. The old me would definitely have headed straight to Afghanistan. It was clearly dangerous, but also a worthwhile cause. It wasn't a matter of 'Oh, it's okay because our side did it,' or 'The Taliban deserved it.' If something like this was true, even if it went against the established narrative, the world needed to know. However, although I wanted to say yes, for some reason I didn't – without even knowing why, and slightly resenting myself for it.

Curiously, within a few days, I had another job offer with the lure of adventure. An old girlfriend, JoJo, called me and said that a mutual friend, Johnny, had gone missing in Eastern Europe. Even though he was married, she and others believed he had done it on purpose – that he wanted to disappear and drop out of life. He'd been prescribed medication for mental health problems, and he had stopped taking it.

Similar to the 'kidnapping stage' of my life, my friends had decided that I might be the right person, both to find him and convince him to go back to his family, who loved him dearly. The family would pay for me to fly to Eastern Europe and my expenses for as long as it took to find him.

Again, this was exactly the sort of challenge I would previously have pursued. But although I sympathised with their awful, heartwrenching pain, I found myself once more saying no. My instinct, which I didn't always understand but always trusted, was that I had to stay in Australia – and that what I needed was not on the other side of the world, but much closer.

CHAPTER 22

Sarah

With the New South Wales state election three months away, the political campaign broke for Christmas 2002. While I had nagging doubts about the direction I was going in, after some quiet reflection I'd concluded that there was nothing left to do but to fight the election to the end as best I could. As for those doubts, it was like navigating through a forest at night with a compass bearing: you might feel you're going in the wrong direction, but you need to trust the needle.

Prayer to my own conception of God was my compass. It wasn't the God of Jesus; it was more some sort of warrior god, but it was the God of Good. For all my black humour and the nonsense of politics, I never lost the desire or the belief that I would do good, both in the short term with the people I met along the way, and in the long term with my country.

Growing up, we had a holiday house at Palm Beach in Sydney's most northern peninsula. It had been a favourite of my father since he'd gone there with his father and joined the surf club at North Palm Beach. Along with the Easter family trip to Dungog, this was the second annual family expedition. We'd take along assorted surf and diving equipment, vinyl records, Christmas presents, and birthday presents for me and my brother as we were both born in mid-December.

We rented various houses for a few summers, then Dad bought a single-storey Spanish-style place, with a lovely courtyard: close enough to hear the sound of the waves at night, and an easy walk to the beach. We played records loud, drank our first glasses of wine and pretty much celebrated the 1970s in that courtyard. But Dad loved his Dungog country dream so much that when he was struck off the register, he sold the Palm Beach house in order to keep the farm afloat. Ultimately it all had to be sold off to pay his debts. Dreams are expensive. He'd wanted to leave each of his children a farm – at one point he owned several – which would then become their family farm in the future. The Debendox rabbits brought all that crashing down.

Dad had sold the house and the farms when I was away making my life in the UK, so it hadn't been traumatic for me. I accepted that change was inevitable, and at least I had the beautiful memories they had provided. I knew I was lucky to have had it at all, rather than bitter that it was no longer there.

The Surf Club had a couple of major parties each year. Usually, there was one on Boxing Day, and another on New Year's Eve. The latter was a typical out-of-control 1970s surf party when I was a club 'fresher' – a trainee – and the former was a little bit more grown up. This was where I had my twenty-first birthday party.

I'm not sure why I decided to go back for the Boxing Day party in 2002. It was a welcome relief, though, from the relentless campaign trail. I didn't know many people up there anymore, so when I saw an old friend from my teenage years, Jo, I went over and chatted to her. She introduced me to her younger sister, Sarah.

I was taking Sarah in, particularly her eyes and arched brows, which were the sort of eyes you'd expected to see peeking out from over a veil in ancient Persia, when another old friend came rushing from the dancefloor, grabbed my hand and said, 'Come on, let's dance.' So we did, with me looking back over my shoulder at the girl I'd just met. I knew I would see her again, and I did.

In fact, I'd met Sarah before. I'd run into the same friend, Jo, buying lunch in Sydney when I was still working on the travel documentaries, and she'd invited me to come to lunch with her and her family at Palm Beach. There was a family connection, as I also knew her father and stepmother, who I'd met at a wedding in India with JoJo, my old girlfriend, in the early nineties when I was still living in the UK. It seemed like a nice way to spend a Saturday afternoon.

David Adams, my old school friend who was the presenter and producer of the documentaries, had also invited me to visit and he lived nearby in Avalon. I didn't stay at Jo's house for long; I was in the early days of not drinking and there were limits as to how much small talk I could manage. I briefly met Sarah that afternoon, although I gathered she had a boyfriend, and while he wasn't there, it seemed they were planning a wedding. Apparently, she noticed me then too, mainly because I was telling Jo and her husband about what I'd been doing on the documentary series.

While I'd been popular enough in my early years in Sydney, apart from those people I now mixed with from the television world, I didn't do a lot of socialising. I was neither invited to a lot of places, nor did I feel I particularly fitted in, and I suppose I was fairly lonely. Sydney seemed to have moved on, and now banking was king. The city was bigger and had lost some of its charm; either that or I had simply lost my place in it. Probably a bit of both. Anyway, I then continued travelling for the documentary series, and Sarah got married to that boyfriend.

By the time of that Boxing Day party, she was newly separated. A few weeks later I got another invitation from Jo to come to her place for a party at Palm Beach, and while all I could talk about was the pitfalls of being a political candidate, my eyes never left Sarah's. Soon, we were the only two people left standing in the garden.

We went on a date for fish and chips a couple of days later. I forgot my wallet, and didn't realise until after we'd ordered. She didn't complain when we had to drive the ten minutes along a winding beach road to get some cash, and go back again. The date turned out to be a lot of fun anyway, which showed the sort of person she is.

She didn't even complain when she visited the apartment I was renting in Coogee. While in a nice enough location, it was basically unfurnished, with a single bed and strewn with old newspapers.

During these months, as my relationship with Sarah was developing, I was up before dawn every day and down to the bus shelter and local coffee shop, where I met some wonderful people. I even managed to briefly give up caffeine, the only time I've been able to do so, which must have meant I was enjoying what I was doing. So, after a dandelion tea, I'd usually spend the day talking to people, and riding my bicycle up the steep hills around Coogee and to the campaign office in Bondi Junction.

My campaign was about to take a turn for the worse. Unbeknowns to me, some party officials – either well-meaning or malevolent – had leaked a story about me to one of the major Sunday newspapers. It wrongly said I had been successful in SAS selection in the British Army, in an article illustrated by a photo of the documentary team in Afghanistan. It didn't seem to occur to these officials that this might create problems for me; nor did they or the journalist bother to contact me to check any details. Ironically, a story like this wasn't likely to impress many swinging but left-leaning voters in Coogee.

In fact, I hadn't claimed to be SAS at any point in the campaign. In my documentation for pre-selection, I said that I'd passed the physical endurance tests and officer week for the SAS.

This was listed as one of the things I had achieved, along with getting a scholarship to Oxford, and winning a boxing Blue.

The newspaper article should have been denied. I asked the campaign team what to do about it, and the general consensus was that since it didn't quote me anywhere, I wasn't under any obligation to correct the record. I knew in my heart that was wrong, and resigned myself to setting the record straight if I was asked about it directly. I didn't expect that to solve the issue, but I wasn't prepared to lie about it for the sake of my campaign staff, or because it was what everybody did in politics.

It was easy enough not to think about the SAS issue, as there was always some other daily bushfire, or fight between campaign staff, or donors, or people outraged about the latest policy - as well as a string of public appearances I needed to make. I should have remembered the lessons from the past that you should never get too exhausted by the small stuff, and then not properly deal with the big stuff.

I think I was too anxious to appear busy, rather than handling the problems that really mattered. Some of the best advice we ever got at Sandhurst was from an eccentric-looking older officer who said simply, 'Officers must sleep. Don't try and impress your men by doing guard duty - impress them by your decisions that keep them alive.'

I'd practised that as a fixer in Africa and Afghanistan, but I didn't have the confidence to do it in this new world. I was exhausted, as any candidate is, and I was largely going from public appearance to door knocking to public appearance to sleep - and then repeat. At night I prayed about it, and everything else.

The weeks and months of the campaign went on, with many old friends, and even more new, contributing a great deal of effort to help me. I was grateful, but felt quite uncomfortable. I didn't particularly like owing favours and being beholden to people. Probably another area where I was out of touch with the modern civilian world was the ability to ask for help.

It was the opposite of the military, where from day one in basic training you were brainwashed that you should do everything yourself and never ask for assistance. Self-reliance and self-discipline were the soldier's gods. Nor did I feel comfortable taking money from people, especially businesses – usually these were property developers who, as I've mentioned, clearly expected favoured treatment in return. There was an acceptable element of 'that's how the world works' about it, but as with the false claims in the newspaper, my conscience knew that – whether it was normal practice or not – it was wrong and could only lead to problems in the future.

There were other issues that made things increasingly fraught. My campaign manager, who had encouraged me to run, and done a huge amount of work, seemed jealous of Sarah coming into my life. When Sarah attended a function as my guest, my manager immediately resigned in a huff, apparently unrelated. She was eventually talked back into the role, and not much damage had been done. I wondered whether it had been my fault in making her feel that we somehow had more than a professional relationship, but I was pretty sure I never had. Again, it was a new problem for me; workplace crushes hadn't really been a thing in my line of work.

I also experienced an early version of online hate, in the form of letters to the editor in a couple of newspapers. Being thin-skinned, I didn't particularly enjoy this. I hadn't found a way to laugh off criticism – I hadn't drunk alcohol for about four years at this stage – and would often stew on negative comments for days, while I barely noticed the positive comments.

Many people seemed to appreciate the fact that I had at least worn a uniform – patriotism and respect for soldiers ran deep in Australia, as it did in the UK. At some point, however, I made a comment that if we wanted peace in Afghanistan, we would have to engage the Taliban in talks. At the time the Western propaganda about the Taliban eating babies was in full swing and some readers of the broadsheet newspapers took this as a sign that I was a fool. It didn't matter that I had actually been to Afghanistan and seen the situation for myself.

I knew the way to survive in politics was to repeat what people wanted to hear, but I felt that politicians had a duty to try to bring the population with them on difficult issues, not simply parrot approved talking points. Speaking of which, as a candidate I had been introduced to the concept of 'daily talking points' – these were arrived at by telephone polling the few people who would decide the election: swinging voters in marginal seats.

This quite scientific method had a number of negative effects on modern politics. Firstly, it meant that there was no real policy based on principles or reality: everything was simply something that sounded good to swinging voters and it played on fears and anger, which was always easier to sell than hope, compassion and optimism. Refugees were bad, because 'they were taking our jobs', and taxes were 'too high', and there was never a reasonable price to pay for the security and services we all enjoyed. While a strategy like this had less effect on a state election than a federal one, it gave me an insight into the reality of politics that I'd remember many years later.

Things were going to get worse. A couple of weeks out from the election, a journalist from the *Sunday Telegraph* called me. I was naïve enough to take the call myself and speak to him directly and off the cuff. After a few pleasantries, he asked if I had been an SAS officer, to which I replied no, as I was anxious to finally set the record straight. I added that the article that had claimed I was didn't quote me. He seemed surprised that I was so forthright.

I knew, as I ended the call, that this would be a big negative story in a major paper a fortnight from the election. For the first time in the campaign I got in contact with a 'flack' – a media consultant – who I knew from working in Peter King's office. She seemed to think it wasn't a big deal. She daily dealt with much worse, involving bribes and sex, and said that if only I hadn't spoken to the journalist, she would have issued a denial that I'd lied in pre-selection paperwork – and waited for the narrative to shift.

Professional as her advice was, ultimately I was more interested in my own conscience than public opinion. While I think it had been an error for me not to set the record straight by asking for a correction of the original story, at least I'd been clear about it when interviewed, and although the story would be painful, my conscience was now pretty clear.

The piece was published on the Sunday, and it did claim that I'd lied in that paperwork. I hadn't, but I knew I couldn't complain, because I also hadn't tried to correct the record of the story that said I was an SAS officer. Negative stories in the media are simply part of the job in politics, but because it struck at my core belief that I was, if nothing else, a good person and a good soldier, it had a big effect on me.

On the upside I didn't have a drink over it. However, I took to having freezing-cold showers at Sarah's place, where I was largely living now, as taking my mind off it was hard. I knew that your conscience – not public opinion – was your best friend and worst enemy, and I realised I could have done better. At the same time, I knew I could handle even the worst criticism if my conscience was clear.

Sarah was a big help. At times like this, you need to be aware of who you are, and she did that without having to say anything. The god of my own understanding helped as did the AA meetings I was attending, because it gave me a chance just to be honest about the situation I was in, in amongst people who were honest about their own pain.

It was a big week. A few days later, my father had a brain haemorrhage while body surfing at his beloved Palm Beach. Body surfing was something simple that always brought a smile to his face, even aged seventy-five. He loved to get out into the surf with me and see who could go further in the shallow clear waters. Like most Australian fathers of that era, it was the simple things like a beach trip, a barbecue, or his country trips with his kids that seemed to bring out the excited teenager in him.

On this particular clear day, Dad said he hit his head on the sand, but it seems more likely that the effort of paddling for a wave caused a small tear in the membrane of his brain. It might have felt like a blow but was internal. He managed to get out and have a shower at his beloved Cabbage Tree Club and drive home along the winding beach roads to where he and Mum lived. He complained of having a headache, and promptly lay down. Mum observed him for a few minutes as he seemed to lose consciousness.

Mum called an ambulance and then called me. She said simply, 'Try to get here, as I think your father is dying.'

Undoubtedly, he would have died if the ambulance service hadn't got to him quickly. They took him to the nearest local hospital, barely alive, then straight to the brain specialists at Royal North Shore. I went straight to RNS and met my mother, as well as a young doctor, who was – like so many of them – the son of one of my parents' old friends from medical school.

The doctor told us that the operation had been successful, and while Dad would be in emergency for a while, they thought he would survive – albeit after a long period of rehabilitation. I did an interview with the ABC the next day about Dad's life, because they wanted to be ready with an obituary story, just in case. I was happy to do it. It was what he would have wanted, and I was proud of him when talking about his achievements and our time together. It was good of the ABC to do it, as it showed they still credited him with his world first on thalidomide, despite his later failures.

For three months he was in and out of consciousness. He could neither write nor walk, nor even remember much about his life or who he was. Dad was still convincing and forceful, though, and one day, very early in his recovery, he convinced me he was able to walk to the bathroom, and he'd done it before. I didn't think he could, and wanted to check with a nurse, but he was insistent and waved away my objections.

So I helped him to his feet, only to feel him drop straight to the floor out of my arms, as soon as I stopped holding him. When he hit the ground with an awful thud, I realised he'd been hallucinating when he said he'd done it before. I quickly picked him up off the floor – which wasn't at all easy as he was a dead weight – and placed him back on the bed before any of the nurses caught us. Fortunately, Dad seemed to find the situation humorous, rather than dispiriting, and we both had to stifle our laughter – being more afraid of the nurses than of any injury.

Later that week, a few days before the state election, the Coalition of the Willing invaded Iraq. Led by US President George W. Bush, the stated aim of the coalition was to disarm the Iraqis of weapons of mass destruction, which the Americans claimed Iraq possessed. John Howard sent Australian naval ships to support the bombardment. There had been large protests in Australia and elsewhere, as a United Nations inspection team had recently been to Iraq and found no evidence of WMD. The media here was divided on the topic, and even some service-men on the ships were asking for advice as to whether they were supporting an illegal war. I had no insider information on the WMD, although I could see the logic of assuming the worst, even if we didn't know for sure.

Then came the state election, which was an anti-climax in many ways. The Labor Government was returned without being troubled, and I failed to win the seat. While we weren't routed, we hadn't made much of a dent on the sitting member's majority in Coogee. However, I was grateful for all the good people I'd met, and I had learnt a lot. Overall, I was satisfied with the way I'd handled things.

It was a blessing in disguise - Dad's brain haemorrhage too, I was later to conclude. Not only had he survived, but when he recovered his memory he was a much softer and happier version of himself.

I needed a job, and I chose to go to the Bar. It seemed like a good way to help people and use one's brains, so with Sarah's help I started studying for the exams. Before that, we took our first trip together, a walking holiday at Cradle Mountain in Tasmania. It was the beginning of winter and the valley was shrouded in mist. We stayed at a different lodge on each of the four nights, and at the end of each day we'd walk in to open fires and hot bread and red wine - for Sarah, at least. I found I got vicarious pleasure from her being relaxed and excited.

We would walk along the duckboards and through the light rain and marshy hills, and we swapped stories of past experiences, successes and perceived failures. It helped restore my soul after the political campaign and reminded me of who I was. I can still see her smile under her white cap, through the mist. We took lots of terrible selfies with an old-school camera, which still have pride of place today.

On our return to Sydney, I sat my Bar exams. Unfortunately, I failed, and had to do them again six months later - this time I passed. In 2004, I started the Bar Readers' Course and began to make friends with people who would be my contemporaries. The course was hard, particularly the mock courts, because most of my fellow students had been in courts for many years - as solicitors - and knew how to play the part. For those of us doing it for the first time, though, it was surprisingly nerve-racking.

I'd read somewhere that one of the original SAS heroes from World War II, Paddy Mayne, who became a barrister, said he was more scared in front of a judge than on the battlefield, and I could now see why. It wasn't so much the public speaking; rather, it was the need to be precise and concise every time you spoke, taking into account both the law and what your opponent might say in response in a few seconds' time. The judge, having been a lawyer for many years, knew exactly what you should say, but was forbidden to help you say it, for fear of displaying bias.

Barristers, being essentially nerds, hate getting things wrong in front of other nerds, the judge being like the teacher. Many a junior barrister would rather be vaporised in a puff of smoke than experience the shame of committing a public legal faux pas, and I was no exception, especially as there were big gaps in my practical legal knowledge. With all the Latin phrases, and overlapping laws, it was surprisingly easy to do.

As with AA, the way to survive as a young barrister was to spend a lot of time sitting in cafes drinking coffee with older barristers. There was a chance they'd give you work that they weren't able to do themselves, because they were double booked, but, far more importantly, whatever tale of woe you had about being berated by a judge, or some such humiliation, they'd proudly trump your story with one involving a far greater degree of chaos and confusion. You'd end up feeling that your day had been surprisingly good in comparison.

While 2003 had been dramatic, it had largely been a dead end. I'd felt like a laboratory rat trying to find its way out of a maze following a path that seems promising, only to realise the path led nowhere, with an electric shock to boot. Luckily, this rat, now in the midst of a Bar Readers' Course, had been able to turn around and head back into the centre of the maze, even if some of its fur was singed.

CHAPTER 23

Birth, Death and Marriages

Sarah and I had been living together in Kings Cross for about a year and decided to try for a baby. We decided not to get married, at least not before the baby. Sarah had already been married, and big weddings, along with big funerals, were pet hates of mine, as they were generally obscene wastes of money, accompanied by often-disingenuous speeches.

I'd never even particularly wanted children. I vaguely imagined they would come at some point, but they'd never been a key goal. I guess that's another side effect of having a soldier's mindset, in that you wouldn't deliberately set out to have children when you were unsure of where you'd be located in six months' time, or the circumstances of you being there.

That all changed when I saw the ultrasound of what was to become James. Everything seemed to change after that – not through any thought on my part, simply by osmosis. At first, Sarah and I decided to get engaged and to have an engagement party. Then, after her stepfather, Maurice, for whom I had a lot of respect, suggested we turn the engagement party into a simple wedding party in the garden in two weeks' time, we both liked the idea.

We wanted to celebrate with our friends and this made it more genuine and with less fuss. On 15 January, which was apparently a date chosen by Elizabeth I's private sorcerer for a successful coronation, we were married on a lovely sunny day in Sarah's parents' garden at Palm Beach, surrounded by about sixty guests and a small jazz band.

Unfortunately, there was an added urgency to get the wedding over and done with. Sarah's father, Robert, had stage 4 cancer, which had started in his stomach and now spread to his other organs. Five years earlier, he'd only been given a few months to live and had held his own 'wake'. However, with the love and care of his second wife, Susie, and the help of Chinese medicine, he was able to be present at our celebration. I still remember his constant smile at the wedding, even though the rest of his body was fading away to nothing.

A few months later, Robert was gone. Luckily, his last memories were of being surrounded by his wife, his ex-wife (Sarah's mother Tina), his son Robert junior, and his two daughters, one of whom was clearly pregnant. I was waiting outside the room in the hospice and almost at the moment of his passing a huge black cat came by, made eye contact with me, and then disappeared.

After I passed my Bar Readers Course, I began working as a junior barrister from chambers in the city. As luck would have it, one of the barristers had, like me, been a soldier before he became a lawyer, and now appeared as defence counsel in court-martials for the Australian Army. He suggested I look into it as a way of surviving financially in my first few years at the Bar.

I wasn't overly keen on the idea at first. I had never wanted to be a military lawyer, and in my time in the British Army I didn't even know such things existed. If there was a problem with a soldier, the sergeant sorted it out – one way or another – and that was the end of the problem. In the Blues and Royals, there was such a high amount of regimental pride it seemed to motivate soldiers to play by the rules or risk losing that place in the world, which was largely for life. Offences were generally minor assaults in the boozer, which were easily solved without need for lawyers' 'objections on the evidence'.

I had had a sort of a vision about rejoining the army, or at least the reserves. After getting sober I'd had low periods and had been recommended a psychologist by a friend in recovery. We talked about what I missed from my old life and I realised I felt unfulfilled without that element of service in my life. Some of my friends had left the army and become everything from real-estate agents to photographers. They'd never looked back, but others, like myself, only felt comfortable in something that was still, in effect, the military.

This had occurred to me in a flash in an AA meeting in early 2004. Sometimes it isn't until you're forced to verbalise things that you see them yourself. A solution seemed to be to join the Australian Army Reserve, so I made up my mind to do so.

There were the usual hurdles of interviews, dinners with senior people, and medical exams, the same as there had been in the UK army all those years ago. But I was more excited about rejoining the army than about making money or buying a house or the usual things other people often got excited by. I seemed to know this was the right track, because it involved doing something positive for the country I'd grown up in, and which had given me such incredible opportunities, even though I now felt like a tourist – having been away, both physically and mentally, for most of my adult life.

I originally felt I'd join the Sydney based 1 Commando Regiment, but this required about six months of continuous training, which was out of the question as I was just starting at the Bar. I opted instead, eventually, for the Legal Corps.

My operational experience would prove to be useful in advising senior commanders on how to deal with problematic legal issues. The job would be a little like being a fixer, but in a mental rather than physical arena.

James was born on 10 August 2005. We chose the name – unusual for a girl – for a number of reasons, but largely it was instinctive. James had been a family name in Sarah's father's family, and as he'd passed away just before she was born, he was still very much on our minds and we wanted to honour his memory. While I felt I'd known James from the moment I saw her turned-up nose in the ultrasound at three months, we didn't confirm the name until she was born and she seemed to suit it. I knew she would be able to carry it off.

Sarah's mum was there soon after James was born, snapping photos as usual, a thankless task but it meant we had priceless memories of an event we'd never have again. Oddly, as I've mentioned, Tina and I had met even before I met Sarah, at that wedding in India. Like most mothers and daughters, they had a relationship that rocked – from unbounded love to extreme annoyance – over things to which I was frequently oblivious.

Tina may have had a touch of the witchy insight. Hours after her birth, James was wrapped up in the crib, sleeping soundly, and Sarah hobbled into the bathroom to have a shower. Tina said quietly, 'Dave, you better go in there. I think she's going to faint.'

I sleepily complied, and the moment I opened the door, Sarah – who was standing in the shower – just collapsed as if she was a puppet with the strings cut. I caught her before her head hit the hard tiles, which would likely have cracked her skull. She had clearly given her all in the delivery room.

James was born around 5 am and my parents came over that afternoon. I'd never really held a baby before but I was given the job of giving her the first bath, and Mum and Dad watched, amused, through the window. Luckily, I'd paid attention during the birthing classes and I was confident enough as to what to do. It seemed a lot like washing a frozen chicken, I joked. From the outset, James and I were very happy together.

James was lucky to have four grandparents, and Sarah and I were lucky that our families, while different, were similar in the ways that mattered, and got on with each other. In fact, the yin and yang nature of Sarah's extended family – they were mainly Jewish and very hospitable – and mine, being very Anglo, Protestant and first-generation wealthy, was good.

They say your first child is the most important because it gives birth to a parent, and that was true of me. Even though I hadn't particularly wanted to be a father, now that I was, I loved it. This was service of a different kind. She seemed to love sleeping on my chest, and the more she gravitated towards me, the more I wanted to be with her and the prouder I became.

I was lucky in that Sarah helped nurture our bond at all times. She always encouraged me to do things alone with James, in my own way. Even before she could talk, we seemed to be able to communicate well. One of the first nights that I had her completely on my own, while Sarah went out with her friends, James would not stop crying. Rather than try to endlessly soothe her, I put her in the Baby Bjorn carrier and took her for a long walk around the streets of Double Bay. The 'adventure' with her dad under the big shady trees and lights of the shops seemed to make her happy. Topped off with a baby-sized cone of vanilla ice-cream from a late-night restaurant, she was all smiles. It probably wasn't the recommended way to deal with a crying baby a few months old but it seemed to work, and it set the tone for our travels together for years to come.

In late 2005, after a seemingly endless wait for the paperwork to be processed, I was accepted as a reservist for the Army Legal Corps, which meant I could do part-time legal advice work and court-martials in Sydney, but it didn't involve being sent to work in the big bases in regional Australia, or deployments overseas. I was given a choice of dates to go into the recruiting office and swear my allegiance to make my membership of the Australian Defence Force official. I chose 15 December, my birthday. In many ways my rejoining the army was a rebirth for me. After years lacking a sense of purpose, I now felt complete. I stood in front of the Australian flag and swore an oath to defend the nation, come what may. It was an oath I took seriously.

The first year as a barrister is spent trying to make ends meet with tiny 'mentions' – asking judges for changes to court dates for $200 a time. However, once the work starts to arrive you become overwhelmed with the stress of trying to manage often-unwinnable cases. These are the cases which no-one else wants, but you're hoping to score an upset win that might boost your reputation. In 2006 I was also travelling to and from Canberra, doing legal work for the Defence Force.

While I'd been a hopeless student as an undergraduate – there were more important things to do than study – now that I was sober and settled, I enjoyed analysing the finer points of the law. The fact that I could do further legal study, a Masters in Law at ANU, probably Australia's leading university for the 'law of war' – that is, rules of engagement and war crimes – was a big attraction for me of the ADF Reserves.

Ironically, considering what was to come, much of my initial work for the ADF concerned whistleblowers, internal complaints and inquiries. Even then, while the 'chain of command' attitude was generally that dissenters should be crushed, I could see that many had legitimate issues that had not been properly dealt with, according to our own regulations, and I refused to whitewash the actions of the senior officers, no matter how annoying the complaining soldiers may have been.

This didn't make me popular of course, as it seemed to be accepted that the chain of command would be found to be right, even if they weren't. I saw something else that concerned me – legal window dressing; namely the throwing around of buzzwords such as 'procedural fairness', while at the same time not actually honouring those stated principles.

While I never lost my operational attitude that the ultimate goal was to keep the wheels of the Defence Force turning (and the country defended), part of that surely involved us being an organisation whose ethics and words mattered. If a soldier had been clearly wronged, it did the ADF's soul no good simply to steamroll them further because it seemed too hard to set things right.

Whether it was called soul or ethos or morale, I knew from my experience in the UK Defence Force that it was a real and tangible thing, and it needed to be protected. Not everybody I worked with felt the same, and I saw even then the beginnings of the 'Whatever the minister wants is what will happen' type of attitude.

There was a plethora of policies in relation to fairness and lawfulness that needed to be applied in everything the ADF did. The problem was that the more of these impressive (although admittedly sometimes ridiculous) policies we had, the more flagrantly they were flouted. There seemed to have grown within the military a mentality in which compliance policies were something that were produced at rapid rates, but whose real purpose was to simply say, 'Look at our amazingly fair policies.' And not that they would actually be followed. It created a culture of dishonesty where it was part of the game to appear to be something, but actually to be something different.

As I was to find with the ADF's interpretation of the law many years later, it wasn't applied consistently; rather, simply used as an excuse to target enemies. If a soldier couldn't be prosecuted on any clear grounds, they would be ejected under spurious subjective standards. Standards that would never be used against senior officers who regularly transgressed against those same standards.

I came across another phenomenon I'd never encountered in the British Army: dishonest officers. My experience in joining the Australian Army had largely been a pleasant one, because I was impressed by the professionalism and education of the junior ranks, as opposed to their UK equivalents. One sour note, though, was the fact that, while they were respectful of my Oxford degree, they considered my British Army service as a bit of a joke.

Largely, this was because of the 'chinless wonder' factor. That is, because so many officers in the British Army – like me – only intended to stay as lieutenants and captains, they were somehow not real soldiers, because Australian officers signed on for a twenty-year career of service. However, while it was true that many British officers couldn't outrun and outshoot their soldiers, that wasn't their job.

A couple of things they did well in the British Army were honesty and integrity. An example of that was an incident while I was at Sandhurst. A group of officer cadets had organised the annual platoon graduation photo and took ten pounds from each cadet to pay for them. The bill was slightly less than what they had taken in; however, rather than take the slightly more difficult course of returning each cadet the fifty pence or so, they pocketed it themselves. They were caught and expelled from Sandhurst within days. They would have had to explain why to their friends and families, which would have been incredibly painful.

And while many of these 'chinless wonders' would return to their estates or family businesses after a few years in the military, this was not an impediment to them being good leaders. It largely meant they were at home looking after their workers, and it certainly meant that they'd never jeopardise their reputations for the sake of some small advantage to themselves, financial or otherwise.

Working in the Legal Corps of the Australian military, though, I was amazed to see how many senior officers, who had passed advanced leadership courses, did things like fudging on their financial allowances. My mind boggled. Why would anyone go to such great lengths to become a military officer, if all they really wanted to do was get rich? It seemed a poor way to achieve that aim. I knew that if senior officers were prepared to exploit opportunities in relation to housing and travel allowances, they were certainly not above covering for their superiors in order to get ahead on the slippery pole of promotion. I would eventually learn a whole lot more about this.

In 2006, in my civilian role, I was the junior defence barrister, under Greg Stanton, in a multiple murder trial for a gang centred around Adnan 'Eddie' Darwiche. There were three co-accused, who'd all grown up together and supported each other in a gang war – the details of which were at times tragic, and at times quite comical. I saw the law working at its best, with both the judge, Virginia Bell, and the prosecutor, Lloyd Babb, polite and professional throughout.

I was pleased to see that Justice Bell was eventually elevated to the High Court. She had risen up from public defender to judge to the High Court, and she knew her way around the foibles of human nature, in a very old-school way. Lloyd Babb too was quite remarkable. He looked like a surfer straight off Narrabeen beach, which apparently he had been. He was never anything but courteous and reasonable in his prosecution, even in crimes as serious as multiple murders.

The trial wasn't particularly stressful for me, as the senior counsel made all the hard decisions, and the gravity of the outcome, and the high-brow arguments on evidence and criminal procedure were fascinating and exciting to me. It was quite consuming, though, and I could see how barristers might let their personal lives unravel. During the case there was only one thing that mattered, and that was the case; and no sooner did one case end than another one started. And the Downing Centre, where the major criminal trials were held, was a world of a thousand stories, but few ever had happy endings.

I did more legal work for the Defence Force, including representing in 2005, again as a junior, a senior naval officer who was facing professional censure for the bad state of repair of an Australian helicopter that had crashed and exploded in Banda Aceh, in Indonesia, while bringing assistance to those affected by the previous year's tsunami.

He was an honest officer, who, when asked why he'd sent helicopters that he knew weren't 100 per cent safe on a mission for the government, said simply, 'If the government asked me to do something, I had a "can do" attitude. It wasn't my role to second guess them. Helicopters will always have a significant chance of crashing, and the only reason we wouldn't fly when asked was if we didn't have enough fuel.' He didn't try to shirk responsibility, but of course the military wanted a scapegoat, and in him they found one.

It was an introduction for me to the 'blame culture'. The military should be one area where deaths in training and operations were more accepted than they were in civilian life, but the political nature of the Australian Defence Force seemed to always demand a culprit. It could never be: 'This is the price of serving as part of Australia's finest.'

Around this time, we decided to have another child, so James would have a brother or sister. When I saw another ultrasound with more or less the same high forehead and same ski-jump nose, once again I was smitten.

Georgie's birth was surprisingly similar to James'. They were both born in winter, and at around 5 am, and both were a little over 3 kilos in weight. Sarah had said that Georgie felt different growing inside her. While James had hardly moved, with the occasional sleepy kick of a leg, Georgie kicked hard. In the same way, she seemed to demand to get out earlier, and came about two weeks preterm.

I can only assume that this was something to do with her being in pain, which she was for the first six months of her life. This was a hard time for Sarah and me. While I didn't realise it then, I believe she had undiagnosed post-natal depression, brought on by Georgie's difficulties and her complete inability to help her. We went from doctor to doctor, and good as they were, they all said something different. Despite all their knowledge, there is more to the world of science and medicine than we can see.

Suddenly, though, when Georgie was almost six months old, we took her to Palm Beach during summer holidays and put her in a little blow-up baby pool. She lay on her stomach, looked up at us and splashed her hands. And smiled. It was her first real smile, but what a smile it was. The pain had gone as mysteriously as it had arrived, and with its disappearance Sarah could start to enjoy life again.

I had a pain of my own. James had been born when I was first at the Bar, and while there was little money to make ends meet, we were basically pretty carefree. At the time, I was supplementing my income with lectures to solicitors wanting to learn more about the law. By the time Georgie was born, we had a mortgage to pay on our first apartment, and I was trying to make that breakthrough – the big case which makes your reputation. This meant I was accepting cases for which I didn't have the experience.

I'd taken on a case for a firm of solicitors which I felt we couldn't lose, as did they, but lose we did. Another case that we settled we probably shouldn't have, as the terms of the settlement were onerous. And while I'd been there with Sarah for Georgie's birth, during the three days she was in hospital I was going back and forth to court for what was – at that point – the biggest case of my life.

It wasn't so much ego that made me hold onto these cases; it was more a sense of duty. I'd said I was going to do something, and people were relying on me, so I did it. And while maybe I could have found them another barrister, new people wouldn't have the same sense of ownership.

I suppose there was also a sense of jealously guarding clients, in case your replacement ended up doing too good a job, and you were replaced as their preferred barrister. This fearful attitude (which I think was largely financial insecurity) has been present every time I've made major mistakes with work. That episode was a lesson for me: don't do things just because you need the money. It's bad for the soul and brings with it bad luck.

Bad luck or good luck, the whole experience of not being present for Sarah and Georgie when they needed me – and losing the case, anyway – made me realise that this wasn't the career for me. As yet, though, I didn't see any alternatives.

However, an alternative did soon present itself. One of the full-time military legal officers at Victoria Barracks in Paddington was going on maternity leave and I took a contract to fill in for them. I enjoyed the work, and got physically fit again. It was great to be advising on things that mattered, rather than commercial law, which was largely two bald men fighting over a comb. Put another way, the problem with criminal law is that most of your clients are professional criminals trying to game the system, and the problem with commercial law is that all of them are.

There had been another helicopter crash in 2006, this time off Fiji, involving the SAS. There had been a coup in Fiji and our government wanted to evacuate all Australians, but a helicopter carrying a number of SAS had crashed trying to land on a ship in a dangerously high wind. The pilot and one SAS member had died.

Sarah and I watched the father of the dead SAS corporal on TV, and looked at the handsome face of the dead soldier on the screen. The predictably bland language of the news report, and the complete ignoring of the bigger-picture questions – for instance, should Prime Minister John Howard have ordered that the SAS storm the island when Qantas flights were still operating – also left a slight feeling of disappointment.

We turned the TV off after the report ended and sat silently. As usual, Sarah surprised me. I thought she might say, 'I don't want you to do so much Defence work,' knowing that the more I did the more places I'd be sent, increasing the risk. She knew that even lawyers could die in Defence helicopter crashes.

Instead, she said with some resignation, 'People like that need people like you to look after them.' She didn't say any more but it was clear what she meant. The 'people' were the two faces who had just faded from the screen: make sure they don't get killed by questionable political decisions, or blamed for doing their job.

I didn't say anything, because while something inside me wanted to join full-time, because I missed the pride of being part of the nation's Defence Force, having been in the full-time army before, I also knew it was a big commitment and a big change. It was a world away from being just a Reservist, and that if I did it I'd have to do it 100 per cent and to the very best of my ability.

It wouldn't necessarily take a greater toll on the family, but what it did confirm – and I didn't quite appreciate at the time – was that Sarah believed that serving Australia was an honourable and worthy thing to do. That meant she also believed that, in turn, Australia would look after me and her and our family. This would be an important factor later on.

Sarah knew me better than I knew myself at times; either that, or the God of my own understanding was speaking through her. We both knew this was the right thing to do, but also that it was going to involve everything that we knew changing, particularly for the two girls.

It was a brave decision on her part, as it would mean she'd have to leave her comfortable Sydney apartment with its white-washed walls, in a beautiful part of the city, and live somewhere that looked very different. Her husband would no longer be a barrister, which held a fair bit of prestige, but simply 'in the army'. She was happy to do it. In more recent times, after all we've been through, Sarah has said she wishes she'd never encouraged me as she did; however, I'm sure it was the right path.

Later that evening, James came into the lounge-room. She'd had a nightmare. Sarah was still suffering from exhaustion from having both a baby and a two-year-old, so James and I sat up and watched our favourite 'Peter Rabbit' videos and snuggled together on the sofa. I never tired of that. I knew it wouldn't last forever, and when it was gone, I'd be able to think of little else.

While I was already a Reserve officer, to be accepted as a full-time officer you had to go through the whole interview panel once more. Again, I went out to Parramatta and was questioned by a panel of three officers, in a classroom under fluorescent strip lights. The team leader was a tall, fit SAS lieutenant colonel. He was respectful but I was a little intimidated by him.

The questions were serious, but I knew the drill by now, and I was in my element as I knew I wanted to contribute, and the sacrifices it involved. I was clearly going to pass. Then, the SAS officer threw a spanner in the works with one last question.

'What,' he asked, looking me in the eye, 'is your biggest regret?'

To this day I'm not sure if he meant anything by it, but it certainly had an effect on me, and caused me to look deep within myself. He said he'd give me three minutes to think about it and left the room.

Suddenly my confidence was gone, and my temperature and heart rate both started to rise, much as I tried to sit perfectly still, and deny that I was thrown. Did he know about me lying by omission about being an SAS officer during the political campaign? On the one hand, it seemed unlikely; but on the other, when you're publicly humiliated like that, there can be an assumption that everyone knows.

As the clock on the wall thudded, with each second like a falling axe, I considered what to do, although there was never really any question. Thoughts of Dad's errors with the rabbits came to mind, coupled with my own experiences that anything less than full honesty usually met with disaster, at least regarding my conscience, which for me was the only thing that really scared me.

The door opened and the officer came back in, alone this time. 'Well?' he asked.

So I told him the story, with as much detail as was necessary, but no more – taking care to put the blame squarely on the one person who deserved it: myself. I had been dishonest, I said, and that was my biggest regret. The officer simply shrugged and left the room again. While I felt deflated, I knew I'd finally been brutally honest with myself, and in a forum that mattered.

He returned about a minute later, congratulated me and shook my hand. I could feel the sweat under my armpits, even though the room wasn't hot. After all the successful applicants had been gathered in the one room, we stood in a row in front of the Australian flag. We were given the choice of the oath – that is, with a Bible, referring to God – or the affirmation.

I had no problem with the latter, and given that I didn't subscribe to the idea of Jesus rising from the dead to cure the world's sins, I wasn't really a Christian. However, I had a strong belief in the God of my own understanding, and while it wouldn't have made sense to anyone else it made sense to me. And not only did I pray to it when the shit hit the fan, my prayers seemed to be answered. I decided to take the oath because it seemed to have a more serious quality that I was looking for. I was about to commit my life to serving my country, perhaps literally, and I was going to do it properly.

The actual words were strangely all related to protecting the Queen, who seemed a long way from Parramatta, but in my mind it was clear what it meant: that I would do everything in my power to uphold the laws, values and defence of this country, and it was an oath I fully intended to follow.

A few years later, I ran into the same SAS officer on my 2011 tour of Afghanistan. He professed to have no memory of our previous meeting, let alone the question he asked me. I couldn't be sure whether he was telling the truth, though, as he seemed to be smiling as he said it. Coincidence or not, in the following years I would often reflect on that day in the recruiting office, and what it meant.

CHAPTER 24

Cane Toads, Rocks and Rockets

Having been accepted for the full-time army, a question arose as to what my rank would be. For legal officers, who were all university graduates with some experience, captain was the usual starting rank. I met with the personnel officer, though, and once he found out about my British Army experience, and that I had been a barrister, and been doing a major's job for the past year while she was on maternity leave, I was promoted straight to major.

I was happy to be back in uniform, and as a new entrant I tried to be enthusiastic and to concentrate on my job: helping people, either senior officers managing major incidents, or soldiers being unfairly punished by the system. Ironically, one of my first tasks as an army legal officer was dealing with someone who was a whistleblower; or at least identified as one.

The man was a Reservist major who had failed to be promoted, and felt it was due to him. In many ways, he had a point, but there was little that could be done for him. His superiors didn't like him and seemed to have done everything they could to thwart his career progression. Every time he complained, they counter-attacked with more complaints against him.

It was a fairly intractable issue, and showed me that despite all the policies claiming to be the world's best practice and committed to procedural fairness, career progression largely seemed to boil down to being obsequious to your boss – and if you were different, you might as well leave. Instead, the major spent years fighting for his promotion, and his detractors spent years fighting back. They were always going to win.

The case was a good lesson for my conscience, however, and it made me reflect upon what the essential elements of my job were, as well as the abuse of administrative processes against whistleblowers.

My days were filled with logistical, as well as legal challenges. Georgie was a year old now, and James three, and they were both doing a couple of days a week at a day-care in Paddington. When I got my first posting, at Holsworthy, a sprawling barracks on the southern edge of the city, we were living in central Sydney. I'd have to fight through the rush-hour traffic during those afternoons, trying to reach the centre by 6 pm. The girls were frequently the last to be picked up. I was dealing with a tricky schedule to the best of my ability, a conflict that would continue, because I was so proud to be back in uniform. Whether I was working for a general or a corporal, I always gave it my all.

One of the key things for me in 2009 was getting to know Paul Brereton. He was a Supreme Court judge, as well as an Army Reserve major general. We'd met briefly when he was my father's junior barrister in his long-running fight to retain his licence. This was before Dad had admitted he lied about the rabbits, and so he had no illusions about Dad's good and bad points.

Brereton and I got on, as he was a good lawyer, and also understood what mattered as an army officer, and I had a great respect for him as a commander. Brigadier (as he then was) Brereton and

I were talking one night and he remarked that my father's case had been his big breakthrough, after which he became a senior counsel. He was a good role model for me, because as a barrister you had very high standards of behaviour to maintain, and a judge even more so. I knew he didn't bend the facts to make the answer he wanted. I assumed at the time that all senior officers in the Australian Army would be like that.

Shortly afterwards, I was posted to Townsville. This was the centre of the military universe in Australia, a plum posting, and one step closer to a deployment to Afghanistan, where I could be at the real coalface, where I longed to be. It's always a mystery as to how one gets posted to a particular place. Sometimes it's because the person who makes the decision is trying to punish someone else more than you. Or maybe you're given a job because they hope you'll fail. Or perhaps Brereton had said some good things about me. Either way, I was heading to North Queensland.

I'd visited Townsville in late winter of 2009, which is when the weather is at its best: clear skies every day, and about twenty degrees. But we moved there permanently in January, high summer, when it's like the Armageddon, and most of the annual rainfall occurs over a period of weeks. Flooding happens every year, and while the intrepid Queensland people just deal with it, taking it all in their stride, for a little family from the Sydney Harbour foreshore it was like stepping into a disaster movie, as we watched cars being carried down the street by raging floodwaters.

The barracks had been rebuilt recently, and we moved into a newish five-bedroom house that was very open, and had a lot of lawn that needed to be cut twice a week in the summer. There were huge cane toads that wouldn't die even if hit with a cricket bat, and delicate green tree frogs that were as gentle as butter-flies. The girls were two and four when we arrived, still small enough for me to take them in the child carrier on the back of my bike.

It was the suburban Australian lifestyle at its best. We lived in a little cul-de-sac, with about ten houses, and every Friday night there was a street drinks, to which people brought a plate. The kids played and the adults made jokes about their week. They were truly very friendly, as we saw when a cyclone came to town, and the neighbours, who we didn't know that well, couldn't do enough to help us get prepared. We made life-long friends just by talking to people in the street. After growing up in Sydney, this was such a breath of fresh air. Everybody lived in pretty much the same kind of house, had the same sort of life, and helped each other. We felt what English people must feel when they visit Australia. When we eventually moved to Canberra in 2012, Georgie said one day, 'I want to go back to Australia,' and we knew what she meant.

While I'd been a specialist in Holsworthy, I wasn't immersed in the army, in that I went home each night to a familiar Sydney suburb. However, this was the full army experience. In Townsville, we didn't wear uniforms every hour of the day, but if you had it wouldn't have been noticed.

I saw some of the best leadership I would ever see in the Australian Army, maybe anywhere. Brigadier Stuart Smith was in charge at the base. His father had been killed serving in the Vietnam War, and he was raised with the help of Legacy. That fact alone would not count for much, but he was also extremely personable. Not everybody 'got him', because even though he was extremely physically fit, he wasn't particularly blokey. Short of stature, he was a giant in character.

One day, we were on one of an endless series of exercises, pretend wars on the huge barren training area a short distance from base. Soldiers in Townsville were ready to be deployed to any part of the world with a few days' warning. They were infantry units, so they were relatively easy to move around by helicopter and trucks. At the headquarters tents, I was called to come and see Brigadier Smith. There was a military policeman there looking hot under the collar. The situation was that the civilian police, a division called the child protection squad, had asked the military police to execute a search warrant, without the normal notifications to the person being issued the warrant. That is, they wanted the military police to secretly search a soldier's house while he was on exercise.

Brigadier Smith asked my advice on it, and while it was not the correct procedure, I could see that, as soon as words like 'child protection' were being thrown around, this was a situation where we needed to be extra careful – no matter what the law said. As with all excellent bosses, he wasn't really looking for my advice, just feeling the vibe. He knew what was right, because I think he truly got what it was to be an army officer. The truth is that soldiers are aliens living in amongst civilians – they never truly fit in.

Perhaps Brigadier Smith knew this because his life was a result of it. If his father had been a civilian who'd been killed in an industrial accident at Port Kembla, or driving a truck in the Pilbara, he would have got a payout, perhaps, but nothing else. He knew it was more than a job. That wasn't just a slogan; it meant being supported through bad times as well as good.

Strange as it might seem to civilians, your soldiers are your family, more specifically your children – whether you're twenty-four and they're forty-four; or whether you're a general and they're a forklift driver in the warehouse who you've never met. It's still the same dynamic: you protect them and defend them as if they're your own children. That doesn't mean lying for them, but it does mean refusing to let the MPs do an illegal search, just because incendiary words like 'child exploitation images' have been thrown around.

The soldier was informed that a search would take place, and was flown down from the exercise to witness it. It was the right decision, but it was still a brave decision. Brigadier Smith treated that soldier like a king might treat a son – whatever the allegations were – and it wasn't the last time I saw him do it.

After the brigadier, the next most important man was the brigade major, Jim Hammett. He was the same rank as me and all the other majors, but as he ran the operations room – where, for instance, at a moment's notice his team might have to put together a plan to move five hundred troops to Fiji in twenty-four hours. He had a status that far surpassed other majors – and even colonels. As his job was truly '24/7, 365', and if his team ever failed to deliver, his career would be over, he didn't bother being overly polite when he spoke, nor did he hold back on his opinions.

Whether he meant to or not, he did me a favour by putting me on the spot once in public. It seemed to be a sport of sorts to embarrass the legal officers, and see them squirm trying to give a straight answer to a question like, 'Do we or don't we shoot them?' Apparently, previous legal officers often couldn't give a straight answer to such a question, inviting derision from the soldiers who were confident in their jobs, and expected those they worked with to be equally confident in theirs.

But not only had I been a platoon commander in Northern Ireland, I'd been in front of some fierce judges, and written a dissertation on rules of engagement (ROE) as part of a Masters degree I'd recently completed. So I wasn't the normal easy target.

I'd only been in Townsville a few months and was making a presentation to the twenty key officers in the brigade for the first time, including Brigadier Smith. At the end of a long meeting, Major Hammett asked me, 'In East Timor, our ROE said we could only open fire if we were protecting embassy staff, so it meant we'd have to stand by and watch while women who weren't staff were raped and murdered in front of us. Isn't that stupid?'

There was a hush as everyone in the room wondered how I was going to handle the pressure moment. I paused for a second, weighing up the question and the atmosphere, and then replied, 'If it was me, I think I would have said, "Isn't that one of our cleaners or our cooks? I think it is. Let's save her."'

The major replied, 'But what if you start a war with Indonesia through your actions?'

This was obviously the trap – the potential no-win situation. I told him, 'At the end of the day you have to answer to your own conscience, not just the ROE. If you really can't live with yourself if you don't act, you should act.'

I don't know whether the major was satisfied with the answer but it seemed to earn a grudging respect. It was at least clear I knew that theory was nothing without you being able to translate into actions of 'yes' or 'no'. And my respect for him grew, as I saw he cared about getting the job done, and not about appearances. When we eventually crossed paths in Afghanistan, we greeted each other like old friends.

When doing the various rules of engagement exercises – in this case, practising for dropping bombs on suspected Taliban members with realistic simulated conditions – I noticed that the commanders were risk averse. This seemed to stem from an understanding that in the real world, you could be in the right legally, but suffer negative career consequences if the issue attracted negative publicity in the media.

This had been borne out ten years before in the wake of the Black Hawk disaster, in which two helicopters on a training exercise near Townsville crashed, killing eighteen SAS troops. It was a tragic event; however, in the subsequent inquiry, no-one seemed to acknowledge that taking reasonable risks during training was an important part of our job. If we didn't practise it in training, we certainly couldn't do it in a war. This applied to commanders and soldiers alike. No-one seemed to be looking out for the long-term interests of the organisation. They were too concerned with the optics.

Despite my reservations, I was happier being a full-time soldier than a lawyer. I was proud of the Australian Army, or at least what I knew it had once been and could be again. I was still focused on my career, and what the next step might be. A posting to Afghanistan was certainly a possibility.

We did a lot of normal suburban things together in Townsville that we hadn't done in Sydney, like visits to koala parks and watching huge crocodiles being fed. I built a swing set for the girls, and Sarah's parents generously bought us an expensive trampoline. I have a lot of sweet memories of that time and we really bonded as a family.

Another development was that, after ten years of not drinking through the help of AA, I had the regression that many people had. My life got busier, with both work and kids, and my AA meetings dropped off. Once that happens, you get less and less out of the meetings you do go to and you seem to forget what brought you to AA in the first place. You also wonder whether you weren't taking things a little too seriously.

One day, while I was still in Sydney, an old friend from my wild days in the UK came to visit. We had a lovely lunch in a restaurant overlooking Bondi Beach on a beautiful clear afternoon and he offered me some aromatic chardonnay. Some of the fun times we'd had together at Oxford came flooding back. It seemed a long way away from my settled life as a barrister in Australia with a wife and two children, and I thought maybe this time it would be okay. So I took a drink.

As I expected, nothing too dramatic happened, and when I mentioned it to Sarah, she didn't mind. She could see how wound up I got over my big legal cases, and could see it helped to make me more philosophical about whether things went right or wrong, in the same way that three beers made me not care about losing rugby games. I'd taken that same attitude to Townsville towards alcohol. So, for now, I was having a few drinks every now and again. And perhaps Sarah tolerated it because having a drink never stopped me finding time for games with the kids.

We began to watch a lot of movies together. Our favourites were the Barbie films. At first Sarah and I enjoyed them because, if we were lucky, we'd get a thirty-minute nap – but we soon came to love them too. It was nice to watch TV as a family, all four of us agreeing to watch the same thing. Almost any spare time I had, I spent with Sarah and the girls.

The one exception was running, which helped me to clear my head when I had more difficult work issues that bothered me. I followed a relatively short route around the flat suburb where we lived: along the river, across a bridge through a park and back home. Townsville is flanked by two huge rocks. In the late afternoon, they'd be lit up by the sun, and I'd look up at them as I sprinted the last 500 metres, listening to the same Coldplay track that I'd eventually listen to all the way to Afghanistan: 'Fix You'. It seemed apt. In some ways, the opportunity that the Australian Army had given me had fixed me from my sense of failure and given me a rebirth. But maybe there was more to it that I didn't yet know about.

In May 2011, after dozens of exercises in the training areas around Townsville during the preceding twelve months, and many weeks away from Sarah and the kids, the time came for me to go to Afghanistan, which we'd been informed about six months before. As Sarah pointed out, while my posting there was for nine months, when you took into account all the preparation exercises, in reality it would be a full year away.

I worked hard. There was a great deal of kudos associated with going to Afghanistan. At the time only a handful of legal officers had been, and they'd return with considerably improved status. They talked in acronyms that the rest of us had never heard of, and wore the coveted desert cams when they came back. Still a rarity, they were a sign you'd taken part in something big, something you could always be proud of. My selection, even though I'd been full-time in the army for not much more than a year, probably put some noses out of joint.

I said goodbye to the girls as best I could. Living in Townsville made it slightly easier, as there was such a big group of us going together. We were a unit who worked together day in, day out, so when we went off to the airport together (complete with our desert cams), it made it a little easier for Sarah and the girls: we, they, were part of a team. James was proud of her soldier father, as it gave her an identity, and she knew it meant her father was brave, and helped people. While it wasn't easy for me and Sarah to explain how it worked, she knew that somehow it did, and as I believed it, and Sarah believed it, James also felt a sense of security about it.

When I'd apologise to James for being a soldier, because it took me away from her so much, and I'd ask her if she wanted me to get another job, she'd say, 'I like you being a soldier. I never want you to be a normal dad.'

While Georgie was only two years younger, it was a significant difference developmentally. She was only three when I left, which in some ways was the worst age. She was old enough to know I was going away, and that it was somehow dangerous, but too young to take it in her stride, or feel a sense of pride about it. While she'd always nod in agreement when I told her I was going away for work and that I'd be back very soon, it was a lot to ask her to understand. I took my hat off to those in the SAS and Commandos who did it again and again and again, simply because their government asked them to.

Australia had participated in the original battles alongside the Americans and other allies against the Taliban in 2001. Prime Minister Howard withdrew our SAS troops in 2003, but in 2006 he decided to send more SAS, this time to help the Dutch in Uruzgan province in southern Afghanistan.

The Dutch were building schools and roads there and fighting the Taliban when they showed their faces to attack those developments. From 2006 to 2010, we were the junior partner, until the Dutch decided to leave Afghanistan and the US asked Australia to take over completely. Our government asked for an American contribution, and this joint Australian US brigade became known as Combined Team Uruzgan. CTU had the responsibility for building infrastructure and training the Afghan soldiers and police. It was a big job, but we were excited to do it.

The first stop on our trip was the Australian military base in the United Arab Emirates. The one good friend I had, the chief intelligence officer, Gav, was sitting near me on the plane. Sarah and his wife were friends and our kids were similar ages.

It was all work and no play in the UAE, except going to the gym and for runs, but that was okay – it's what I had joined for. It was a dry base, and for the next nine months there would be no drinking at all: for me and the officers, anyway. There were rumours of drinking in various hidden spots, but I had no more intention of drinking on the tour than I would have in the jungle. This was a serious time and I was determined to do the job well.

A week later we took a Hercules to the Tarin Kot military base in Uruzgan. There was a little bit of banter from people who'd known each other for a while, but it was basically pretty tense. We walked onto the tarmac in the middle of the day in summer, and felt the dry heat. There were a lot of aircraft of different types coming and going, but no sign of civilians at all. They were many kilometres away behind wall after wall, wire after wire.

We got to work at once meeting our counterparts in the previous rotation. They talked us through our individual jobs in their final three or four days before they left for their well-earned rest.

Once they'd departed, each day was busy and long. Before we left Australia, the main danger we'd been told about was the dreaded IEDs – improvised explosive devices – clever handmade bombs that were placed under the surface of a road, which exploded with enough force to split an armoured vehicle clean in two. Soon, though, getting killed by 'green on blues' was becoming a greater danger: the Afghan soldiers we were training turning on us and shooting us in the barracks.

We were the headquarters staff. There were about five thousand soldiers here – half American, half Australian, in two separate units – and we were in charge of what they did each day. There was also a big Afghan Army group with about as many soldiers again, who were just on the other side of one of the inner fences. The base was huge, with the circumference about 30 kilometres. When we ran a charity marathon and half-marathon later that year, it was simply one or two laps of the base perimeter.

There was a full-size airport too, with a single landing strip that could accommodate the biggest planes in the world. There was a separate helicopter base off to the side, which housed both types of transport helicopters, Black Hawk and Chinook, and the attack helicopters, Apaches: those flying death machines that had been so deadly to enemy soldiers eight years before in the invasion of Iraq.

On the slight hill above the airfield was a constantly spinning radar-type device, about ten metres off the ground, which was our ever-vigilant eyes for incoming rockets. This clever piece of equipment was linked to the loudspeakers on every building and inside every room, which blared out in a mechanical voice, 'Incoming, incoming, incoming.' When we heard that dreaded noise, wherever we were we had to lie in the dust, and wait until we heard the explosion.

The idea was that the rockets exploded largely upwards when they hit the ground, and if you were lying flat, and it didn't land within a hundred metres of you, the chances of a bit of shrapnel catching you were minimal. Not non-existent, but minimal. We lost two people to rockets, so it was a little like the chances of a shark attack in Australia: unlikely, but if you were in deep water on your own, you couldn't rule it out.

One of my day-to-day tasks in our office was watching the units moving around on the four big flatscreen TVs in the Ops Room, which was a bit like a mini-version of a control room for the lunar landing. The key staff – legal officer, intelligence officer and gunnery (weapons officer) commander – would decide whether to get Apache helicopters to shoot an Afghan who looked like he was setting off rockets or digging in IEDs. I had a lot of additional jobs, like liaising with the civilian administration – both our Department of Foreign Affairs and Trade (DFAT) and Afghan – and going outside to the Afghan prison down in the city of Tarin Kot, to check on the Taliban prisoners we'd arrested. This meant an armoured escort of about three vehicles, either driven by the Australians or the Americans.

The whole place was covered in a thin layer of yellow dust, and stank of shit. It was the overriding smell of the place, because of bad drainage, and a massive number of portaloos that were always being emptied on rotation, as well as a large open sewage plant.

Gradually, I began to make friends with the other people there, although it was pretty much work 24/7. I slept, but even then, I was still pretty much at work. After I cleaned my teeth at night, there was a short amount of time when I might watch a bit of a movie on my laptop with headphones, escaping to the fantasy land of what I was going to do when I got home.

That said, this was what soldiering was all about, and all of us had fought to get here, so we weren't complaining. But there would be few people who wouldn't be happy to go home; we knew that from the very first day we stepped off the Hercules. This was nine months to be endured, like being on a colony on the moon. It was very different to when I'd been in Afghanistan in 2000, and was actually moving amongst the people. It felt a bit detached from reality.

Speaking of which, one of the most frustrating aspects of being in Afghanistan was the daily meetings, held by every unit in every base. They helped foster my increasing lack of faith in our military leaders telling us the facts about how our mission was progressing. It was becoming clear to me that things weren't going well – not that you'd know it from the meetings.

All you'd hear, from the various different heads of the different projects we were conducting, was good news. There didn't seem any genuine attempt simply to tell us the truth. It was like a company endlessly claiming to generate massive profits. It didn't seem credible to me, or to others I spoke with.

It was hard to be sure whether the colonel believed what he was being told, or was just happy he in turn had good news to relay to his boss, the US General in Kandahar, who ran the whole south of the country. There was certainly political pressure on the military leaders to paint the situation to be as rosy as possible. And, in fact, when the real politicians arrived – and both the prime minister and the leader of the opposition came for separate visits while I was there, and I sat in on both briefings – they too were taken in by the rhetoric. Or again, perhaps they weren't but they didn't care.

Approximately halfway through the 2011 deployment, all personnel were given a two-week holiday, which could either be in Europe or a return home. Sarah and I decided it would be too disruptive for the girls if I came home for a week, then left again.

Deployments are notoriously emotional experiences. Sarah and I would talk to each other every day in a strange wooden room with banks of phones and graffiti. It was before Skype and Zoom and the quality was poor. I often left the call feeling worse than before it. I shared an office – a converted shipping container – with one other officer, and while we weren't meant to use the work phones to call home, in frustration I eventually did.

Sarah and I arranged to meet in Dubai. When I saw her, I could tell she was at breaking point. Her connecting flight had been a little late, but only a little; however, the tension of being delayed in seeing me because of some sort of mix-up was considerable. When she finally saw me through the crowd, she hugged me and cried.

My deployment had been tougher for her than me, because she'd had to live with the worry that one day she'd see the 'padre' walking towards our front door holding a Bible and looking grim. While she'd enjoyed the whole Townsville experience, with us as a little family, being the partner of deployed personnel was a very different experience.

We booked a stylish small hotel on the Left Bank, which she loved but I hated, as I'd forgotten how small Parisian hotels were. We moved a couple of times and eventually found something on the Right Bank, named after an American general from the First World War, which had a chic bar. We had fun walking the streets and managed to simply walk into L'Atelier, one of the great Parisian restaurants, and get a table – we were paid well on deployments.

We took the train to London and arranged a dinner with four close friends, which was a beautiful bittersweet night. It reminded me how lucky I was to have such incredible people in my life. It was lovely that Sarah got to meet them, joining the two quite separate strands of my life, and she warmed to them and they to her.

While I was talking with the group about being a military lawyer, one of my wisest and most beautiful friends said, 'That's the perfect job for you.' However, I was conscious of my lack of status. I was a soldier, but contemporaries of mine from the SAS and Oxford were running the whole military effort for the UK in Afghanistan.

I was a single rank higher than I'd been when I left the British Army almost twenty years before, and I was living in a suburban house, in a remote regional city in Australia. It was exactly what I'd thought I never wanted. But for the first time perhaps I had to agree that, despite its lack of status, this *was* the perfect job for me.

The next night we went to another dinner party and saw some more old friends, Sarah eventually went home but I stayed, so excited not just to have got out of Afghanistan, but also to be seeing these people I was so fond of. The combination of excitement and frustration meant I drank too much and was sick, which was embarrassing. Again, though, because my friends were such lovely people, they couldn't care less.

I got a taxi home to Sarah at dawn. She was happy to see me and not the least bit bothered by the state I was in. She'd wanted me to let off steam, and now held me in bed like you might a child who's had way too much cake and red cordial.

I was back in London but not really back. Getting a few planes from Uruzgan for a few days in London, before returning to Uruzgan, was almost too surreal to be enjoyable. We took the train to Gloucestershire the next day for a cricket match between some other friends; then it was back to Paris for a final few days together, and a teary goodbye at Dubai. Before I knew it, I was in Tarin Kot again, running on that treadmill.

The post-ROCL (Relief Out of Country Leave, pronounced 'rockel') blues were well known and I got them bad. I found it hard to leave the cargo container where I slept, and if there wasn't time during the day to get to the gym, I'd just go to the sleeping quarters and sit in the quiet for ten minutes or so.

I was able to get some relief via Jack Reacher, a series of escapist books recommended by a friend, about a former American Military Police major fighting high-level corruption. I also started watching TV series on my laptop every night. I enjoyed the shows with glossy backdrops and ridiculous storylines to make me laugh and take my mind off things.

I didn't look at photos of the girls. That was too painful. I missed them very much and, while they were brave, I knew they didn't quite understand why I had to be away. It was time to start counting down to the next leave.

It was eventually work, or more specifically violence, that jolted me out of my dark space – and it did so instantly. Ever since we'd arrived there had been rocket attacks on the base, sometimes once a week. One contractor, a civilian worker from another country, had been killed by one, apparently while he was having a shower. In one of the smaller patrol bases in the regions of Uruzgan, a young Commando had been killed by a direct hit. And while we hadn't suffered any casualties from them yet on this tour, we'd had plenty of narrow escapes, with shrapnel landing in both buildings and vehicles.

Gav, my friend who ran the intelligence cell, took it upon himself to catch the attacker in the act. He established a set of drills for us to counter-fire at him from the Control room, as soon as he fired at us. It wasn't easy, and we failed many times.

One day when I was feeling most down, the rocket alarm went. I grabbed my rifle and webbing and ran for the Control room, even though we were meant to wait until the all-clear sounded. It's funny how the chance to fire back can overrule any sense of self-preservation. I got there just in time to confirm that the rules of engagement had been complied with for return fire from the Apache helicopter. The crucial question was whether 'Rocket Man' had been under constant surveillance since he'd fired that rocket. The pilot confirmed that he had. The commander gave the order to open fire, and two seconds later, our attacker was a cloud of red dust.

We didn't exactly high-five each other, as there was always a chance there'd be an inquiry. However, I was satisfied we'd got the right person and that the engagement was legal. I no longer felt down about being back in Uruzgan. I realised I'd rather be here than London or Paris. This is what we had trained to do: take the fight to those who would kill us, and protect the lives of our fellow soldiers.

I continued to travel outside the base each week to visit the Afghan prison, always in that convoy of three armoured vehicles. The prison was about five kilometres from the base perimeter, on the other side of Tarin Kot. We had to take pretty much the same route each time, so we were exposed to an IED strike. The Australians who ran the armoured escort teams were competent and I never felt unsafe, although it wasn't a journey you'd take if you didn't need to.

The prison – in fact, the whole legal system – symbolised so much of what was wrong with the mission. They'd been using it since before the war. It was basically a big house, in Afghan terms, that is a large walled compound with a courtyard and a double storey main building with ramparts on the corners. It looked more like a small castle from Britain in the Dark Ages, or a Roman fort in Jerusalem.

The prisoners wore loose chains and their traditional robes and spent their days wandering around the courtyard chatting and drinking tea, while the guards watched from above. It worked – and I didn't hear any complaints. However, because it didn't look like a Western prison, it was considered bad, and needed to be replaced. A new prison was built along Western lines, at great expense, but the Australian Government was only too happy to pay for it because, when it was finished, it provided a suitable photo opportunity that showed both progress and largesse.

Unfortunately, the new prison had been designed without any attempt to make it sustainable. It required large amounts of diesel fuel to run the lighting, air conditioning and heating necessary to stop the large concrete building with small barred windows becoming a death trap – for guards and prisoners alike. A simple assumption had been made that the Afghans would supply the diesel themselves; but they had no fuel, and no trucks to transport it. Emergency fuel was found, but it wouldn't last long.

The toilets too were a disaster. The designers and builders had insisted on putting Western-style toilets in a building where the end users didn't even know what they were. The toilets were completely blocked within days of opening.

Down the road, the even bigger police academy was equally impractical. In fact the whole of Afghanistan at that time seemed to be swamped with these flawed projects. The Western nations were saying to the Afghans, 'Look! We've saved you!' However, it was also Western contractors who profited from the construction, paid for by Western taxpayer money.

I increasingly felt uncomfortable about the mission, and the way it was being sold as a success. When Tony Abbott visited Afghanistan as leader of the opposition in November 2011, we spoke briefly. Later that day, I got a message that I'd been invited to the VIP dinner put on in his honour by the senior Australian general. I couldn't bring myself to go. I wasn't a VIP or a general. Nor did I want to be a performing seal for a cause I was losing faith in. That didn't mean I wouldn't do the job to the best of my ability: my love for the military, and personal pride, would always demand that. But I couldn't bring myself to mouth platitudes with generals and politicians about the mission, a few days after we'd buried some soldiers, and a few days before we'd bury our next.

I went to the base gym instead and ran ten kilometres on the treadmill, listening to my favourite trance tracks. Hard as it was, that always worked, and it worked again that day. Somehow, someday, I was going to get out of this, and make it back home, and I didn't mean just Afghanistan.

CHAPTER 25

Harriet, Vegemite and Iron Bars

I've mentioned the problems associated with the Western approach to bricks and mortar issues in Afghanistan. Unfortunately, the legal system we introduced was just as bad. Afghanistan's existing judicial structure was largely tribal based. As such, we considered it ridiculous, and replaced it with a simplistic European one. Court buildings were built and judges appointed.

Under this new system we'd enacted, strict standards of evidence were required for criminal convictions. The problem was the country simply wasn't developed enough to apply these standards, which meant they were largely fudged. This, in turn, fostered a distrust of them by the local people.

The police didn't have the ability to take fingerprint evidence properly; nor did the courts have the ability to properly test the veracity of that evidence. Yet incriminating fingerprints miraculously turned up on Taliban weapons, and convictions were imposed as a result. In reality, and very ironically, we created a system that taught the Afghans that the reality didn't matter, as long as the appearance was one of world's best practice.

There was no possibility of arresting Taliban suspects under the cover of night in remote villages, then transporting them through a number of staging points to eventual court, with anything approaching the required Western standards of evidence. We did anyway, and the long-suffering prosecutor and judges were strongly encouraged to ensure convictions. Because they were appointed by us, if they didn't convict the people we brought before them, we could just as easily appoint someone who would.

At the same time they were told to watch out for corruption, even though it was us who were promoting the corrupt systems to them. We needed to be able to tell our audiences back home that, despite *outrageous* Taliban propaganda, our systems were squeaky clean, and this meant having judges who did what we said, and told the very lies we expected them to.

When prisoners were considered high value, which meant there was some evidence they'd been somewhere near a firearm, they were sent to a place called DFIP, the Detention Facility in Parwan, formerly known as Bagram. A number of suspicious deaths and incidents of torture had taken place in Bagram, thus it received a name change. There may have been some other cosmetic changes, but the fact that no major journalists or media outlets seemed to draw much attention to this duping of the public is indicative of the level of media complicity.

One day in November, my local Afghan liaison, someone called Dr Stanikzai, who worked for a tiny organisation called the Afghan Independent Human Rights Commission, came to see me with two older men. Dr Stanikzai and I had a good relationship. He said the men were from the north of Uruzgan province and their two sons had disappeared, presumed dead. They'd last been seen visiting the US base a week earlier, the notorious FOB Ripley/Cobra, FOB standing for Forward Operating Base.

The fathers had walked and hitched rides all the way to our base, which was a significant journey. All they had with them were the clothes they stood up in, and they were likely relying on the kindness of strangers to feed them. They had a hollowed look about them, but no bitterness. Because they assumed their sons were dead, they simply wanted to bury them. Unlike the negative stereotype favoured by many of those in the coalition forces, they were not seeking compensation, or even blame, just a moment with their sons. They reminded me of the grieving fathers I'd met in the refugee camps in 2000 with the bodies of their dead children.

I said I'd look into it, and they thanked me, bowing with gratitude and holding their hearts. They would wait, sheltering where they could for however long it would take me. That would probably be at some tiny makeshift mosque, where they might get some dry bread – with the local mullahs, most of whom were considered Taliban by us simply on account of being mullahs.

Because I was always overwhelmed with work, I'd never been particularly polite to Dr Stanikzai, but it seemed he'd recognised in me someone who cared. I made some inquiries and, at first, received point-blank refusals from the American Navy Seals that anything remotely resembling what I was asking about had occurred at the base in the last few weeks. I smelt a rat. Something about the certainty of their reaction didn't seem right.

After persistent questioning, the story changed. I was told that the two men were informants for the coalition forces, and had not been seen after they left the base one night after giving infor-mation to the US. The Seals suggested they must have been killed by the Taliban. I accepted this at the time, although I resented them having lied to me when I first asked.

Up until that point I had great faith in the Seals, who were all good looking and charming. As the years have gone by, and more atrocities have emerged, I suspect that rather than being informants the two men were probably just captured, tortured and killed, then buried.

There was a perception that the local Afghans, because of their broken English and dishevelled appearance, were stupid.

They were anything but. They rarely moved more than a few hundred kilometres away from where they were born, so if something happened in their area, they noticed. If the men had been killed by the Taliban, their fathers would have known, and they wouldn't have made the trek to our base. They came to the base because they believed that those in the base had been responsible.

While I doubt these old men would have taken up arms against us – they were too broken by grief – their stories would be told, and our mission was increasingly doomed by the weight of them. We lived behind high walls, only venturing out in armed vehicles, and anyone taken by us back into our bases never returned. But we were making terrorists as fast as we were killing Afghans.

After I reported back to the fathers what I had found, they again bowed deeply with respect, although I could see their hearts were breaking. They wouldn't be able to bury their sons, and this was shaming for them. For my part I was angry that my own forces had lied to me. Trust between soldiers was sacrosanct. These were US, though, and I knew that Australians, at least the ones I worked with, wouldn't do this. But it gave me a new attitude when dealing with the US Special Forces, and that was not to simply trust them because they looked the part.

There were some good moments, though. While I took my job seriously, that didn't mean we couldn't have a little adventure along the way. Most of the people at the base wanted nothing to do with the Afghans, but occasionally you met someone who wanted to see the country for themselves – and in Harriet, one of the DFAT advisors, I found my partner in crime.

Like me, Harriet had no problem in rewriting her own job description to include 'finding out what was really going on'. She was brave and didn't mind taking a risk to do so. Each week or so we'd search for excuses to get out of the base and meet the various key personalities of the Afghan prison, judicial and security services. After we'd visited the new prison in Tarin Kot, we went to the home of the Chief Afghan Prosecutor, where I ate his fresh pistachio nuts, and we shared a lunch with the chief of the secret police, another Shiite. Harriet gave him some Vegemite to try. He politely bit into it, but didn't take a second bite.

The high-ranking Afghan officials were enthralled by Harriet, because they could see she was smart and brave enough to travel around Tarin Kot, which most weren't, and they gave her gifts of Afghan traditional robes. I was a bit concerned they might try to marry her, as had almost happened to another similarly intrepid DFAT advisor on a visit to a village leader.

While Harriet and I were having fun, we were also doing something useful: cutting through the 'CCTV lens' and seeing the real Afghanistan. Of the thousands of people on the base, few had been outside in anything but an armoured vehicle, let alone had any normal interaction with the Afghans.

The head of the secret police seemed very competent to us both. He was neither bombastic, nor too smooth. It was a hard job, and almost the equivalent of being a construction union leader: stuck in between the 'suits' and the 'tradies', and all the while being sniped at by the media.

He told us that there weren't secret prisons in the province anymore, although there used to be. He'd shut them down because he had no control of them. He went on to say that one of the officers in the secret prisons had used jump-leads to give electric shocks to a suspect who'd turned out to be an innocent taxi driver. The offender had been demoted, although we smiled in a black-humoured way when we realised that he was now cooking us lunch.

Dark as this version of events was, it had a ring of truth to it and matched what we heard from other sources. We knew the Afghan police were never going to be perfect. The sorts of things Harriet and I were on the lookout for, though, weren't individual acts of violence, but systematic and premeditated murders. We would eventually find them, slightly closer to home, but that was a few years away.

The highlight of our fact-finding tours was when Harriet and I flew up to the neighbouring province, Dai Kundi, to visit a prison. There was no base in Dai Kundi because there was no Taliban there. Like Bamiyan, which we had visited in 2000, it was a Shiite Muslim area. Located between Bamiyan and Uruzgan, it was considered a backwater, but as far as the war went it was a paradise.

There was an element of summer holiday about our trip, especially as it was not really necessary. The helicopter ride to Dai Kundi was by Black Hawks, which were smaller than the usual carriers, and they had taken the doors off permanently. This meant you were exposed to the wind and the engine noise, which was deafening.

We were wearing body armour and a helmet, and in my case a rifle and pistol, but that was pretty much all I took, apart from a small backpack with some books. The route was directly north over high and desolate shale mountain-tops with no signs of life on them, and the tips of which we only just cleared. From my flying experience, twenty years before, I knew that the hot dry conditions meant the pilots were pushing the limits of the aircraft, but I was glad to be escaping Tarin Kot.

In Dai Kundi we entered a parallel universe of what Afghanistan could have been like without war. It was a peaceful-looking valley with undulating hills and poplar trees. The compounds dotted around the place were much bigger and better maintained than Uruzgan, and often had high turrets, giving them the appearance of mini-castles. The helicopter dropped us right next to the houses where we were staying.

There was no base, just a low-walled compound with two buildings, about the size of a scout hall. There were no armoured vehicles or heavy machine-guns pointing out at the populace. There were only four US soldiers there, and I liked them immediately. They were Rangers – Operational Detachment Alphas, simply called ODAs – which meant their job was to live as a small unit, without support, in a remote place and try to win the locals over to their side by sheer force of personality. By and large, they had done so.

It was the sort of thing that the fictional character Colonel Kurtz, made famous by Marlon Brando in *Apocalypse Now*, one of my favourite movies as a teenager, had done. The leader of this team looked more like Nick Nolte. He was dishevelled, but friendly to us. His second-in-command, Felipe, was small, Hispanic and camp, and wore a Palestinian scarf jauntily angled on his head. He had a cheeky smile on his face, no matter how much the major swore at him, which was constantly.

Supplies were dropped in on heavy pallets by parachute, and sometimes they landed on Afghan houses, but the major seemed to be able to placate the locals if that happened. No doubt with cash.

The major took Harriet and me out in a four-wheel-drive with the windows wound down, as if he was driving around his local town in the US. We didn't bother with helmets or body armour. He and I simply had our pistols. It reminded me of the Afghanistan of 2000, when, even under Taliban occupation, there was no great danger to Westerners travelling.

He took us to the prison, which was about the size of an old police station in an Australian country town. There was only one prisoner, a woman, and her crime wasn't terrorism related. She had killed her husband. Her family came each day and gave her food, which was the custom. She didn't appear to be mistreated, but had a wild look in her eyes. She wasn't going to be executed, but I'm not sure how long she was going to be locked up. Even in this relative idyll, not everything was a fairytale.

To our surprise, even the Dai Kundi mayor was a woman, which completed the topsy-turvy nature of this place. We went to the council buildings, which were newly built and not unlike a local council building in Australia, although largely empty. Harriet and I posed for joint selfies on the council steps, a memento of our small rebellion.

Back at the accommodation, Felipe cooked us up lobster tail, which I picked at gingerly, and I seem to remember red wine, but didn't try any. All through dinner, the major kept swearing about some local disagreement, and Felipe kept on smiling and making sure we had enough to eat. For once we could see the stars out the window of our bedrooms. The next day, all too soon, we flew back to miserable Tarin Kot and our normal lives.

The trip to Dai Kundi was a good reminder to me of a number of things. Firstly, don't make the mistake of assuming all Americans are the same. While the Navy Seals at Tarin Kot were smooth liars, the dishevelled cursing Rangers team were the real deal. I'd had a similar experience in the US when I was there rowing during the summer holidays back in 1987. No sooner had I dismissed it as a ghetto of broken dreams, I was transported to places of beauty by equally kind and beautiful people. It was a country that couldn't be categorised. Perhaps because of its incredible size, its personality was changeable, like a squid changing colours when it senses danger.

The second thing was the question of why Dai Kundi was so placid, and Uruzgan such a mess. The conventional answer was that it was because, like the equally peaceful Bamiyan, the area wasn't populated by Sunni Pashtuns – the dominant race of Afghans from eastern and southern Afghanistan from whom almost all the Taliban was drawn – but by the more moderate Shiite Hazara.

It said a lot about the whole war effort that even with trillions of dollars being spent, that was about as sophisticated as the reasoning got and it was never second guessed.

However, I had been to the border areas of Pakistan where it was equally Pashtun dominated, and these places didn't look like Uruzgan. In Peshawar, I'd played that 'polo' game, and walked openly through the weapons bazaars and the labyrinth-like covered market. It's true that the Pashtun areas were the most destroyed. But the major international players bore some of the blame for that by arming anyone who was prepared to fight the Russians, indifferent to what would happen afterwards.

The reason the Afghans were fighting us now, as Gav, the intelligence chief, quietly pointed out one night over a chat session in his room, was because we were here. The more bases we built, the more people came to fight us for invading their land, just as we would have done if they'd sent an army to Australia. Our invasion was proving to be counterproductive. By sending more troops, as President Obama had done in 2011, we didn't quell the violence, we increased it.

I continued to speak to Sarah about once a day in the room where the phone calls were made and she shared news about the kids. It was getting hard for both of us to maintain the façade that everything in Afghanistan was okay. By this stage about six soldiers had been killed, two of them shot in the back as they were walking around the base. Sarah would have seen their faces on the television screens in the gym, or on morning TV.

One time, there was a rocket attack while I was on the phone to her, and she heard the deafening sirens blasting 'Incoming. Incoming. Incoming.' I quickly told her not to worry but that I had to go.

The first thing that told you someone was dead was that the phones didn't work. In order to make sure the padre got to the widow's house before the gossip did (and in 2011 they all were wives), the phone lines between Tarin Kot and Australia were cut off.

Jonesie was the first to die on our tour, although another young officer had fallen out the back of a helicopter on his way into Tarin Kot. Jonesie, though, had been shot. He'd been standing, pissing at a makeshift outdoor urinal in the middle of one of the small bases, which were only as big as about two football pitches, surrounded by thick mud walls about three metres high, when one of the Afghans looking down on him from the guard tower had turned his rifle on him, shot him a couple of times, jumped over the wall and disappeared into the fields and houses around the base.

Jonesie was one of the salt-of-the-earth-type soldiers who made you proud to be in the Australian Army. Young, handsome and fit, he was a cook for a small satellite base an hour or so drive from Tarin Kot by armoured vehicle. I was sent to do a short legal report on his death. When I arrived there, I could see his kitchen was well organised and a relaxed kind of place, where the soldiers got some relief from the danger and boredom of their patrols.

While there was no suggestion he was deliberately targeted, I could see that if you wanted to really break the morale of a small base, killing the cook was a good place to start – with the mess hall being where people went to let off steam, and now they couldn't even do that without being reminded of their loss.

While it was always sad to be looking at the 'crash scene' where some young person had lost their life, this was our job. The base was jumpy now, because, while the day before the Afghans and Australians had been laughing and joking together and had even played cricket together, today both sides eyed each other warily with their backs to the wall, and their hands on their rifles.

One interesting thing came out of the incident; namely the ease with which the shooter had managed to escape the area, even though we'd put drones in the sky, and had helicopters and patrols everywhere. I found out later that he'd hidden in some bushes near the river and asked a local farmer for help. He told him straight up, 'I've just killed an Englishman,' and help was given – not just to be hidden but to be transported all the way out to Pakistan.

While we were slightly bemused that he'd described Jonesie as 'English', it wasn't because he was ignorant. He – and others – called us English, not caring whether we were or not, seeing us as simply the latest in a long line of foreign invaders. It was clear that when the Allied Forces left Afghanistan – as we would – the shooter, and others like him, would be considered heroes who'd fought against the foreign enemy.

They found the shooter eventually. After a month or so in Pakistan, he returned to his family home in the north-east of Afghanistan. I don't know whether it was informants or the eye-in-the-sky satellite spying, but it seemed to be known exactly where the shooter's family lived, and that he'd made it home, and told his father what had happened. A US team was dispatched, with an Australian SAS soldier embedded, and one night he was shot dead.

Our approach was always to maintain that we'd acted under international law, and if we hadn't, to lie about it. The problem was that two groups of people knew the truth: the SAS and the local Afghans. One concluded that it was not just okay, but required for us to lie, while the other concluded we were full of shit. At least the Taliban were honest about who they murdered.

One of the worst green-on-blue killers was the Afghan sergeant, Hekmatullah. He struck in 2012 after I was back in Canberra, killing three Australian soldiers. They'd been playing cards after a hard day's patrolling in 40-degree heat.

After a few years in prison, he was eventually released as part of negotiations to end the war. His freedom was traded for that of an American soldier, who had been captured but not killed, or even tortured by the Taliban. They treated him better than we treated those in Guantanamo Bay and elsewhere, although we still maintained the moral high ground at all times. The families of those killed by Hekmatullah were outraged that he'd been set free with Australian Government consent – as I would have been in their position.

In early December 2011, I took another visit to the now not-so-shiny new prison – which, as I've said, was becoming more of a health hazard each day, black mould now growing due to poor hygienic conditions. I was brought in to see a new captive. It was routine practice that I'd meet the new captives and ensure they hadn't been tortured. Generally, they were rather bemused, as the decades of violence had made them stoic. Nor did it seem to be in the nature of the staff to abuse prisoners just for the sake of it.

I got to know the prison staff and I liked them. The prison director and his deputies were proud Pashtuns. They seemed to have agreed to work with us because they didn't like the excesses of the Taliban. However, they were becoming increasingly frustrated, since we weren't giving them the tools to keep it in working order, which set them up for failure.

I was only required to interview prisoners who'd been taken by the Australian forces, or by the Afghan soldiers we were training. They were all assigned numbers and were brought to me in a room with a guard. Each of them told me their story, then returned to their cell. They seemed to be surprisingly honest, and when I asked them if they'd been treated badly, or if the food and conditions were adequate, they'd say things like, 'Oh, I lost a tooth when I was captured, but that's only to be expected really. As for the food, it's pretty good – no complaints.'

I also had to check on those who'd been in the prison for some time. I could tell, from the photos I'd take of them each month for my records, that they were putting on weight, and generally looking better each time.

It turned out that one prisoner I interviewed had been brought in mistakenly, because he hadn't been captured by Australian soldiers, and was therefore beyond my jurisdiction. With everything being done through a translator, it took a few minutes before we resolved the confusion.

By then, he'd already said that, after being captured by the Afghan police and before he was bought to the prison, his hands had been manacled to the roof of a holding cell in another building. He'd been left hanging by his hands in agony for a day, then beaten with an iron bar around the head. He showed me his scars and bruises, and I duly took photos of them with the camera required for the purpose. I wasn't particularly shocked, but under our training and protocols it had to be reported. I put together a brief detailing what I had seen, including the photos, and stating that his story had the hallmarks of truth about it.

What happened next was another step in my belief that something was seriously not right in the Higher Command. Immediately after I'd made the relatively mild report, the phone started ringing from panicked political advisors. It didn't seem to be the beating they were concerned about; rather, that I hadn't 'got the memo' and that reporting of abuse was not something that one did. While no one was expressly saying it, they seemed angry that I didn't just look the other way.

What I was equally incensed about was that I'd done many weeks of training in legal standards, much of it paid for by the ADF, and it had all told me the opposite. There now seemed to be an assumption that we were meant to pretend to do things properly for the public appearance in Canberra, but in practice you should cover bad things up if you saw them.

'Just send a report to Kabul,' the political advisor said to me, referring to the US headquarters, 'and then it's no longer your problem.'

But I knew this was bullshit. Under the Geneva Conventions, I had a positive duty to ensure that the report wasn't just made, but that an investigation followed. Ignored reports were the same as no report at all. US headquarters might make a decision not to investigate, but I wanted to see that in writing. However, I knew they wouldn't dare investigate, preferring the idea of plausible deniability, in order to later claim they had no knowledge of the incident. But I knew that if the story came out, I'd be in the frame if it seemed that I'd known of the torture and done nothing about it.

I got a call from the highest-ranking Australian officer in Afghanistan, a major general, who was widely tipped to be chief of army. She oozed charm with me, and said, 'What a terrible experience,' and tried to reassure me that no-one was suggesting to cover it up.

I thanked her for her call and played along, but my mind was made up. I would put in a confidential report to the Red Cross representation in Tarin Kot, a charming Dutchman who I got along well with, and who was brave enough to live in the city with only a sleepy local guard. There was no danger that he'd misuse the information, and I believed he'd do the right thing – namely, that he'd speak confidentially to the Afghan police and ask them not to string people up and hit them with iron bars. Giving my report to the Dutchman might well have no effect, but turning a blind eye to such things, which the Afghans knew we knew about, gave them the message that we secretly thought torture was okay, whatever we said in public.

So you might say that my informing the Red Cross representative of possible prisoner abuse, despite being told not to, was probably my first piece of whistleblowing. It didn't make me feel superior; if anything, it made me quite nervous, as I knew the POLADs, the Political Advisors from the Department of Defence, and the major general could damage my career if they found out. It was a risk I decided to take. I knew the law, and I knew I was right.

CHAPTER 26

Special Operations Headquarters

The 2011 deployment, which had originally been planned to finish before Christmas, was extended to February 2012. I had divided feelings about that. If the government needed us to stay, we stayed. But underneath my commitment to the job at hand was a growing sense of frustration that the whole mission was really a pointless waste of lives and money. It was hard for Sarah at home as well, but neither of us wanted to burden the other with our increasing disillusionment.

One upside of the extended deployment was that I was entitled to a second ROCL, before a final six-week stint in Tarin Kot. This time I decided to go home. The night before I left for Australia in mid-December, I got a call from the major general. Generals don't usually call majors to have a chat. Perhaps it was to sound me out about whether I was likely to say anything to anyone in the military about the torture, or to check whether I was still angry with the advisors who'd told me to forget about it. I wanted to get back to Australia to see Sarah and the girls without any drama, so I told the general I'd finalise the matter after I returned to Afghanistan. I knew what I was going to do, though. Perhaps she did too.

Because it was individual leave I flew on civilian airlines, although I was sitting next to a lieutenant colonel on one side and a corporal on the other. The rule for us was no drinking, even on civilian airlines. When the attendant came around and asked us whether the lieutenant colonel wanted a drink with dinner, the corporal and I held our breath to see what he'd say. He ordered a Cab Sav. We silently cheered, while pretending not to notice. I tentatively asked for a beer, while the corporal didn't hold back and got a rum and Coke.

Although Sarah and the kids were still living in Townsville, we met at her family's beach house at Palm Beach. Sarah was thin, and her face a little drawn, and while the girls were pleased to see me, there was an air of unreality about it, because they knew I'd soon be going back to Afghanistan. Still, we were grateful to have ten days together. We enjoyed swimming at the beautiful Pittwater beaches, and Sarah's extended family were extremely pleased to see us all.

Most Australians are proud of their soldiers, and I felt a little humbled by the attention and love. There was an assumption by a lot of people in this country that, in a military sense, we were doing everything right. The media control had achieved something. I shudder to think of what it must have been like to be a Vietnam veteran, and to have to come home to friends and family who criticised what you'd done there.

Much too soon, the holiday was over and I was back in the daily grind of Afghanistan. But there was some good news to come. One peculiarity of being an Australian military officer is that, once you pass the rank of captain, you're being trained for executive jobs. This involves moving to different postings every two years. Even when you were overseas on an operation, the posting cycle continued.

In early 2012, those of us for whom this was our second year posted to Townsville (even though I spent that whole second year in Afghanistan) received our posting orders to our next Australian location. As I wanted to experience everything I could in the army, and, like everyone else, plotted out possible career progression, I'd been waiting anxiously for the news. The call finally came from a senior legal officer, who asked me, 'Do you want to go to Special Forces?'

This was exciting. I told her I did, and from that moment I was walking on air. This was what I'd most wanted, because it gave me the chance to advise on the very things I'd written about in my Masters paper – on targeted killing or kill/capture missions.

It was a sought-after position, although not for the faint-hearted. Special Forces Command, or SOCOMD, as they were called, didn't suffer fools, and had rejected some other legal officers, because they didn't think they were good enough military lawyers. Famously, they'd rejected the officer who was now head of the whole army Legal Corps, and it seemed to have created a quietly brewing 'blood feud' between her and them, and a whispering campaign to go with it.

Being offered this job felt like some sort of vindication for my decision to join the army. It was why I'd been so drawn to the British SAS, and one of the things that had drawn me back to the Australian Army was the evocative photos of our SAS troopers walking resolutely into an Afghan valley, with steep mountains towering over them, dust clouds rising from their footsteps, their weapons at their sides, as if to say, 'Putting our lives on the line for Australia is all in a day's work for us.' It seemed to personify the best of this country that had given me and my family so much. I wanted to be part of that picture, and now I would be.

I told Sarah and she was excited for us. The prestige of the Special Forces had reached the families as well. She probably sensed that the job wouldn't be straightforward, but she was happy. We'd be moving to Canberra, and as much as Sarah had loved her North Queensland experience, she wanted to be close to the museums, restaurants and cafes that the capital had to offer.

So in a very clunky way – using the ancient computer systems in Afghanistan that seemed steam-powered – the two of us tried to select an army house in which to live. As luck would have it, someone knew someone who'd recently completed their tour in Canberra. They'd been living in one of the few military houses near the centre of the city, i.e. normal civilian townhouses that were leased long-term by the military.

Sarah spent many hours hovering over the computer, ready to press 'Accept' (as in, take the available house) the second the military computer system changed the listing of the place we wanted from 'unavailable' to 'available'. Fortunately, she managed to get it. Sarah could be as tenacious as any army wife, when she set her mind to something. And while we didn't know anything about the suburb we were moving to, coincidentally the house was also in close proximity to a very good public school and local shops – so we were very lucky.

For Sarah, that was only the beginning of the challenge. Single-handedly co-ordinating the move from Townsville to Canberra was obviously stressful. During our daily phone calls, she spoke as if it would all be fine, not wanting to complain to me while I was on operations, but I could tell she was nearing breaking point.

It was nice to have something to look forward to after the deployment ended, but, again, it hadn't been easy settling back into life at the base at Tarin Kot. I still had a few weeks left, and while that mightn't sound like a long time, by the end of the deployment I wouldn't have been in my family home for nine months. This had taken its toll mentally. The US troops did a full year of deployment in Afghanistan, and it's likely why they had such problems reintegrating into the civilian world on their return.

I found out from Sarah after I'd returned to Australia that she found the move to Canberra even more difficult than I'd imagined. This period of more than nine months managing the children on her own – the whole time worried about me not coming back – had been traumatic, and the army's stringent requirements for cleaning the place, and moving house according to their specific regulations, pushed her to the edge.

Old hands had warned us about the pitfalls. When either Sarah or I said that she'd pack up the house and kids while I was still in Afghanistan, so we could get to Canberra in time for the girls to start the school year, they asked, 'Are you sure?', or more mischievously said, 'Sounds like fun.'

In any case, Sarah went back into that dark place that had been Georgie's first months. To her credit she didn't act out in any way, but she had been scarred, like a twig being snapped off a young tree. It would grow back, and after a few months together as a family she was fine again. But she would never move house without me again. Or so she thought.

When you get back from deployment, things aren't easy. Like all partners in a similar situation, the one who has been at home alone has worked out a system of dealing with everything. And when the partner returns, instead of making things easier they throw the system out of kilter. Both partners want relief, but they want it for different things: the soldier from rules, regulations and army 'shit'; the other from the endless workload of being a single parent, with worried kids, who are themselves sick from worry, without necessarily knowing it.

The kids want to see Daddy, but it takes a few months for Daddy actually to be on the same mental plane as them. You can hug but you can't really communicate. We found that the best way to deal with the homecoming was for Dad to take the kids for a week, and Mum to go to a yoga retreat, or have a night out with the girls, followed by a health retreat. It wasn't very romantic, but the reality of deployments is not romantic, which is why so many army marriages fail. I was home in Australia with Sarah and the kids, though, and that's all that mattered. For the moment.

One good thing about the military was that the actual house move was carried out by a national carrier, who also unloaded everything at the other end. The unpacking took a few weeks, and we learned that there were plenty of people who didn't get to unpack all their boxes until their next two-year rotation came up.

Luckily, our best friends from Townsville, Gav the intelligence chief and his family, were living only a few doors down from us. James started school in Year 2 and Georgie did a couple of days at the local day-care, while Sarah started volunteering at Red Cross. It was a good decision on her part, following her instinct, as that volunteer job led to a paid job – conveniently not far from where we lived.

James' was a good little primary school, and while she'd been in a private school for her first two years, the principal told us matter-of-factly that this school was better, and after a year we agreed with him. It was my first experience of Australian public schools, and I was impressed with the dedication of the teachers and the good nature of the children it produced.

I was working at the new purpose-built, high-security Special Operations Command base near Canberra, and each day I'd do the forty-minute commute each way. The girls went to after-school care, or drama classes, and I was often late to pick them up, driving madly through the traffic to find them standing on their own, waiting for me.

One thing during our time in Canberra was to change all our lives for the better. During one weekend we went to the country around Merriwa, in the Hunter region, for a party thrown by one of my oldest friends, James, who lived on a beautiful property that had been in his family for at least three generations. Extremely kind and likeable, James had managed to go through two stints at boarding school without ever having anyone seriously dislike him, which is almost impossible.

His kids were a few years older, and while staying at their house we saw a Wii machine for the first time. We fell in love with it – in particular 'Just Dance'. When we got back to Canberra, Sarah agreed that we could buy one, as well as a (not very big) TV to go with it.

From then on, each weekend saw James, Georgie and me spending hours competing to imitate Rihanna and Justin Bieber, or even dancing to old school 1950s tracks. Wii led to Xbox, and the family soon reached a new level of competition and happiness. James was very good, considering she was only seven, and she and I would have long, exhausting contests. I managed to be the champion at imitating Beyoncé, but no matter how hard I tried, she had me beaten at the tough moves of the male rappers on screen. Georgie, at only five, struggled to keep up, and would be so heartbroken when she never won that we devised ways to let her have the occasional victory without letting her know.

There was high security at my workplace. The building was low slung with only two storeys, and from a distance looked like a warehouse. I was happy to be here, however, because working at Special Operations Command had been one of my life's ambitions. This was the pinnacle, the best of the best: the people who carried out the most dangerous operations for Australia, often under the cloak of complete secrecy.

I liked the people I worked with and respected their abilities. My boss, Aaron, was someone I had a fair bit in common with. He'd been a full-time legal officer but had left the army to pursue a career as an advocate against the military, acting for those who were entitled to compensation. Eventually, he'd rejoined. I had respect for his legal brain, and his high-level work for military inquiries meant that his interpretation of statutes was very good.

He appreciated the fact that I had been a barrister and had completed my Masters. In fact, about this time, my Masters dissertation on targeted killing was published in one of the better international law journals, the *Australian Yearbook of International Law*.

Townsville had been a big army base since World War II. Canberra was different. There were some older bases for air force and navy, but apart from Duntroon it wasn't really an army town. Even those army people based here largely worked in offices, and no-one lived on base, or even near their HQ. It was as if they were all pretending not to be in the military, but public servants who put on a particular suit each day. However, soldiers are different, as they're aliens in the civilian world. They can enjoy it, but they never really understand it – any more than a civilian understands why someone would volunteer to die for their country.

The base was newly built in a farm paddock. The idea of running operations from one central headquarters – with big screens showing the locations on digital maps on the walls of all army, air force and navy units – was a logical one. But politics had apparently intervened in its implementation. We couldn't just build a new headquarters – that would be considered a waste of money, in the jaundiced view of the politicians, anyway. It needed to be built in a way that benefited the politicians who'd signed off on it. Under Prime Minister Howard it seemed that government spending, on every department, even Defence, had been weaponised. Probably both parties did it, but it didn't work when it clashed with military capability, which it did in this case.

The site that was chosen was outside Canberra in a neighbouring electorate. It was a swinging seat. The rumour was that the location for this new building had been chosen by the government because it was in this electorate, in an attempt to say, 'Look how many jobs we brought to your area.'

That was okay, but in the same way that it was a good idea to group all those involved in an operation in one building – a concentration of all our planners and decision makers in one small place – for other reasons, it was a bad idea to build the base there. Firstly, rather than make it secure, it made it an easy target. This supposed top-secret base, which controlled all of Australia's secret operations, was clearly visible on Google Maps.

Secondly, there was that forty-minute drive from Canberra. While some chose to live nearby, if everybody had moved there state secrets would soon become the town's secrets. As it was, the general in charge of Special Operations Command also had an office in Canberra, and sometimes had to attend both. This meant that, like me, he spent six hours a week, thirty a month, three hundred a year in his car, on trips that could have been avoided had the base not been built in a location to help a particular political party win an election. Having said that, I was new in the job, and excited to be here, so I didn't dwell on it. I had other concerns in those first few months.

Georgie had always been a bit different to James. She was more introspective and nervous. She was our baby, so we loved her all the more. A soldier's life is a hard one, and disappearing is unfortunately necessary. James seemed to get it. She had had me to herself for the first two years; perhaps that's why she seemed to take my comings and goings in her stride. She liked me being a soldier, and noticed how her carers at day-care would stiffen up a little, as if to salute me, when I arrived in uniform.

Unfortunately, I wasn't there for Georgie in the same way. Subsequently, in her first five years, she seemed to have some sort of child version of depression and/or anxiety. It first really became apparent when she started school in 2013. She had done the first year in day-care a couple of days a week, and seemed okay. But when she started school, something about the bell ringing struck her with fear. She'd immediately cling to the nearest fencepost and wouldn't let go, absolutely refusing to go inside, as if she knew something terrible would happen in there.

Admittedly, the bell was extremely loud and jarring, designed to reach the far corners of the grounds, and it would give me a start as well. There was too much of a similarity to the missile warning in Tarin Kot. It felt somehow as if Georgie and I were connected, her tiny body a reflection of my own fears. It broke my heart to have to pull her fingers off me and hand her to the teacher, as she held on, grim faced and terrified. Some days it was too much for me, and we'd simply go home together.

When Georgie would cry because of loneliness at school, I would as well, feeling both bad for her and guilty that I'd somehow caused her this pain. She had liked Townsville and had friends there. However, me going to Afghanistan had taken a toll, and she didn't like this new place. As well, the sight of me in my uniform seemed to make her think I was about to disappear again, maybe worse.

This was a tough time for the family, but I had no regrets about joining the military. It gave me the purpose I'd lacked as a barrister. As a barrister, your purpose is largely related to your own career, with maybe a small amount centred upon being an upstanding lawyer. A soldier always had a purpose, though. It involved truth, bravery and protecting those who couldn't protect themselves. And if I had a purpose, it made me a better father.

The Skype scandal from the previous year – in which a cadet at the Australian Defence Force Academy filmed himself having sex with a female colleague, then broadcast it on Skype to several male colleagues – was still reverberating around the ADF in 2012. Having seen some of my fellow officer cadets get expelled from the British Army for pocketing the equivalent of about $30 between them, the idea that future Australian officers would devise a plan whereby they'd watch one of their classmates having sex was a quantum leap in questionable ethics.

To me, the scandal typified so much of what was wrong with Defence. The whole ADFA program seemed a little misguided – something that had sounded like a good idea, but in practice didn't really work. There were plenty of perfectly good universities in Australia, and nothing cadets learnt at ADFA couldn't be learnt elsewhere. One of my classmates at Oriel had been an air-force officer. Unless they were engineers, army officers didn't really benefit from a degree, as it was the leadership that was required, and education was 'leadership neutral'. I had a law degree when I went to Sandhurst, but it didn't help me in any way – nor did I expect it to.

The defence minister vowed to leave no stone unturned, and although the three cadets had only been at ADFA for a few weeks, and were not even in the Defence Force in any real sense, an inquiry into the culture of the ADF was commissioned. There was nothing wrong with that; however, from the beginning it looked to me like window-dressing, hatched simply to boost the minister's popularity, not to improve the actual conditions in the ADF. This was the modern world, though, where everything had a real-time price – sometimes in morale, sometimes in credibility, sometimes in soul.

The Skype scandal did say something about the sort of people they were recruiting for officers, and the fact that they needed to tighten psychological recruiting standards. What made it typical of everything that was wrong with the ADF was that there were females in the ADF who complained that not only had they been sexually assaulted, they were victimised later for even making a complaint. It appeared to me that the only reason the minister and his staff cared about this particular case was that it had hit the media, and their response was equally focused on the media, rather than dealing with the actual assaults. It seemed to be putting out fires with image consultants.

When I arrived at the Canberra base in 2012, all the way up the stairs I was confronted with posters proclaiming the minister's latest initiative: 'Pathway to Change'. To me, it felt like a typical slogan dreamt up by Canberra consultants. The section on officers' behaviour summed up how far off track we'd gone. It was entitled 'Beyond Compliance' and was almost breathless in its exhortation that officers must not just do what was required by law, we should have an extra safety measure between us and the legal compliance.

While that sounds great, it was actually silly and unworkable. It wasn't always smart or even necessary to do things 'beyond compliance', however worthy that sounded delivered from the pulpit of public adoration. Compliance standards were there for a reason. We didn't wear two seatbelts or two helmets. New policies were meaningless without enforcement, and it was impossible to enforce: how could we rule that someone hadn't gone far enough beyond compliance?

The intended meaning was probably: 'Do more than the minimum.' But it didn't say that, and the fact that no-one seemed to care that it didn't make sense added to my impression that this initiative was just for show for the civilian media – and I seemed to be the only one who hadn't got the memo.

At the same time as this very visible campaign, women who alleged they suffered serious sexual assaults were denied compensation, bullied out of the service and gaslit, by the same people paying for the expensive posters featuring purposeful-looking models in uniform, gazing towards the sky, holding folders: contemplative, hopeful, resolute. After the inquiry, there was no change to ADFA's selection process. It would have made more sense to direct resources to a dedicated sexual assault unit with some qualified female staff. It seemed to me that convictions, or at least charges, for rapes would change behaviour better than brochures.

Meanwhile, at Special Forces Command, there were plenty of women who were self-assured and doing fine. In terms of its impact on my work, 'Pathway to Change' was little more than that array of posters I'd see on the wall. They seemed almost like murals on the side of Soviet public buildings. A brighter future. Together. Today.

In any case, at Special Forces we were focused on the important work with which we'd been entrusted. In 2012 there were many significant firefights with the Taliban, and a number of deaths of our own people in combat, all which had to be carefully considered to see what, if anything, the soldiers had done wrong, and if the rules of engagement had been misused, misunderstood or misinterpreted. We had to consider the rules of engagement, and whether they needed to be adjusted. Closer to home, we were training the counterterrorism team on the correct use of force in hostage-rescue operations.

Aaron was the most qualified lieutenant colonel in the Legal Corps, and we both considered it a privilege to be at Special Forces Command. But it was hard work. I left home about seven each morning to get to Headquarters Joint Operational Command (HQJOC), where Special Forces was located, and usually didn't get home until seven at night, by which time Sarah would be exhausted.

In September, Aaron told me he'd be deploying to Afghanistan later in the year as the lawyer for our Special Operations Task Group. He asked me to fulfil his role as senior advisor to the Special Forces Command General for about four months. It was a big responsibility, but I was confident I could do it.

It was what had drawn me back into the military: the chance to use my brains to contribute to what I saw as taking the fight to those who fought democracy by terrorism. There was something satisfying about giving advice to those who were putting their lives on the line for this country, time and time again, and I was proud that Aaron had confidence in me. After my disillusionment with the window-dressing of my first deployment to Afghanistan under a US commander in 2011, Special Operations seemed to be the only soldiers really fighting the war, and I was proud to contribute to making them more effective in some small way.

Day-to-day family life was presenting its challenges. One weekend, when Sarah was away on a training course and the girls and I were visiting an old friend of mine from the Sydney Uni rugby club who'd just moved to Canberra, James fell awkwardly in their backyard and broke her arm. This was the strangest of accidents, in that she simply tripped over the family cavoodle, who was jumping up on her, and as she came down on the soft lawn she fell awkwardly.

It was a Sunday and my friend drove us to the hospital as I cradled James in my arms in the front seat. She was incredibly brave, and I was more upset than she was, feeling the parent's responsibility for not keeping my child safe and not being able to prevent this pain. As Canberra's is a regional hospital there was no guarantee that James would get operated on immediately, and it looked as if she'd have to wait until Monday. I called an old friend, again from the rugby club, who was head of orthopaedics in Canberra, and we got the last slot that night. I knew how fortunate we'd been.

Eventually, we met the doctors at around 11 pm. The anaesthetist was about sixty and when he came and said hello, he told me he was a big fan of my father, which made me feel proud. They treated James like a VIP and she left the operating room an hour later with pins in her arm. Back at school, she became a minor celebrity as everyone signed her cast, which was pink.

We took Georgie to a child psychologist to try to help with her feelings of anxiety. The psychologist said that when she asked her to draw a picture of Daddy at work, she drew me in a battle, with bullets flying and bombs going off. She suggested Georgie come to my work one day to show her that it was all quite safe. We did that and it helped, but I think her concerns were more instinctive than literal. She knew I dealt with death, whether it was via email, or in real life, and thought that I was somehow in danger. She seemed to know, before I even told Sarah, that next year I'd be going back to Afghanistan.

CHAPTER 27

The ROEAMP

By 2013, I knew something was seriously wrong. I believed it went to the very core of the Defence Force, such that it was no longer fit for purpose. There'd been other things I'd noticed before then, such as the daily meetings in Afghanistan and the way the Skype incident had been handled. These were uncomfortable and slightly embarrassing failures. The ROEAMP was another good example of the rot setting in.

This curious document – the Rules of Engagement Amplification, to give it its full name; pronounced 'ro-amp' – was shown to me in early 2013. With Aaron away, I was the acting Command Legal Officer and was given the right to comment, although it soon became clear that I was expected simply to rubber-stamp the ROEAMP and move on.

The ROEAMP was a one-page document, while the existing rules of engagement ran to twenty pages. What was it for? It was claimed to be simply a summary of the rules, but this was the first strange thing: it wasn't. It misquoted the original – mistakenly replacing the word 'practicable' with 'practical' – and added some phrases that, in reality, made no sense to a soldier under fire from the Taliban. These included 'reasonable and necessary' and having a 'high degree of confidence' that the person you encountered was directly participating in hostilities.

While, on the face of it, this terminology mightn't seem unworkable, it was. In court, with a prosecutor arguing with you and no benchmark by which to prove you were right, if it was entirely up to the judge's interpretation of those terms, what confidence could you have that you wouldn't be convicted?

And puzzlingly, according to this new document those who shot a person by mistake in the heat of battle might be found guilty of murder. This was simply inaccurate.

In addition to the ROEAMP, the existing ROE had its share of problems. I was determined to help fix them, so, based on my criminal law experience and time in Northern Ireland, I wrote an internal paper aimed at making the ROE both clearer for the soldiers and, if necessary, easier to prosecute.

Rather than subjective and imprecise terminology, it had simple numerical guidelines, outlining the exact circumstances in which a soldier could open fire, with a proviso that small variations were possible: 1. You see a man carrying a weapon; 2. They fail to heed commands; 3. Their movements make you suspect they are evading you, or attempting to use the weapon.

I submitted my recommendations, but the office of the Chief of Defence Force, which had produced ROEAMP, refused to budge on any of the amendments at all. I couldn't work out why there had been the need to produce this pointless, impractical – potentially dangerous – document.

In late April there was another incident that made me believe the organisation was losing its way. This matter is one that is relatively difficult for civilians to understand. After a Taliban had been killed, an SAS corporal had removed his hand, in order to identify him by DNA. While it might seem like a savage thing to do, it wasn't.

From the beginning my sympathies lay with the corporal, not the senior leadership. They went into a state of panic, the likes of which I'd never seen. It showed how our wars had become so distorted that the way the public back in Australia perceived events was not simply a factor in the way our military behaved, it had become the single most important factor.

In many ways, this epitomised the nature of honour: while people were baying for the corporal's blood, I was defending him. To me, the real crime was not the cutting off of a Taliban's hand, but the way we abandoned a soldier who was just doing his job, and making a reasonable decision on which lives depended. It was a tough decision I had to make; however, sometimes you must defend what most people see as indefensible, and sometimes you must call out what most people think is acceptable. It's not a way to become popular. My general from Townsville got it right, though, when he refused to let the police secretly search a soldier's house. The nature of honour requires you to stand firm in the face of panic, because you respond to values, not appearances.

It was clear to me that this was not a crime, as the US Standard Operating procedures allowed such practice. It wasn't the war crime of mutilation, as was suggested by some senior ADF lawyers, because that relates to disfigurement of live victims. The corporal gave evidence that he'd been told by the military police that it was acceptable, and in fact the procedure is not unknown to civilian police, if they can't recover the full body, but need to identify it.

About four years after the investigation commenced, the corporal concerned was finally told he would not be charged. In the meantime, he'd been denied promotion, postings, courses, as well as any peace of mind, because he was a person awaiting charges.

The ADF neither knew the applicable laws, nor were prepared to front the media and defend him. It was wrong to abandon a soldier simply because it was politically expedient to do so. A quiet anger was continuing to grow inside me. While it's normal in any large organisation that you won't agree with how everything is handled, the events I would witness later that same year led me to believe it was no accident.

A conference on international law was coming up in Houston, Texas. Organised by a group of academics, it centred around a legal blog called Lawfare, which I skimmed most days. Because my paper on rules of engagement had been published and well received in academic circles around the world, I was invited to speak. I wanted to visit my US counterpart in Joint Special Operations Command, but they seemed too busy to see me. It was disappointing that, for so called allies in the war, we weren't *that* welcome. I couldn't even get into the United States without a fair bit of rigmarole over visas. It seemed being an ally of the US didn't count for much, except at press conferences.

I enjoyed the international law conference and afterwards went to Washington D.C. for a few days. I took the time to go to the Lincoln Memorial, as well as Arlington National Cemetery. There, I found the graves of the three US Army soldiers who'd drowned when their armoured vehicle had overturned in a river on my 2011 deployment to Afghanistan. They'd been unable to release their seatbelts and open the doors with all their body armour on. There were a few flowers and tiny American flags by little white headstones.

While I was at the cemetery, I saw a funeral. Among the mourners were a young widow and children. It was a sad sight. Soldiers in the US seemed to be largely quite poor, and, if they lost their lives, I'm not sure there was much left for their family, either in state support or public understanding.

I wondered where she would go now, and what life she and her kids would have.

Some of the gravestones simply had 'G.W.O.T.' on them: the Global War On Terror. It seemed strange for me that this phrase – so glib, so vague – would end up on people's graves as if it was a real thing. Perhaps the grieving families wanted it to be real.

A few weeks later, in early June, I was back in the Special Operations Command office near Canberra. We were all told to go and watch the TV for an obligatory message from the Chief of Army, Lieutenant General David Morrison. This was peculiar in itself. The only time this happened was if there was a death, and I knew that wasn't the case, because the Command Element at Special Forces, of which I was part, hadn't been informed.

When I got to the nicely appointed breakout room, with SAS memorabilia over the walls, I felt saddened as he unfolded sketchy details of some terrible sounding group sex crime. I couldn't help but nod in agreement when, speaking about female soldiers and officers, he said, 'They are vital to us maintaining our capability now and into the future. If that does not suit you, then get out.' He looked outraged, and while I didn't know the details I felt a sense of embarrassment to be a man.

As I returned to my desk, though, the lawyer in me returned to my body. I had some nagging doubts. Why had this been broadcast on national TV, when the investigations weren't even complete, and this would clearly prejudice the trials? The general had mentioned that he'd been forced to make a public announcement because an internal video for the army's consumption had been loaded onto YouTube and apparently gone viral. But I'd never heard of it. This wasn't exactly the world's best practice procedural fairness of which the Defence Force brochures boasted.

While Morrison attempted to partly justify his speech as a message to men who didn't want women in the military, I knew this was a distortion of the reality. I'd now been in the ADF since 2005, and seen Reserve service, as well as service on two of the biggest bases, and deployment to Afghanistan. I'd never seen anything to suggest that men had a problem with women in the military. Why would they?

He must have rehearsed his speech many times in front of a professional film crew, until he got it just right; practising his 'avenging glare' and delivery, so it seemed like he had just heard the news. In the version that supposedly was made for the troops, which I saw later, he talked in a way that didn't feel authentic for a general addressing his troops. It was almost as if the video had been made to show the public all along.

As with the reaction to Skype, I suspected this was a big smokescreen for the public's benefit. But at the time I had plenty of immediate issues to deal with, relating to my core duties, so I put my nagging doubts to the back of my mind, and got back to bullets and basics.

A few months after the ROEAMP issue, I made another proposal to the office of the Chief of Army. I suggested greater use of computer gaming software to train the troops and commanders alike. The idea was rejected. It annoyed me because the same senior ADF commanders and their political masters who refused to simplify extremely complex and confusing rules of engagement were the loudest in calling for the soldiers to be put on trial for transgressing them.

It was particularly frustrating as the ADF already used similar computer-based programs for tactical exercises, and even things as minor as the responsible service of alcohol, but they weren't interested in using the technology to address a potential liability to their reputation on a much larger scale.

In terms of the ADF's priorities, as always, the risk of a soldier being hung out to dry by poor training and leadership seemed to be near the bottom.

CHAPTER 28

The Last Dance

I'd known for a few months now that I had to go back to Afghanistan, and the day had arrived. I'd already said goodbye to Sarah and James. I'd bought them a little pug-cross puppy the week before I left as a distraction while I was away. Sarah took it bravely, rationalising that this was both my job, and who I was. She had friends who were also military wives and, mercifully, this trip would only be half as long as the nine-and-a-half months of the previous deployment.

James, even at only eight years old, was the family's optimist, always seeing the glass as half full. While she knew she'd miss me, she looked forward to the fun we'd have when I returned, and the presents of exotic dresses and jewellery that I'd send her from the far-off parts of the world that Sarah would show her on the map. In her sunny childlike way, one day she imagined she would go with me.

Georgie wouldn't find it so easy. When I went to her primary school to say goodbye, I saw that the walls in the corridor were covered in children's paintings, and as Father's Day was approaching, the theme was 'Daddy and me'. The individual white sheets bore the child's name, as well as two stick figures – one large, one small – both with big smiles on their faces, holding hands. I felt a pang of guilt, and maybe shame. An accurate picture from Georgie's point of view would have been a single, small stick figure, arms outstretched, but with no big stick figure there. There'd be a crumpled frown on her face; maybe with a tiny little figure of Daddy way up in a far corner, in clothes of green and black, wearing a helmet and carrying a stick-like gun. Out of reach, on a cloud, almost imaginary.

While we had talked about me going away again for a little while, it seemed Georgie didn't want to take it in, and was remote and aloof every time either Sarah or myself brought it up. But on my departure day, although the plane that would eventually take me to Dubai was only a few hours away, I wanted one last hug from her. So I got the taxi to detour to her school on the way to the airport.

Georgie was brought out of class by the teacher. She ran to me excitedly, as she always did, although this time the action seemed a little forced. She knew this was what she was meant to do, but her face said otherwise. I knelt on one knee to hug her. The teacher was watching us both, behind Georgie's back, twisting her hands together.

'I love you very much, and I'll be back very soon,' I said, choking back the tears, and gripping her far too tightly.

She was still only about four feet tall and tiny in my arms. I'm sure she remembered me leaving on my first deployment, when she about to turn four years old. When I got back, she was almost five, and now that she'd just turned six I was going again. It wasn't much of a birthday present.

Whenever we were together, she always wanted me to carry her on my back. Even when watching TV together on the sofa, she insisted on sitting on my shoulders. The child psychologist we'd taken her to suggested it was because she was worried that each time I left, I'd never come back.

Long before I was finished hugging her, Georgie released her grip, and turned away with a fixed smile on her face. 'Bye, Daddy,' she said over her shoulder, and, without making eye contact, started skipping back towards the classroom. I let her go for a few steps and then was overcome with emotion. I was thinking that possibly – just possibly – this would be the last time we'd ever see each other.

'Wait!' I said, and ran after her for a few steps. I knelt down and grabbed her for one last hug, lifting her off the ground.

Georgie said nothing and her body was stiff and unresponsive. I put her down. She turned and ran off, apparently as unaffected as before. As I turned to get back into the taxi, the tears started flowing and I noticed the teacher was crying too.

I sat silently in the cab as it drove towards the airport. I knew that despite her brave face Georgie would have eventually cracked and wept huge sobs when she was alone in the school bathroom. After that, she'd bottle the pain up inside of herself, shutting down that part of her brain and not discussing my absence again. I felt I had abandoned her. When faced with a choice between my work and being there for her, I had chosen my work. She was right. I'd be on the plane to Afghanistan in a few hours. As I waited at the traffic lights in the cab, I had a brief premonition that I wouldn't make it back, then put it out of my mind. I had a job to do.

I'd been keen to go to Afghanistan for a number of reasons. Firstly, I wanted to be a part of the direct targeting process, killing key Taliban from a distance with drones and helicopters. I'd written a paper on it, and wanted to make it my speciality. I could also see that something was amiss over there. As with my unofficial missions with Harriet on the 2011 tour, I wanted to see things for myself, and work out what was mere rumour and what was true.

I thought I was the best person for the job, and it was frustrating to have to be a backseat driver, when what I really wanted to do was take the wheel. This may seem like arrogance, but I had been there two years earlier, I'd been there in 2000, I was the only person who'd written a paper on the type of missions we did, and I had a genuine love of the army and those who put their life on the line for Australia.

My new boss wasn't keen to send me. No bosses wanted their subordinates to deploy, because it would mean more work for them. However, I pushed and pushed, and eventually she agreed, as long as I found a replacement to do my job while I was away, which I duly did.

I'd be lying if I said I wasn't partly driven by knowing that Australia's mission in Afghanistan would be ending soon, as Prime Minister Julia Gillard had said we were ceasing combat operations at the end of 2013 (although our troops would continue to train the Afghans after that date). I was wanting to be a part of it once more, while the opportunity was still there. If you didn't feel like that, why would you join the army?

In Afghanistan, I'd be working for Special Operations Task Group, Task Force 66, which was the ultimate for a military lawyer. Being an operational lawyer for the military was probably the best job in the world for me: half-lawyer, half-soldier. Task Force 66 was the code name for Australia's special forces taking the war to the Taliban. They were the door-kickers. The bomb-droppers. They were the desert equivalent of the men who abseiled off the Iranian Embassy roof in London, swinging through the glass windows, firing machine-guns and smoke grenades at the same time. The people on whom so many thrilling fictional on-screen characters, from James Bond to Jason Bourne, were based. Except this was real.

We'd killed many hundreds of Taliban by 2013, and they in turn had killed about twenty of our elite war fighters. My attraction to the job was heightened because in TF66 there was less bullshit, more bullets than anywhere else in the Australian Army. They were professional soldiers, but as the designation implied, with its hint of Route 66, they were undeniably a little bit rock and roll. And there was nothing wrong with that, if you made sacrifices that were very much on the scale of the original mud-soaked ANZACs. I also never forgot that, while my two deployments in two years were hard for my family, most of these guys had done six in six, and plenty even more.

Arriving in Tarin Kot, I got to work. Being the TF66 legal officer might have looked easy to an outsider, but it wasn't. You basically hung around in the gym, or wherever, waiting to be called – but when you were called, it was crucial that you get it right. And 'right' meant that, even under the critical microscope of people 10,000 kilometres away, who'd never been anywhere near a war zone and who were looking for a scapegoat, you could defend your decision. Plenty of my predecessors had ended up being forced to justify decisions they signed off on in relation to TF66 in military enquiries. Some careers were ended by it.

Thousand-pound bombs might be dropped on houses; hellfire rockets launched at a couple of people on a motorbike; someone shot dead on the basis of what they said in a recorded conversation. Each of these instances of the infliction of death needed to be signed off by the legal officer, and it wasn't a matter of simply saying 'yes' all the time or 'no' all the time. The presence or otherwise of civilians, the individual characteristics of the weapon systems and the quality of the intelligence, among other factors, were all interpreted and quantified according to some fairly complex flow charts. You needed to have big cojones to stand up to the SAS people on one side, and the overly risk-averse legal arse-coverers on the other.

It didn't take long for my good mood to fade. The new improved ROEAMP and the restrictions it imposed drove me up the wall, and the new atmosphere within the Australian Government of suspicion towards the SAS was deeply concerning.

It seemed that every time I asked for approval from the coalition Middle East HQ or Canberra for a strike by the SAS, it was denied. This had a twofold effect. It not only stopped whatever mission we were on from going ahead, it was a chilling warning that anything the SAS did was, at some point in the future, likely to be analysed negatively by people who had never been on operations.

On one occasion, we called for fire support for a local police station that was being overrun by the Taliban. However, as soon as it became clear that no Australians were in danger, the request was denied. The ugly truth of our mission here was becoming exposed like a rock in low tide: we weren't here to help the Afghans, we were here to help ourselves by pretending to help the Afghans.

It was hugely frustrating to have to be bearer of the news: 'No, we can't carry out that strike.' Nor was this no-strike policy to guard against war crimes. But when we had plenty of safeguards, such as a room full of people in the operation control centre, including myself and the CO, calling for a strike, and despite there being no chance of an extrajudicial execution, it would likely be denied.

Something was up.

The mission that started it all occurred on 23 September, an SAS section going out with an Afghan National Police patrol – the ANP being, in effect, simply another regiment of the Afghan Army – to arrest a suspected key insurgent. It was a grey, windy day. They had all been dropped off by two Black Hawks, which left immediately. It seems their arrival was not unexpected, as they came under fire from the high ground as soon as the helicopters disappeared.

'Beachy' (not his real name) was an SAS corporal who was patrol second-in-command. He'd done four tours of Afghanistan and a couple of East Timor, and had a record of exemplary service to his country. He returned fire in the direction from which the shots came, and pursued the shooter up the hill. Such was the wild west nature of Afghanistan, you came under fire, returned fire, and if that didn't come to anything, you'd simply get on with what you were originally there to do.

In this case, that was to locate and arrest a suspected Taliban member, who was meant to be in the area. It was like so many of the hundreds of previous missions the SAS had done, but with an important difference. Three months out from the US withdrawing, everything was Afghan led; that is, the ANP were in charge of the mission – officially, at least.

I had seen this ANP platoon up close because I'd had to deliver them a lecture on human rights. It was basic: the usual PowerPoint, with comical-looking stick figures illustrating the key issues: don't kill prisoners, do arrest. After the lecture a couple of them wanted to pose for selfies. They had hardly any English but looked at me and gave me the thumbs-up sign, smiled and said, 'Women's rights good.' I doubted they believed it, but they knew to say it and to give the thumbs-up and smile. I feared we'd taught them a little too well.

The 'Afghanisation' of the coalition forces was having a tipping-point effect regarding the danger levels for the SAS soldiers. There were now fewer SAS in relation to the locals, so they had to watch their backs for potential green on blue. Any of these raw Afghan recruits, who were largely only there for the money, might be considering becoming a hero by shooting you in the back. The Taliban had struck gold with green on blue, because it meant that the Afghanisation was particularly hindered.

In order to withdraw our forces without it being a rout – which would gain the attention of the Western media – we needed, at least temporarily, for the Afghan Army to be able to hold against the Taliban. Therefore, they needed some practice at actually leading while we were still here. Time was running out, so the gradual shift from a single Afghan on our patrols to those patrols being led by Afghans, with a few SAS people present as advisors, needed to be accelerated. In short, political considerations put extreme pressure on the people at the coalface – the SAS soldiers on the ground.

The rules of engagement hadn't changed. The shooter was required to decide whether someone was directly participating in hostilities, according to a tortured definition with many inappropriate, subjective phrases such as 'reasonable', 'necessary', 'if possible' and 'high degree of confidence'.

The Afghan-led patrols of late 2013 were just like the ROEAMP. Although the risks for the SAS soldiers had increased, if anything went wrong it would likely be blamed on them, rather than the unrealistic pressure they were being put under. It was possible that a really good journalist might have gone in to bat for the soldiers, but they were being embedded with the defence forces, further away from the frontline. Their war would be dangerous enough to get kudos when they returned, but not so dangerous that they might not make it back.

Despite all the requirements that an SAS soldier had to fulfil to do the job properly, there seemed to be little backing of people if they made an understandable mistake. However, on the flipside there was often a naïve acceptance of stories that were a stretch. The leadership rewarded and therefore encouraged dishonesty. In six years not a single soldier was charged with disingenuously claiming an unarmed person was a Taliban battlefield informant, nor was anyone ever called out over placing weapons and radios on dead bodies.

Yet the honest soldier who shot a farmer holding a shovel who suddenly appeared in the dark skyline could face trial for murder. He might not be convicted, but his life could be destroyed. The reason? Politics. So many mediocre military lawyers seemed only too happy to pick the low-hanging fruit and charge a soldier who was defending himself, while not being streetwise enough to see bullshit that was right in front of them. Maybe they knew but simply didn't care; like the rest of the war, it was all about appearances, getting promoted and moving on. But it wasn't about appearances for me, and it wasn't for most people on Task Force 66.

Which brings us back to this particular mission. Beachy pursued the firer up the hill, but gave up after a short chase. The soldiers returned to the area of the landing zone, and got on with the task they were sent to undertake. The actual arrest was like herding cats, because the Afghans were supposedly in charge; however, the SAS was there, telling them how to be in charge, without taking charge. All the while, there was the danger of being shot in the back, not just as a calculated green on blue, but occasionally due to some argument or slight over an order or an action.

Despite the wind, and lack of inspirational leadership, the joint patrol managed to arrest – or, rather, 'detain' – three locals who were suspected of being Taliban. Even the obligatory use of the word 'detain' rather than 'arrest' indicated the nature of this political war. There was no difference in the legal meaning. It was not the same as being charged, but the lawyers who advised Defence had largely never been near a courtroom, and they didn't understand this, so they put out an edict saying we must be careful to call them detainees, or Persons Under Control – PUCs, as the SAS called them. Detainees, PUCs, however they wanted us to label them, they were clearly arrested in that they certainly weren't free to go. They were coming with us back to base, and they weren't allowed a phone call.

The three PUCs were questioned individually with the aid of an interpreter, and their mugshots were taken, each holding a board with their details. They were compliant, and there was no reason to be on heightened alert – from the detainees, anyway.

It was decided to take all three detainees back to our base. The PUCs had their hands tied behind them by plasticuffs. In order to get them seated in the Black Hawks, the plasticuffs needed to be cut and new ones refastened in front. It was a two-man job, one to cut and reapply the plasticuffs, one to stand guard.

There had been incidents in the past in which PUCs had grabbed for weapons in that split second. While small and malnourished, they were wiry and had a fire about them that meant that, in a one-on-one wrestle, they weren't easily subdued, even by the SAS. And as far as they knew, they might not be leaving our base once we took them there.

In a tiny cow shed, the only structure in the area, next to which the helicopters were to land, the first two had their cuffs removed and reapplied. An Afghan Army soldier was meant to be covering Beachy as he redid the cuffs for the third, but he'd walked outside the hut, leaving Beachy and the PUC alone, with the unarmed interpreter looking on through the door.

Having been completely compliant during his arrest, questioning and now detaining, the PUC had lulled Beachy into a false sense of security. As he was doing the job, Beachy was aware of the risk, but with the helicopters returning shortly, he cut the plasticuffs off on his own. The suspected Taliban saw his chance.

As far as plans go it wasn't too bad, and it almost worked. There was a mighty struggle for about ten seconds, during which Beachy and the PUC battled for control of the rifle. Beachy couldn't break the PUC's grip entirely, but he managed to pull the trigger while, at the same time, angling the barrel towards the Afghan's body. Three rounds made sure he was dead.

Who could blame Beachy in the circumstances? He would have experienced a mix of emotions in a matter of milliseconds. The strongest of these was probably anger for letting himself get into this position. The SAS have incredibly high standards of soldiering, and they are harder on themselves than anyone else. Secondly, he would have been disappointed that he'd given the Afghan the benefit of the doubt, even though he was a suspected Taliban, and had been rewarded by almost being killed by him.

Thirdly, he would have been in a mild state of shock, having had a desperate, heart-racing struggle when he least expected it.

Beachy's near-death experience went unnoticed by the other soldiers. No-one realised what was happening, except the interpreter, who stood watching open-mouthed from the doorway, knowing if the Taliban got hold of the weapon, he'd probably be shot next.

Beachy was honest and took photos of the scene, in which the Taliban was not holding a firearm, a knife or a radio. When Beachy made it back to base, he ran into me soon afterwards, but didn't tell me what had happened. In retrospect, perhaps his reluctance to do so wasn't that surprising. After all, when the well-intentioned SAS corporal had cut off the hand of the dead Taliban for DNA testing, and the legal officer had found out, it didn't end well.

I came out of the sleeping accommodation in a bit of a daze. It was early evening and already getting dark. I'd had a sleep in the afternoon and dreamt I was back in England many years before. I woke disappointed that I wasn't. I went to get coffee. As I left the building and crossed the dirt road to the office block, I saw the Afghan Army commander getting a pat on the back from one of the SAS corporals. He was clearly trying to boost his confidence, but the Afghan looked as sour as ever.

Against the wall of the accommodation block were two people in Afghan dress. I didn't remember seeing handcuffs on them, but generally there were few people in Afghan dress in the Special Forces base. They must be prisoners. They weren't meant to be here, although I wasn't particularly bothered. I trusted that they were about to be moved, and I knew they were safer here than with the Afghan National Police.

Typically, the only reason prisoners weren't allowed within the walls of the Special Forces camp was that the politicians didn't want the headline. If they were killed in the Afghan base, well, that wasn't our fault.

There was nothing urgent going on in the office, and after the coffee, I thought I'd go back to the gym. I needed the weights and music. After the session, and after showering, someone came to tell me to see the CO. After ten years in the army, I could read the body language of the messenger. I decided to get into uniform for once.

When I got to the CO's office, he told me to close the door.

'Dave, you know those prisoners we took today ...?'

I nodded and said I'd seen them outside the accommodation block.

'Well, there used to be three.'

I looked from him to the regimental sergeant major.

When soldiers have to give and receive news like this, there's never pretend outrage. It is, after all, just a bad day at work for us, and it could be worse.

'They shot one.'

He didn't have to say that they'd only just told him, because that was obvious.

The regimental sergeant major didn't make a joke and say, 'You'd think they might have remembered that,' but his expression said it. Both the funniest and angriest moments between experienced soldiers were by looks, not words.

There was a moment's silence while I looked back at them. I'd seen Beachy and he didn't mention it. Seemingly, they'd waited till they got their story straight – a period of a few hours. Despite Beachy's exemplary record, it didn't look good.

I sighed and said, 'Cunts.'

The commanding officer said he'd asked one of the SAS staff captains to do a quick gathering of the facts. He wanted me to look at it when it was finished and draft a letter to headquarters. No doubt people in Canberra were getting excited. It would be a long night. Lucky I'd had a nap.

Soon afterwards, I received the incident report from the staff captain. It was well written and its conclusions were logical. It seemed there was nothing to suggest that Beachy hadn't acted in self-defence. I gave the report to the CO, who agreed with its findings. He then sent it to Canberra.

Hours later, there had been significant developments. I called the SAS sergeant major and asked him to send Beachy up. Beachy knocked on the thick steel door and came into my cargo-container office. I explained to him that despite the fact that the CO had argued strongly against it, and that the CO had supported him, the generals in Canberra were sending a team to investigate him for murder. There was no easy way to put it.

He didn't say anything, but just gave me a look. It was only a look, but I'd been around enough to know what it meant.

'Yes, it's political bullshit,' I said with a sigh, not taking the easy option of looking away. While I didn't bother saying anything to win his approval, it burnt me all the more that I'd been fighting hard against the same political bullshit for the last six months. But I didn't need to tell him about fighting. He'd done six long, dangerous deployments for his country, so whatever efforts I'd made weren't much in comparison.

Then he said the words that I'll never forget.

'Isn't it your job to stop the political bullshit?'

I sighed, dropping eye contact for the first time. All sorts of defensive answers were lining up in my brain, but before I could choose any of them, I gave in to the only one that was true. I knew he was right.

'Yes, it is.'

We discussed a few of the details about the interviews with the police that would take place when they arrived. But from that moment on, I knew exactly what my duty was.

ACKNOWLEDGEMENTS

To Deborah Bibby, who took me to Penguin Random House. There are other publishers but I'm not sure this would have been a reality – and the book it is – without them. To Meredith Curnow, the General, who had incredible faith in me, and without whom there would be no book at all. To Patrick Mangan, the pilot, who turned a pile of pages into something I'm very proud of, working coolly under incredible stress, day in, day out, seven days a week, landing the book like an overloaded 747, with one engine, in a hurricane.

To all the proofreaders, particularly the unpaid ones such as Rosie Jacobs and her assistant Frenchie, and the whole team at PRH, including Veronica Eze, who got the audiobook going so beautifully, and the voice actor, Hazem Shammas.

To Ben McKelvey and Antony Loewenstein, who befriended me and inspired me and showed me it was possible. To Sean, Abdullah and Bill, who kept me fighting the good fight, and all the incredible donors, especially Edward from Roach Maxam Family Foundation, and Suelette Dreyfus from Blueprint

Whistleblowing Prize, without whom I doubt this book would ever have been finished. To my lawyers at both Xenophon Davis and LS Legal, who had to be very patient while they took second place to 'the bloody book'.

To my friends who encouraged me, especially those in the fellowship; my brother John and his family; Dan Droga, Dave Adams and Jim Munro; and anyone who takes that leap of faith to read my story.

Finally, to the people of Afghanistan.

Discover a
new favourite